How Should One Live?

Essays on the Virtues

Edited by
ROGER CRISP

CLARENDON PRESS · OXFORD

NOTES ON CONTRIBUTORS

LAWRENCE BLUM is Professor of Philosophy at the University of Massachusetts at Boston. He is the author of *Friendship, Altruism, and Morality, A Truer Liberty: Simone Weil and Marxism*, and *Moral Perception and Particularity*.

JOHN COTTINGHAM is Professor of Philosophy at the University of Reading and editor of the journal *Ratio*. He is author of *Rationalism, Descartes, The Rationalists*, and *A Descartes Dictionary*. He is a co-translator of *The Philosophical Writings of Descartes* and the editor of *The Cambridge Companion to Descartes*.

ROGER CRISP is Fellow and Tutor in Philosophy at St Anne's College, Oxford. He is an associate editor of *Utilitas* and a member of the *Analysis* Committee. He is currently working on a book on J. S. Mill's *Utilitarianism*.

JULIA DRIVER is Associate Professor of Philosophy at Brooklyn College and the Graduate Center of the City University of New York. She is currently working on a book titled *Uneasy Virtue*, which presents a consequentialist account of the virtues.

BRAD HOOKER teaches in the Philosophy Department at the University of Reading. He is an associate editor of *Ratio* and *Utilitas*, and is currently writing a book on rule-consequentialism.

ROSALIND HURSTHOUSE is Head of the Philosophy Department at the Open University. She is the author of *Beginning Lives* and recently wrote 'Applying Virtue Ethics' for *Virtues and Reasons*, a book edited by her, Gavin Lawrence, and Warren Quinn.

TERENCE IRWIN is Susan Linn Sage Professor of Philosophy, Cornell University. He is the author of *Aristotle's First Principles, Classical Thought*, and *Plato's Ethics*, and has translated and edited Plato's *Gorgias* and Aristotle's *Nicomachean Ethics*.

ANDREW MASON is Lecturer in Philosophy at the University of Reading. He is the author of *Explaining Political Disagreement*, and is currently working on a book on the notion of community.

SUSAN MOLLER OKIN is Professor of Political Science at Stanford University. She is author of *Women in Western Political Thought* and *Justice, Gender, and the Family*.

ONORA O'NEILL is Principal of Newnham College, Cambridge. She writes mainly on ethics, political philosophy, and in particular conceptions of practical reason. She is the author of *Faces of Hunger: An Essay on Poverty, Development and Justice*, and *Constructions of Reason: Explorations of Kant's Practical Philosophy*.

MICHAEL SLOTE is Professor of Philosophy at the University of Maryland. He is the author of *From Morality to Virtue*, and is currently collaborating with Marcia Baron and Philip Pettit on a book debating the merits of Kantian ethics, consequentialism, and virtue ethics.

MICHAEL STOCKER is Guttag Professor of Ethics and Political Philosophy at Syracuse University. He is the author of *Plural and Conflicting Values* and *Valuing Emotions*.

GABRIELE TAYLOR was formerly Fellow in Philosophy at St Anne's College, Oxford. She is author of *Pride, Shame, and Guilt*.

DAVID WIGGINS is Wykeham Professor of Logic at New College, Oxford. He is author of *Sameness and Substance* and *Needs, Values, Truth*.

I

Modern Moral Philosophy and the Virtues

ROGER CRISP

1. AN ANCIENT QUESTION

Should I go into business or into politics? Should I live the contemplative life, or seek after pleasure? Should I be just? These were among the questions Aristotle tried to answer over two thousand years ago in his lectures on ethics in Athens. Aristotle was working through an agenda already laid down by Socrates and Plato; in one of Plato's dialogues, Socrates asks, 'What would even a person of little intelligence be more concerned about than this: how should one live?'[1]

Our question, then, is an ancient one; but, on one view of the history of moral philosophy, it has in the modern era faded into the background. Our morality is heavily influenced by the Judaeo-Christian tradition, and has its roots in conceptions of divine law. This has had two results. First, the primary question has been not 'How should I live?', but 'How should I *act*?' Secondly, answers to the question about how to act have been put in terms of *obligations*. Morality is seen as a lawlike set of principles which binds us to perform or not to perform certain actions.

The two moral traditions which have come to dominate modern philosophy certainly fit this description. One tradition begins with the German philosopher Immanuel Kant (1724–1804), according to whom the right *action* is the one performed out of respect for the moral *law*. The other tradition, utilitarianism, has also focused almost without exception on the *act* which one is *required* to perform by morality (the act, in this case, that will produce the greatest overall good).

This view of the legalistic turn in ethics was stated first in one of the most influential philosophy articles of the twentieth century, Elizabeth

---

[1] Plato, *Gorgias* 500ᶜ2–4.

Anscombe's 'Modern Moral Philosophy', published in 1958.[2] Anscombe charged all contemporary moral philosophers with seeking foundations for pseudo-legalistic moralities of obligation that make little sense in the context of disbelief in the authority of a divine lawgiver.

Anscombe's remedy for the modern malaise was that moral philosophy be put aside until an adequate philosophy of psychology, including analyses of notions such as action, intention, and pleasure, became available. 'Eventually,' she claimed, 'it might be possible to advance to considering the concept "virtue"; with which, I suppose, we should be beginning some sort of a study of ethics.'[3] Anscombe believed that a return to an Aristotelian view of ethics, in which norms are founded not legalistically but on a conception of human flourishing with virtue at its centre, provided for moral philosophy the only hope of its retaining any significance.

Why did utilitarianism and Kantianism dominate moral philosophy for so long? Anscombe's reference to the attraction of legalism undoubtedly has something in it, as do many of the alternative explanations that have been offered: the need for a *rapprochement* between various points of view facilitated by the notion of natural rights, the fact that it was Kant's earlier ethics that came to dominate discussion, the increasing complexity of society and the consequent need for rules, diminishing personal relations and increasing commercial and individualist relations, the simplicity and unity of some versions of utilitarianism and Kantianism, the modern emphasis on the voluntary, and so on.[4]

But whatever the reasons, it is hard to deny that the predominance of utilitarianism and Kantian ethics is at least under threat, and possibly already over. For Anscombe's challenge has been taken up by many philosophers, most of them intent on developing or meeting it. One effect of this work has been the emergence, or perhaps re-emergence, of what is now called 'virtue ethics' or 'virtue theory'.

Although virtue theory does have ancient roots, it is far from mere revivalism. Modern writers on the virtues, however keen they are on

---

[2] G. E. M. Anscombe, 'Modern Moral Philosophy', *Philosophy* 33 (1958), 1–19.
[3] Ibid. 15.
[4] See J. Schneewind, 'The Misfortunes of Virtue', *Ethics* 101 (1991), 42–63; E. Pincoffs, 'Quandary Ethics', *Mind* 80 (1971), 552–71; M. Stocker, 'The Schizophrenia of Modern Ethical Theories', *Journal of Philosophy* 73 (1976), 453–66; A. MacIntyre, *After Virtue: A Study in Moral Theory* (London, 1981); A. Flemming, 'Reviving the Virtues', *Ethics* 90 (1980), 587–95; H. Alderman, 'By Virtue of a Virtue', *Review of Metaphysics* 36 (1982), 127–53; G. Hartz, 'Desire and Emotion in the Virtue Tradition', *Philosophia* 20 (1990), 145–65.

bridge-building, are not unaware of the vastness of the gulf that lies between us and the ancient Greeks. One of the central contrasts between ancient and modern virtue ethics is brought out nicely in Chapter 3 by Terence Irwin. Having noted that any Greek answer to the question of how one should live would most naturally be couched in the language of virtue (or *aretē*, 'excellence'), Irwin goes on to show how Greek philosophers rejected many common-sense views of the virtues: that they are concerned primarily with action, that different social roles require different virtues, that one can possess one virtue while lacking others, that they may be bad for the person who possesses them, and that they require not knowledge but the correct intuitive response. There is an interesting contrast here with the modern move in the direction of the virtues, which can be seen partly as an attempt to close a yawning gap between common sense and moral theory opened up by the ethical theory of the last few centuries.

2. ABOUT THIS BOOK

Comparisons between ancient and modern treatments of the virtues, then, must be treated with care. But so must all generalizations about virtue theory. The idea for this book came to me while trying to teach Oxford undergraduates, who have less than a week to work on any one topic, about virtue ethics. So many philosophers have become involved, so many issues have been discussed from so many points of view, that I found myself unable to recommend a set of readings which would allow the students to see the main lines of argument, their subtlety and importance. This book, then, is in part an attempt to fill the gap in my reading list. Each contributor was commissioned to write on a specified topic central to virtue theory. The result is that the main strands in virtue theory have been teased out and woven together in such a way that even a reader without a philosophical background will be enabled to grasp them.

Much of the writing in virtue theory has been negative, and the wide-ranging critique of Kantianism and utilitarianism will be further developed in this book (see especially the papers by Michael Slote, John Cottingham, Michael Stocker, and David Wiggins). But the second main aim of the book is positive: to suggest a broad agenda for future thought. This aim is achieved largely because the contributors themselves have played an important part in the debates which they clarify and continue in this volume.

In this introduction, I shall offer my own account of virtue ethics and virtue theory, providing an overview of the main areas under debate and placing each paper in the volume on the philosophical map that emerges. But let me first briefly describe the structure of the book.

In Chapter 2, Rosalind Hursthouse characterizes virtue ethics, and demonstrates how it can offer practical guidance. Terence Irwin in Chapter 3 puts virtue ethics into historical perspective, and in Chapter 4 John Cottingham brings out the importance of Aristotelian partiality in contrast to modern impartialist accounts of ethics.

Focus then shifts to modern history, and the relationships between virtue ethics and its two main rivals, Kantianism and utilitarianism, are covered by Onora O'Neill and Michael Slote in Chapters 5 and 6 respectively. Aristotle grounded his virtue ethics in a conception of human nature, and in Chapter 7 Julia Driver discusses this idea, linking it to a utilitarian or consequentialist theory of the virtues (hence her place in the volume after Slote). Human nature was also appealed to by David Hume (1711–1776) as the foundation for the 'natural' virtues, and David Wiggins provides in Chapter 8 an authoritative account of how these virtues are to be distinguished from others.

Human nature and the human good are closely linked. In Chapter 9, Brad Hooker considers the claim, central to Greek ethics, that a flourishing human life will involve the virtues. Gabriele Taylor in turn shows in Chapter 10 how certain vices are incompatible with living a good life.

In their accounts of the place of virtue in the good life, both Plato and Aristotle put a great deal of emphasis on reason. But both were also concerned with the emotions, and many modern writers have claimed that this concern is lacking in modern ethics. Michael Stocker offers one version of such a claim in Chapter 11.

The book ends with three papers more or less in the political realm. In Chapter 12, Andrew Mason provides an interpretation of Alasdair MacIntyre's critique of modern liberalism and his advocacy of a return to virtue in public life. In Chapter 13, Susan Moller Okin criticises MacIntyre, and indeed Aristotle, from a feminist point of view, and proceeds to object also to those feminists who have attempted to create a special place for the feminine in moral education. In the closing chapter, Lawrence Blum places virtue soundly in its social context, where it must be learned and practised, and considers the importance of community in understanding the virtues.

in the ethics of modernity is the notion of an ideal of excellence around which we can shape our lives.[19]

Narrowing the scope of morality and moral reasons has several advantages. First, morality will no longer appear unreasonably demanding. Secondly, it makes room for agents to pursue their own good and the good of those close to them independently of the support of any background principle. As Williams suggests, if I justify my saving my wife from a burning building by appealing to an impartial background moral principle, such as utilitarianism or Kantianism, I am having 'one thought too many'.[20] And it can be argued that even sophisticated versions of utilitarianism and Kantianism which allow alternative motivations at the point of action nevertheless unnecessarily require the background principle to be present as justification for what is done. Thirdly, as the fire example shows, it increases the likelihood that morality can play a part in the agent's good.

These advantages are pursued on behalf of virtue ethics by several contributors. In Chapter 6, Slote points out that virtue ethics, unlike utilitarianism, allows the agent to put herself on one side of the balance and the interests of others collectively on the other, thus making for a more plausible account of the relation between morality and self-interest. Cottingham suggests in Chapter 4 that, whatever we say in our more reflective moments, we are in fact Aristotelians, who see morality, the good life, and reasons generally in terms not of impersonal duty or impartial maximization of well-being, but of a life of personal flourishing bound up with others in special relationships. He shows how philosophical ethical theory can first be seen coming apart from an everyday virtue-based ethic in the work not of Kant but of Descartes.

Stocker's seminal paper, 'The Schizophrenia of Modern Ethical Theories', advanced the critique of utilitarianism and Kantianism considerably. In Chapter 11, he demonstrates how a virtue ethics which introduces the emotions as an important constituent of what is itself valuable in life and in our understanding of it can, through eschewing reference back to some further goal or principle, avoid the kind of schizophrenic split between evaluation and motivation typical of the competitors to virtue ethics.

In Chapter 8, Wiggins approaches the related issues of motivation

---

[19] See A. Cua, *Dimensions of Moral Creativity* (State College, Pa., 1978); L. Blum, 'Moral Exemplars', in P. French, T. Uehling, and H. Wettstein (eds.), *Ethical Theory: Character and Virtue*, *Midwest Studies in Philosophy XIII* (Notre Dame, Ind., 1988), 196–221.   [20] Williams, 'Persons, Character and Morality', 18.

and justification in ethics via the important Humean distinction between natural and artificial virtues. Wiggins wonders whether the Platonic approach to justifying morality—in which one starts out, with nothing, to convince a self-interested moral sceptic—gives too much away. Why should we not begin our account of morality, as does Hume, with the observation that benevolence is natural to us? The Platonic approach also, perhaps, asks too much of reason: why expect theoretical reason, in abstraction from the human context, to supply a foundation for a morality which must be lived by us?

But, it may be asked, how can weak natural benevolence explain or justify virtues such as justice, which seem to involve a respect for convention independent of its relation to human well-being? The answer depends on the origin of such conventions themselves. Their being generally beneficial results in their being approved by benevolence or self-love, and so a moral motive for the artificial virtues takes root and flourishes naturally in a civilized society.

Wiggins's chapter brings out the explanatory power of an account of the virtues based on a realistic understanding of human nature, practical rationality, and practical life in general. His elucidation should encourage those interested in the virtues to turn as readily to Hume for inspiration as they now do to Aristotle.

6. UNIVERSALITY, TRADITION, AND PRACTICE

The questioning by writers such as Foot and Williams of the utilitarian and Kantian view that morality provides reasons independent of the agent's desires or her conception of her good is just one of the considerations that have led various philosophers to doubt the claim of morality to universality. Interestingly, certain views in this area can again be seen to be at once Aristotelian and distinctively modern. The emphasis on the importance of context, for example, is quite Aristotelian, as Cottingham shows in Chapter 4; but when this is used, as it is in MacIntyre's *After Virtue*, to support relativistic claims about the grounding of moral reasons in traditions, conflicts between which are irresolvable, we have returned to a distinctively modern theme.

The antagonism to universality, in particular the universality of utilitarianism and Kantianism, has emerged especially clearly in the debate between liberals and communitarians in political philosophy.[21] As

[21] See MacIntyre, *After Virtue*; S. Hampshire, *Morality and Conflict* (Cambridge, 1983); M. Walzer, *Spheres of Justice* (Oxford, 1983).

representative of modernity, the liberal conception of the self and moral agency is criticized for its lack of content, while, as yet another tradition, liberalism is attacked not only for its thinness, but for its advocates' lack of awareness that the Archimedean standpoint they claim to occupy is unobtainable. The thin emotivist or existentialist self is replaced in MacIntyre's work with a narrative conception of self-hood.[22] This richer notion of the self, unified as it is over time, provides another route for the reintroduction of the notion of character into moral philosophy.

MacIntyre also takes into account the development of social practices over time. The concept of tradition, and particularly that of a neo-Aristotelian tradition based on the virtues, enable MacIntyre to answer the question of what can ground the good when a teleology based on human nature has been rejected. Further, the good of the agent, as I noted above, can be closely tied in an Aristotelian manner to the good of others through the notions of practice and community. In Chapter 11, Stocker develops this account of the nature of valuable practices, spelling out how emotional engagement is an important constituent in activities we find worth while, such as playing with our children.

In Chapter 12, Andrew Mason examines MacIntyre's critique of modern work practices, and finds that, despite the exaggerated pessimism of MacIntyre's overall account, he has posed a genuine challenge to liberals who allow a place for the market within social arrangements. Practices supply the conditions for goods, and modern work is often insufficiently complex to allow the exercise of the virtues and the consequent enjoyment of internal goods. Mason's concluding pages offer an example of practical virtue ethics in a political context. Rather than MacIntyre's feudal communities centred on households, Mason suggests the far more plausible solution to the problem of alienation at work of rotation of tasks within a co-operative framework. Market socialism might permit workers to develop and exercise the excellences which modern emphasis on the pursuit of external goods has banished from many workplaces.

7. COMMUNITY AND GENDER

Practices are communal. In Chapter 14, Blum examines the possible connections between virtue and community itself. Such connections are

---

[22] See MacIntyre, *After Virtue*, 202; C. Taylor, *The Sources of the Self* (Cambridge, 1989).

often gestured at, but rarely analysed in detail. Blum looks at a number of claims: that virtue is learned in a community, sustained by a community, provided with content or meaning by a community, and so on. He proceeds to clarify the sustaining and content-conferring roles of community with the example of Le Chambon, a French village which offered a refuge to many Jews during the Second World War. In so doing, Blum provides an alternative account of the nature of moral agency to those forms of Kantian liberalism which ground it in the reflection and choice of the free and rational individual. He suggests that any dualism between categorical and supererogatory duties will fail to capture the phenomenon he is studying, since what is expected of an agent in any community will depend on the standards of that community. The standards in Le Chambon were high, and their very presence in the community provided the villagers with motivation.

Okin, in the first section of Chapter 13, provides a feminist critique of the grounding of the virtues in communal practice by Aristotle and MacIntyre. Neither, she claims, shows equal concern and respect for women. In the case of Aristotle, she argues, the modern attempt to 'rehabilitate' his philosophy by attempting to hive off his ethics from his inherently sexist biology and politics will fail. In the *Politics*, Aristotle makes it clear that virtues are relative to social position, which implies that those in an inferior position are not capable of the 'higher' virtues. And these higher virtues as they are depicted in Aristotle's *Ethics* are themselves male-oriented. Okin goes on to suggest that Aristotle's influence on MacIntyre is evident in the fact that his virtues too revolve around the lives of males with a high status in society. Neither Aristotle nor MacIntyre sees the importance of traditional 'women's work' and the virtues or excellences it involves.[23]

8. PRACTICAL REASON, MORAL KNOWLEDGE AND MORAL EDUCATION

Utilitarianism and Kantianism have frequently been put forward as ethics of rules, that is, as sets of explicit and systematic principles on the basis of which agents can make moral decisions. Morality presents itself as a series of isolated problems or dilemmas to be resolved by the theory as

---

[23] Patricia Scaltsas pointed out to me that Aristotle does nevertheless offer the love of a woman for her child to illustrate that the value of the virtue of love or friendship (*philia*) lies in loving rather than being loved; see Aristotle, *NE* $1159^a27–33$.

each case arises. I have already suggested that the focus of these theories can be broadened to include lives and characters as well as acts. Utilitarians may take a line similar to Driver's in Chapter 7, advocating the acquisition and practice of the virtues; and attempts have been made by Kantians, including O'Neill in Chapter 5, to bring Kantian practical reason more into line with an Aristotelian model. Many of these moves can be seen as a response to arguments from virtue theorists.

One of the oldest arguments against founding morality on rules is based on Aristotle's account of the legal virtue of equity.[24] Rules are inevitably too simple to cover every eventuality, human life being of sufficient complexity and unpredictability that hard cases will always arise. A judge requires equity to apply universal law to particular cases, and in the same way the virtuous person requires practical wisdom (*phronēsis*), that is, a sensitivity to the salient features of situations which is not to be characterized as a capacity to apply explicit rules.[25]

John McDowell has revived this argument in a Wittgensteinian context in his important article 'Virtue and Reason'.[26] McDowell argues against a conception of moral agency according to which the world as seen by the virtuous person can be neutrally characterized, and some special desire postulated to explain her being motivated. Any such object of desire could not be made explicit, since moral principles always meet with exceptions. McDowell introduces Wittgenstein to support his claim that acting rationally does not require guidance by articulable rules. Sometimes there is no further foundation for our going on in the same way than human practices. Again, we are brought back to practice and community.

The virtuous person's sensitivity, then, constitutes a kind of knowledge. Here we find traces of both the Socratic conception of the 'unity' of the virtues (virtue *is* knowledge) and the Aristotelian notion of their 'reciprocity' (the possession of any one virtue requires the possession of all, since the possession of any one depends upon the intellectual virtue of practical wisdom, a capacity which both is partly perceptual and itself depends upon the moral virtues as an organized whole).[27] In Chapter 11, Stocker claims that this knowledge comes largely from a capacity to engage emotionally in certain practices. These practices are often not rule-governed, in the sense that those who understand them cannot fully articulate their knowledge; think again of the parent playing with her

---

[24] *NE* 1137ᵃ31–1138ᵃ3.   [25] *NE* 1142ᵃ11–15.

[26] J. McDowell, 'Virtue and Reason', *The Monist* 62 (1979), 331–50.

[27] See, e.g. Plato, *Protagoras*; Aristotle, *NE* 1144ᵇ17–1145ᵃ2.

child. Stocker goes on to suggest that such practices in fact *constitute* practical knowledge, and that this knowledge is importantly prior to articulated and reflective theory. Here, 'knowing that', in a full-blooded sense, requires first 'knowing how'. For Stocker, Aristotle's virtuous person enjoys exercising the virtues in the sense that he can engage emotionally in the right way in virtuous practice or activity.

Aristotle puts a great deal of stress on the developmental aspect of the virtues. Stocker's 'knowledge that' is the articulable understanding of the virtuous person. For Aristotle, this stage can be reached only by 'knowledge that' of a kind which does not require moral sensitivity. This knowledge is of the common morality of one's culture, and arises at least partly through education.[28]

In recent years studies have been made of moral education in our own culture which suggest that women develop morally in a way different from men.[29] It has been argued that women tend to see morality in a more Aristotelian, particularist, contextual way than men, who are inclined to adopt a moral framework bounded by explicit universal principle. In the final section of Chapter 13, Okin offers an account of these arguments, and subjects them to a wide-ranging critique. She notes that there are important differences between the feminist ethics based on this research and many versions of virtue ethics, in particular that in the so-called 'ethics of care' the central virtue of justice is eschewed. Okin also charges the 'different voice' theorists with unclarity and exaggeration: is partiality always laudable, and do men—including male philosophers—really see morality differently from women?

Virtue theory is more important than many philosophers have yet realized. Its significance lies not so much in its offering, in the form of virtue ethics, a normative alternative to utilitarianism and Kantianism, but in its reviving absolutely central questions concerning morality and its role in human life. Now is an exciting time in moral philosophy, and this book shows why.[30]

[28] *NE* 1098^{a}33–1098^{b}8.

[29] See especially Carol Gilligan, *In a Different Voice* (Cambridge, Mass., 1982).

[30] I am grateful for comments on earlier drafts to Diego Gambetta, Brad Hooker, Susan Khin Zaw, Peter Momtchiloff, and an assessor for Oxford University Press.

2

Normative Virtue Ethics

ROSALIND HURSTHOUSE

A common belief concerning virtue ethics is that it does not tell us what we should do. This belief is sometimes manifested merely in the expressed assumption that virtue ethics, in being 'agent-centred' rather than 'act-centred', is concerned with Being rather than Doing, with good (and bad) character rather than right (and wrong) action, with the question 'What sort of person should I be?' rather than the question 'What should I do?' On this assumption, 'virtue ethics' so-called does not figure as a normative rival to utilitarian and deontological ethics; rather, its (fairly) recent revival is seen as having served the useful purpose of reminding moral philosophers that the elaboration of a normative theory may fall short of giving a full account of our moral life. Thus prompted, deontologists have turned to Kant's long neglected 'Doctrine of Virtue', and utilitarians, largely abandoning the old debate about rule- and act-utilitarianism, are showing interest in the general-happiness-maximizing consequences of inculcating such virtues as friendship, honesty, and loyalty.

On this assumption, it seems that philosophers who 'do virtue ethics', having served this purpose, must realize that they have been doing no more than supplementing normative theory, and should now decide which of the two standard views they espouse. Or, if they find that too difficult, perhaps they should confine themselves to writing detailed studies of particular virtues and vices, indicating where appropriate that 'a deontologist would say that an agent with virtue X will characteristically . . . , whereas a utilitarian would say that she will characteristically . . .' But anyone who wants to espouse virtue ethics as a rival to deontological or utilitarian ethics (finding it distinctly bizarre to suppose that Aristotle espoused either of the latter) will find this common belief voiced against her as an objection: 'Virtue ethics does not, because it cannot, tell us what we should do. Hence it cannot be a normative rival to deontology and utilitarianism.'

This paper is devoted to defending virtue ethics against this objection.

1. RIGHT ACTION

What grounds might someone have for believing that virtue ethics cannot tell us what we should do? It seems that sometimes the ground is no more than the claim that virtue ethics is concerned with good (and bad) character rather than right (and wrong) action. But that claim does no more than highlight an interesting contrast between virtue ethics on the one hand, and deontology and utilitarianism on the other; the former is agent-centred, the latter (it is said) are act-centred.[1] It does not entail that virtue ethics has nothing to say about the concept of right action, nor about which actions are right and which wrong. Wishing to highlight a different contrast, the one between utilitarianism and deontology, we might equally well say, 'Utilitarianism is concerned with good (and bad) states of affairs rather than right (and wrong) action', and no one would take that to mean that utilitarianism, unlike deontology, had nothing to say about right action, for what utilitarianism does say is so familiar.

Suppose an act-utilitarian laid out her account of right action as follows:

U1. An action is right iff it promotes the best consequences.

This premiss provides a specification of right action, forging the familiar utilitarian link between the concepts of *right action* and *best consequences*, but gives one no guidance about how to act until one knows what to count as the best consequences. So these must be specified in a second premiss, for example:

U2. The best consequences are those in which happiness is maximized,

which forges the familiar utilitarian link between the concepts of *best consequences* and *happiness*.[2]

---

[1] Kant is standardly taken as the paradigm deontologist, but Stephen Hudson argues he is much closer to Aristotle on the act/agent-centred point than is usually supposed. See 'What is Morality All About?', *Philosophia* 20 (1990), 3–13.

[2] Variations on utilitarianism are not my concern here. I am ignoring rule-utilitarianism, and assuming my reader to be well aware of the fact that different utilitarians may spe-

Many different versions of deontology can be laid out in a way that displays the same basic structure. They begin with a premiss providing a specification of right action:

> D1. An action is right iff it is in accordance with a correct moral rule or principle.

Like the first premiss of act-utilitarianism, this gives one no guidance about how to act until, in this case, one knows what to count as a correct moral rule (or principle). So this must be specified in a second premiss which begins

> D2. A correct moral rule (principle) is one that . . . ,

and this may be completed in a variety of ways, for example:

(i) is on the following list (and then a list does follow)

or

(ii) is laid on us by God

or

(iii) is universalizable

or

(iv) would be the object of choice of all rational beings

and so on.

Although this way of laying out fairly familiar versions of utilitarianism and deontology is hardly controversial, it is worth noting that it suggests some infelicity in the slogan 'Utilitarianism begins with (or takes as its fundamental concept etc.) the Good, whereas deontology begins with the Right.' If the concept a normative ethics 'begins with' is the one it uses to specify right action, then utilitarianism might be said to begin with the Good (if we take this to be the 'same' concept as that of the *best*), but we should surely hasten to add 'but only in relation to consequences; not, for instance, in relation to *good* agents, or to living *well*'. And even then, we shall not be able to go on to say that most versions of deontology 'begin with' the Right, for they use the concept of moral rule or principle to specify right action. The only versions

cify *best consequences* in different ways. See the introduction to A. Sen and B. Williams (eds.), *Utilitarianism and Beyond* (Cambridge, 1982), from which I have (basically) taken the characterization of utilitarianism given here.

which, in this sense, 'begin with' the Right would have to be versions of what Frankena calls 'extreme act-deontology'[3], which (I suppose) specify a right action as one which just *is* right.

And if the dictum is supposed to single out, rather vaguely, the concept which is 'most important', then the concepts of *consequences* or *happiness* seem as deserving of mention as the concept of the Good for utilitarianism, and what counts as most important (if any one concept does) for deontologists would surely vary from case to case. For some it would be God, for others universalizability, for others the Categorical Imperative, for others rational acceptance, and so on.

It is possible that too slavish an acceptance of this slogan, and the inevitable difficulty of finding a completion of 'and virtue ethics begins with . . .' which does not reveal its inadequacy, has contributed to the belief that virtue ethics cannot provide a specification of right action. I have heard people say, 'Utilitarianism defines the Right in terms of the Good, and deontology defines the Good in terms of the Right; but how can virtue ethics possibly define both in terms of the (virtuous) Agent?', and indeed, with no answer forthcoming to the questions 'Good *what*? Right *what*?', I have no idea. But if the question is 'How can virtue ethics specify right action?', the answer is easy:

> Vі. An action is right iff it is what a virtuous agent would characteristically (i.e. acting in character) do in the circumstances.

This specification rarely, if ever, silences those who maintain that virtue ethics cannot tell us what we should do. On the contrary, it tends to provoke irritable laughter and scorn. '*That*'s no use', the objectors say. 'It gives us no guidance whatsoever. Who are the virtuous agents?' But if the failure of the first premiss of a normative ethics which forges a link between the concept of right action and a concept distinctive of that ethics may provoke scorn because it provides no practical guidance, why not direct a similar scorn at the first premisses of act-utilitarianism and deontology in the form in which I have given them? Of each of them I remarked, apparently *en passant* but with intent, that they gave us no guidance. Utilitarianism must specify what are to count as the best consequences, and deontology what is to count as a correct moral rule, producing a second premiss, before any guidance is given. And similarly, virtue ethics must specify who is to count as a virtuous agent. So far, the three are all in the same position.

---

[3] W. Frankena, *Ethics*, 2nd edn. (Englewood Cliffs, NJ, 1973), 16.

Of course, if the virtuous agent can only be specified as an agent disposed to act in accordance with moral rules, as some have assumed, then virtue ethics collapses back into deontology and is no rival to it. So let us add a subsidiary premiss to this skeletal outline, with the intention of making it clear that virtue ethics aims to provide a non-deontological specification of the virtuous agent via a specification of the virtues, which will be given in its second premiss:

> V1a. A virtuous agent is one who acts virtuously, that is, one who has and exercises the virtues.
>
> V2. A virtue is a character trait that . . .[4]

This second premiss of virtue ethics might, like the second premiss of some versions of deontology, be completed simply by enumeration ('a virtue is one of the following', and then the list is given).[5] Or we might, not implausibly, interpret the Hume of the second *Enquiry* as espousing virtue ethics. According to him, a virtue is a character trait (of human beings) that is useful or agreeable to its possessor or to others (inclusive 'or' both times). The standard neo-Aristotelian completion claims that a virtue is a character trait a human being needs for *eudaimonia*, to flourish or live well.

Here, then, we have a specification of right action, whose structure closely resembles those of act-utilitarianism and many forms of deontology. Given that virtue ethics can come up with such a specification, can it still be maintained that it, unlike utilitarianism and deontology, cannot tell us what we should do? Does the specification somehow fail to provide guidance in a way that the other two do not?

At this point, the difficulty of identifying the virtuous agent in a way that makes V1 action-guiding tends to be brought forward again. Suppose

---

[4] It might be said that V1a does not make it clear that virtue ethics aims to provide a non-deontological specification of the virtuous agent, since it does not rule out the possibility that the virtues themselves are no more than dispositions to act in accordance with moral rules. And indeed, it does seem that the belief that the virtuous agent is nothing but the agent disposed to act in accordance with moral rules is often based on that assumption about the virtues. (See, for example, Frankena, *Ethics*, 65 and A. Gewirth, 'Rights and Virtues', *Review of Metaphysics* 38 (1985), 739–62.) Then we must say that V2 aims to clear that up by saying that the virtues are character traits, assuming it to be obvious that someone's being of a certain character is not merely a matter of her being disposed to do certain sorts of acts in accordance with a rule.

[5] 'Enumeration' may connote something more explicit than is required. Deontologists and virtue ethicists actually engaged in normative ethics may well do no more than take it as obvious in the course of what they say that such-and-such is a correct moral rule or virtue, neither stipulating this explicitly, nor attempting to list other rules/virtues which have no bearing on whatever issue is under discussion.

it is granted that deontology has just as much difficulty in identifying the correct moral rules as virtue ethics has in identifying the virtues and hence the virtuous agent. Then the following objection may be made.

'All the same,' it may be said, 'if we imagine that that has been achieved—perhaps simply by enumeration—deontology yields a set of clear prescriptions which are readily applicable ("Do not lie", "do not steal", "do not inflict evil or harm on others", "Do help others", "Do keep promises", etc.). But virtue ethics yields only the prescription "Do what the virtuous agent (the one who is honest, charitable, just, etc.) would do in these circumstances." And this gives me no guidance unless I am (and know I am) a virtuous agent myself (in which case I am hardly in need of it). If I am less than fully virtuous, I shall have no idea what a virtuous agent would do, and hence cannot apply the only prescription that virtue ethics has given me. (Of course, act-utilitarianism also yields a single prescription, "Do what maximises happiness", but there are no *parallel* difficulties in applying that.) So there is the way in which Vɪ fails to be action-guiding where deontology and utilitarianism succeed.'

It is worth pointing out that, if I acknowledge that I am far from perfect, and am quite unclear what a virtuous agent would do in the circumstances in which I find myself, the obvious thing to do is to go and ask one, should this be possible. This is far from being a trivial point, for it gives a straightforward explanation of an aspect of our moral life which should not be ignored, namely the fact that we do seek moral guidance from people who we think are morally better than ourselves. When I am looking for an excuse to do something I have a horrid suspicion is wrong, I ask my moral inferiors (or peers if I am bad enough), 'Wouldn't you do such and such if you were in my shoes?' But when I am anxious to do what is right, and do not see my way clear, I go to people I respect and admire—people who I think are kinder, more honest, more just, wiser, than I am myself—and ask them what they would do in my circumstances. How utilitarianism and deontology would explain this fact, I do not know; but, as I said, the explanation within the terms of virtue ethics is straightforward. If you want to do what is right, and doing what is right is doing what a virtuous agent would do in the circumstances, then you should find out what she would do if you do not already know.

Moreover, seeking advice from virtuous people is not the only thing an imperfect agent trying to apply the single prescription of virtue ethics can do. For it is simply false that, in general, 'if I am less than fully virtuous, then I shall have no idea what a virtuous agent would do', as the objection claims. Recall that we are assuming that the virtues have been enumerated, as the deontologist's rules have been. The latter have been enumerated as, say, 'Do not lie', 'Do not inflict evil or harm', etc.; the former as, say, honesty, charity, justice, etc. So, *ex hypothesi*, a virtuous agent is one who is honest, charitable, just, etc. So what she characteristically does is act honestly, charitably, justly, etc., and not dishonestly, uncharitably, unjustly. So given an enumeration of the virtues, I may well have a perfectly good idea of what the virtuous person would do in my circumstances despite my own imperfection. Would she lie in her teeth to acquire an unmerited advantage? No, for that would be to act both dishonestly and unjustly. Would she help the naked man by the roadside or pass by on the other side? The former, for she acts charitably. Might she keep a deathbed promise even though living people would benefit from its being broken? Yes, for she acts justly.[6] And so on.

2. MORAL RULES

The above response to the objection that V1 fails to be action-guiding clearly amounts to a denial of the oft-repeated claim that virtue ethics does not come up with any rules (another version of the thought that it is concerned with Being rather than Doing and needs to be supplemented with rules). We can now see that it comes up with a large number; not only does each virtue generate a prescription—act honestly, charitably, justly—but each vice a prohibition—do not act dishonestly, uncharitably, unjustly. Once this point about virtue ethics is grasped (and it is remarkable how often it is overlooked), can there remain any reason for thinking that virtue ethics cannot tell us what we should do? Yes. The reason given is, roughly, that rules such as 'Act honestly', 'Do not act uncharitably', etc. are, like the rule 'Do what the virtuous agent would do', still the wrong sort of rule, still somehow doomed to fail to provide the action guidance supplied by the rules (or rule) of deontology and utilitarianism.

But how so? It is true that these rules of virtue ethics (henceforth 'v-rules') are couched in terms, or concepts, which are certainly 'evaluative'

---

[6] I follow tradition here in taking the virtue of fidelity, or faithfulness to one's word, to be part of the virtue of justice, thereby avoiding a clumsy attempt to manufacture an adverbial phrase corresponding to 'fidelity'. But nothing hangs on this.

in *some* sense, or senses, of that difficult word. Is it this which dooms them to failure? Surely not, unless many forms of deontology fail too.[7] If we concentrate on the single example of lying, defining lying to be 'asserting what you believe to be untrue, with the intention of deceiving your hearer(s)', then we might, for a moment, preserve the illusion that a deontologist's rules do not contain 'evaluative' terms.[8] But as soon as we remember that few deontologists will want to forego principles of non-maleficence or beneficence, the illusion vanishes. For those principles, and their corresponding rules ('Do no evil or harm to others', 'Help others', 'Promote their well-being'), rely on terms or concepts which are at least as 'evaluative' as those employed in the v-rules.[9] Few deontologists rest content with the simple quasi-biological 'Do not kill', but more refined versions of that rule such as 'Do not murder', or 'Do not kill the innocent', once again employ 'evaluative' terms, and 'Do not kill unjustly' is itself a particular instantiation of a v-rule.

Supposing this point were granted, a deontologist might still claim that the v-rules are markedly inferior to deontological rules as far as providing guidance for children is concerned. Granted, adult deontologists

---

[7] Forms of utilitarianism which aim to be entirely value-free or empirical, such as those which define happiness in terms of the satisfaction of actual desires or preferences, regardless of their content, or as a mental state whose presence is definitively established by introspection, seem to me the least plausible, but I accept that anyone who embraces them may consistently complain that v-rules give inferior action-guidance in virtue of containing 'evaluative' terms. But any utilitarian who wishes to employ any distinction between the higher and lower pleasures, or rely on some list of goods (such as autonomy, friendship, knowledge of important matters) in defining happiness, must grant that even her single rule is implicitly 'evaluative'.

[8] It might be thought that the example of promises provided an equally straightforward example. This would not substantially affect my argument, but in any case, I do not think that this is so. The *Shorter Oxford* defines the verb 'to promise' as 'to undertake or . . . , by word or . . . , to do or refrain . . . , or to give . . . : usu. to the *advantage* of the person concerned' (my italics), and the qualification containing the word I have italicized seems to me essential. Its significance has been highlighted in the many stories and myths whose tragic point turns on someone wicked doing what they literally undertook to do, to the horror and despair of 'the person concerned'. ('Promise me you will fearfully punish the one who has done so and so', the person concerned says, not realizing that the one in question is her long-lost son.)

[9] I cannot resist pointing out that this reveals a further inadequacy in the slogan 'Utilitarianism begins with the Good, deontology with the Right' when this is taken as committing deontology to making the concept of the Good (and presumably the Bad or Evil) somehow derivative from the concept of the Right (and Wrong). A 'utilitarian' who relied on the concept of *morally right*, or *virtuous*, action in specifying his concept of happiness would find it hard to shrug off the scare quotes, but no one expects a deontologist to be able to state each of her rules without employing a concept of *good* which is not simply the concept of *right action for its own sake*, or without any mention of *evil* or *harm*.

must think hard about what really constitutes harming someone, or promoting their well-being, or respecting their autonomy, or murder, but surely the simple rules we learnt at our mother's knee are indispensable? How could virtue ethics plausibly seek to dispense with these and expect toddlers to grasp 'Act charitably, honestly, and kindly', 'Don't act unjustly', and so on? Rightly are these concepts described as 'thick'![10] Far too thick for a child to grasp.

Strictly speaking, this claim about learning does not really support the *general* claim that v-rules fail to provide action-guidance, but the claim about learning, arising naturally as it does in the context of the general claim, is one I am more than happy to address. For it pinpoints a condition of adequacy that any normative ethics must meet, namely that such an ethics must not only come up with action-guidance for a clever rational adult but also generate some account of moral education, of how one generation teaches the next what they should do. But an ethics inspired by Aristotle is unlikely to have forgotten the question of moral education, and the objection fails to hit home. First, the implicit empirical claim that toddlers are taught *only* the deontologist's rules, not the 'thick' concepts, is false. Sentences such as 'Don't do that, it hurts, you mustn't be *cruel*', 'Be *kind* to your brother, he's only little', 'Don't be so *mean*, so *greedy*' are commonly addressed to toddlers. Secondly, why should a proponent of virtue ethics deny the significance of such mother's-knee rules as 'Don't lie', 'Keep promises', 'Don't take more than your fair share', 'Help others'? Although it is a mistake, I have claimed, to define a virtuous agent simply as one disposed to act in accordance with moral rules, it is a very understandable mistake, given the obvious connection between, for example, the exercise of the virtue of honesty and refraining from lying. Virtue ethicists want to emphasize the fact that, if children are to be taught to be honest, they must be taught to prize the truth, and that *merely* teaching them not to lie will not achieve this end. But they need not deny that to achieve this end teaching them not to lie is useful, even indispensable.

So we can see that virtue ethics not only comes up with rules (the v-rules, couched in terms derived from the virtues and vices), but further, does not exclude the more familiar deontologists' rules. The theoretical distinction between the two is that the familiar rules, and their applications in particular cases, are given entirely different backings. According to virtue ethics, I must not tell this lie, since it would be dishonest, and

---

[10] See B. Williams, *Ethics and the Limits of Philosophy* (London, 1985), 129–30.

dishonesty is a vice; must not break this promise, since it would be
unjust, or a betrayal of friendship, or, perhaps (for the available virtue
and vice terms do not neatly cover every contingency), simply because
no virtuous person would.

However, the distinction is not merely theoretical. It is, indeed, the
case that, with respect to a number of familiar examples, virtue ethicists
and deontologists tend to stand shoulder to shoulder against utilitarians,
denying that, for example, this lie can be told, this promise broken, this
human being killed because the consequences of so doing will be generally happiness-maximizing. But, despite a fair amount of coincidence in
action-guidance between deontology and virtue ethics, the latter has its
own distinctive approach to the practical problems involved in dilemmas.

3. THE CONFLICT PROBLEM

It is a noteworthy fact that, in support of the general claim that virtue
ethics cannot tell us what we should do, what is often cited is the 'conflict problem'. The requirements of different virtues, it is said, can point
us in opposed directions. Charity prompts me to kill the person who
would (truly) be better off dead, but justice forbids it. Honesty points
to telling the hurtful truth, kindness and compassion to remaining silent
or even lying. And so on. So virtue ethics lets us down just at the point
where we need it, where we are faced with the really difficult dilemmas
and do not know what to do.

In the mouth of a utilitarian, this may be a comprehensible criticism,
for, as is well known, the only conflict that classical utilitarianism's one
rule can generate is the tiresome logical one between the two occurrences
of 'greatest' in its classical statement. But it is strange to find the very
same criticism coming from deontologists, who are notoriously faced
with the same problem. 'Don't kill', 'Respect autonomy', 'Tell the
truth', 'Keep promises' may all conflict with 'Prevent suffering' or 'Do
no harm', which is precisely why deontologists so often reject utilitarianism's deliverances on various dilemmas. Presumably, they must think
that deontology can solve the 'conflict problem' and, further, that virtue
ethics cannot. Are they right?

With respect to a number of cases, the deontologist's strategy is to
argue that the 'conflict' is merely apparent, or *prima facie*. The proponent
of virtue ethics employs the same strategy: according to her, many of
the putative conflicts are merely apparent, resulting from a misapplication

of the virtue or vice terms. Does kindness require not telling hurtful truths? Sometimes, but in *this* case, what has to be understood is that one does people no kindness by concealing this sort of truth from them, hurtful as it may be. Or, in a different case, the importance of the truth in question puts the consideration of hurt feelings out of court, and the agent does not show herself to be unkind, or callous, by speaking out. Does charity require that I kill the person who would be better off dead but who wants to stay alive, thereby conflicting with justice? Not if, in Foot's words, '[a] man does not lack charity because he refrains from an act of injustice which would have been for someone's good'.[11]

One does not have to agree with the three judgements expressed here to recognize this as a *strategy* available to virtue ethics, any more than one has to agree with the particular judgements of deontologists who, for example, may claim that one rule outranks another, or that a certain rule has a certain exception clause built in, when they argue that a putative case of conflict is resolvable. Whether an individual has resolved a putative moral conflict or dilemma rightly is one question; whether a normative ethics has the wherewithal to resolve it is an entirely different question, and it is the latter with which we are concerned here.

The form the strategy takes within virtue ethics provides what may plausibly be claimed to be the deep explanation of why, in some cases, agents do not know the answer to 'What should I do in these circumstances?' despite the fact that there *is* an answer. Trivially, the explanation is that they lack moral knowledge of what to do in this situation; but why? In what way? The lack, according to virtue ethics' strategy, arises from lack of moral wisdom, from an inadequate grasp of what is involved in acting *kindly* (unkindly) or *charitably* (uncharitably), in being *honest*, or *just*, or *lacking in charity*, or, in general, of how the virtue (and vice) terms are to be correctly applied.

Here we come to an interesting defence of the v-rules, often criticized as being too difficult to apply for the agent who lacks moral wisdom.[12] The defence relies on an (insufficiently acknowledged) insight of Aristotle's—namely that moral knowledge, unlike mathematical knowledge, cannot be acquired merely by attending lectures and is not characteristically to be found in people too young to have much experience of life.[13] Now *if* right action were determined by rules that any clever

---

[11] P. Foot, *Virtues and Vices* (Oxford, 1978), p. 60, n. 12.

[12] This could well be regarded as another version of the criticism discussed earlier, that the v-rules somehow fail to provide action-guidance.

[13] *Nicomachean Ethics* (= *NE*) 1142^{a}12–16.

adolescent could apply correctly, how could this be so? Why are there not moral whiz-kids, the way there are mathematical (or quasi-mathematical) whiz-kids? But if the rules that determine right action are, like the v-rules, very difficult to apply correctly, involving, for instance, a grasp of the *sort* of truth that one does people no kindness by concealing, the explanation is readily to hand. Clever adolescents do not, in general, have a good grasp of that sort of thing.[14] And *of course* I have to say 'the sort of truth that . . .' and 'that sort of thing', relying on my readers' knowledgeable uptake. For if I could define either sort, then, once again, clever adolescents could acquire moral wisdom from textbooks.

So far, I have described one strategy available to virtue ethics for coping with the 'conflict problem', a strategy that consists in arguing that the conflict is merely apparent, and can be resolved. According to one—only one of many—versions of 'the doctrine of the unity of the virtues', this is the only possible strategy (and ultimately successful), but this is not a claim I want to defend. One general reason is that I still do not know what I think about 'the unity of the virtues' (all those different versions!); a more particular, albeit related, reason is that, even if I were (somehow) sure that the requirements of the particular virtues could never conflict, I suspect that I would still believe in the possibility of moral dilemmas. I have been talking so far as though examples of putative dilemmas and examples of putative conflict between the requirements of different virtues (or deontologists' rules) coincided. But it may seem to many, as it does to me, that there are certain (putative) dilemmas which can only be described in terms of (putative) conflict with much artifice and loss of relevant detail.

Let us, therefore, consider the problem of moral dilemmas without bothering about whether they can be described in the simple terms of a conflict between the requirements of two virtues (or two deontologists' rules). Most of us, it may be supposed, have our own favoured example(s), either real or imaginary, of the case (or cases) where we see the decision about whether to do A or B as a very grave matter, have thought a great deal about what can be said for and against doing

---

[14] In defending the thesis that virtue ethics is a normative *rival* to utilitarianism and deontology, I am not simultaneously aiming to establish the far more ambitious thesis that it beats its rivals hollow. Utilitarians and deontologists may well take the Aristotelian point on board and provide an account, appropriate to their ethics, of why we should not consult whiz-kids about difficult moral decisions. For example, Onora O'Neill's sophisticated version of Kantian 'maxims' rules out their application by (merely) clever adolescents.

A, and doing B, and have still not managed to reach a conclusion which we think is the right one.[15] How, if at all, does virtue ethics direct us to think about such cases?

4. DILEMMAS AND NORMATIVE THEORY

As a preliminary to answering that question, we should consider a much more general one, namely 'How should any normative ethics direct us to think about such cases?' This brings us to the topic of normative theory.

It is possible to detect a new movement in moral philosophy, a movement which has already attracted the name 'anti-theory in ethics'.[16] Its various representatives have as a common theme the rejection of normative ethical theory; but amongst them are numbered several philosophers usually associated with virtue ethics, such as Baier, McDowell, MacIntyre, and Nussbaum. This does not mean that they maintain what I have been denying, namely that virtue ethics is not normative; rather, they assume that it does not constitute a normative *theory* (and, mindful of this fact, I have been careful to avoid describing virtue ethics as one). What is meant by a 'normative theory' in this context is not easy to pin down, but, roughly, a normative theory is taken to be a set (possibly one-membered in the case of utilitarianism) of general principles which provide a *decision procedure* for all questions about how to act morally.

Part of the point of distinguishing a normative ethics by calling it a normative 'theory' is that a decent theory, as we know from science,

---

[15] I have chosen this description of the sort of dilemmas with which I am concerned deliberately, mindful of Philippa Foot's paper, 'Moral Realism and Moral Dilemma', *The Journal of Philosophy* 80 (1983), 379–98. As she points out, some cases that are discussed as 'conflicts' or 'dilemmas' are taken to be resolvable, that is, taken to be cases in which we do reach a conclusion we think is the right one; these are my cases of 'apparent' conflict. Commenting on Wiggins (see below, n. 18), she also points out that undecidability may exist 'in small moral matters, or where the choice is between goods rather than evils, only it doesn't worry us' (395); I am concentrating on the ones that worry us.

[16] See S. Clarke and E. Simpson (eds.), *Anti-Theory in Ethics and Moral Conservatism* (New York, 1989), containing, *inter alia*, articles by Baier, McDowell, MacIntyre, and Nussbaum, as well as Cheryl N. Noble's seminal 'Normative Ethical Theories' (49–64). It is noteworthy that, in the latter, Noble explicitly denies that she is attacking the idea of normative *ethics*. Her criticisms of the idea of normative ethical *theory*, she says, 'are aimed at a particular conception of what normative ethics should be' (62, n. 1).

enables us to answer questions that we could not answer before we had it. It is supposed to resolve those difficult dilemmas in which, it is said, our moral intuitions clash, and, prior to our grasp of the theory, we do not know what we should do.[17] And a large part of the motivation for subscribing to 'anti-theory in ethics' is the belief that we should not be looking to science to provide us with our model of moral knowledge. Our 'intuitions' in ethics do not play the same role *vis-à-vis* the systematic articulation of moral knowledge as our 'observations' play *vis-à-vis* the systematic articulation of scientific knowledge; many of the goals appropriate to scientific knowledge—universality, consistency, completeness, simplicity—are not appropriate to moral knowledge; the acquisition of moral knowledge involves the training of the emotions in a way that the acquisition of scientific knowledge does not; and so on.

Clearly, many different issues are involved in the question of the extent to which moral knowledge should be modelled on scientific knowledge. The one I want to focus on here is the issue of whether a normative ethics should provide a decision procedure which enables us to resolve all moral dilemmas. Should it, to rephrase the question I asked above, (1) direct us to think about moral dilemmas in the belief that they *must* have a resolution, and that it is the business of the normative ethics in question to provide one? Or should it (2) have built into it the possibility of there being, as David Wiggins puts it, some 'absolutely undecidable questions—e.g. cases where . . . nothing could count as *the* reasonable practical answer',[18] counting questions about dilemmas of the sort described as amongst them? Or should it (3) be sufficiently flexible to allow for a comprehensible disagreement on this issue between two proponents of the normative ethics in question?

If we are to avoid modelling normative ethics mindlessly on scientific theory, we should not simply assume that the first position is the correct

[17] As Noble points out, a normative theory may also be expected to say something about cases 'where we have no intuitions or where our intuitions are inchoate or weak' (ibid. 61); and, to some of us, it is indeed one of the oddities of utilitarianism that certain states of affairs, concerning which we may have no moral intuitions at all, emerge from it as so definitively 'morally better' than others. I would like to argue for the incoherence of the idea that a theory could attach a truth-value to a sentence (employing a moral term) which lacked a sense outside the theory, but space does not permit. See, however, P. Foot, 'Utilitarianism and the Virtues', *Mind* 94 (1985), 196–209.

[18] D. Wiggins, 'Truth, Invention and the Meaning of Life', *Proceedings of the British Academy* 62 (1976), 371, my italics. I have omitted the phrase that attracted Foot's criticism (see above, n. 15), in which Wiggins seems to imply that undecidable questions are undecidable *because* the alternatives are particularly terrible.

one. But rejection of such a model is not enough to justify the second position either. Someone might believe that for *any* dilemma there must be something that counts as the right way out of it, without believing that normative ethics remotely resembles scientific theory, perhaps because they subscribe to a version of realism (in Dummett's sense of 'realism').[19] More particularly, someone might believe on religious grounds that if I find myself, through no fault of my own, confronted with a dilemma (of the sort described), there must be something that counts as the right way out of it.[20] The belief in God's providence does indeed involve, as Geach says, the thought that 'God does not require of a faithful servant the desperate choice between sin and sin.'[21] Should a normative ethics be such that it cannot be shared by a realist and an anti-realist (again in Dummett's sense)? Or by an atheist and a theist? It seems to me that a normative ethics should be able to accommodate such differences, and so I subscribe to the third position outlined above.

Which position utilitarians and deontologists might espouse is not my concern here; I want to make clear how it is that virtue ethics is able to accommodate the third.[22]

Let us return to V1—'An action is right iff it is what a virtuous agent would characteristically do in the circumstances.' This makes it clear that if two people disagree about the possibility of irresolvable moral dilemmas, their disagreement will manifest itself in what they say about the virtue of agents. So let us suppose that two candidates for being virtuous agents are each faced with their own case of the same dilemma. (I

---

[19] M. Dummett, *Truth and Other Enigmas* (London, 1978), 1–24 and 145–65. For a brief but helpful discussion of the distinction between Dummett-type realism and cognitivism in ethics, see Foot, 'Moral Realism and Moral Dilemma', 397–8.

[20] I am assuming that the qualification 'through no fault of my own' is all-important, since I cannot imagine why anyone should think (except through oversight) that there must always be a right action I can do to get myself out of any mess that I have got myself into through previous wrongdoing.   [21] P. Geach, *The Virtues* (Cambridge, 1977), 155.

[22] I had hitherto overlooked the possibility of this third position, and hence had emphasized the fact that virtue ethics could occupy the second. But I subsequently heard Philippa Foot point out that Aquinas, Anscombe, and Geach should surely be classified as virtue ethicists, notwithstanding their absolutist stance on many of the familiar deontological rules; and, given their consequent stance on the clear resolvability of some dilemmas that others find irresolvable, this prompted me to look at what a commitment to resolvability (with respect to dilemmas *as described*) might look like within virtue ethics. I am grateful to the editor for reminding me of the further possibility of his own 'realist' position. (Aristotle is clearly an absolutist too, at least with respect to 'adultery' (*moikheia*), theft, and murder (see *NE* 1107ᵃ11–12), but where he stands (or should stand, to be consistent) on irresolvable dilemmas of the sort described is, I think, entirely unclear.)

do not want to defend the view that each situation is unique in such a way that nothing would count as two agents being in the same circumstances and faced with the same dilemma.) And, after much thought, one does A and the other does B.

Now, those who believe that there cannot be irresolvable dilemmas (of the sort described) can say that, in the particular case, at least one agent, say the one who did A, thereby showed themselves to be lacking in virtue, perhaps in that practical wisdom which is an essential aspect of each of the 'non-intellectual' virtues. ('If you can *see* no way out but a lie, the lie may be the least wicked of the alternatives you can discern: it is still wicked, and you should blame yourself that you lacked the wisdom of St. Joan or St. Athanasius, to extricate yourself without lying. It is not a matter of foxy cleverness; "the testimony of the LORD is sure and giveth wisdom to the simple".'[23] Thus Geach, discussing the absolute prohibition against lying in the context of the claim that God 'does not require of any man a choice between sin and sin'.) Or they can say that at least one agent must have been lacking in virtue, without claiming to know which.

But those who believe that there are, or may be, irresolvable dilemmas can suppose that both agents are not merely candidates for being, but actually are, virtuous agents. For to believe in such dilemmas is to believe in cases in which even the perfect practical wisdom that the most idealized virtuous agent has does not direct her to do, say, A rather than B. And then the fact that these virtuous agents acted differently, despite being in the same circumstances, *determines* the fact that there is no answer to the question 'What is *the* right thing to do in these circumstances?' For if it is true both that *a* virtuous agent would do A, and that *a* virtuous agent would do B (as it is, since, *ex hypothesi*, one did do A and the other B), then both A and B are, in the circumstances, right, according to Vi.

The acceptance of this should not be taken as a counsel of despair, nor as an excuse for moral irresponsibility. It does not license coin-tossing when one is faced with a putative dilemma, for the moral choices we find most difficult do not come to us conveniently labelled as 'resolvable' or 'irresolvable'. I was careful to specify that the two candidates for being virtuous agents acted only 'after much thought'. It will always be necessary to think very hard before accepting the idea that a particular moral decision does not have one right issue, and, even on

---

[23] Geach, *The Virtues*, 121.

the rare occasions on which she eventually reached the conclusion that this is such a case, would the virtuous agent toss a coin? Of course not.

No doubt someone will say, 'Well, if she really thinks the dilemma is irresolvable, why not, according to virtue ethics?', and the answer must, I think, be *ad hominem*. *If* their conception of the virtuous agent—of someone with the character traits of justice, honesty, compassion, kindness, loyalty, wisdom, etc.—really is of someone who would resort to coin-tossing when confronted with what she believed to be an irresolvable dilemma, then that is the bizarre conception they bring to virtue ethics, and they must, presumably, think that there is nothing morally irresponsible or light-minded about coin-tossing in such cases. So they should not want virtue ethics to explain 'why not'. But if their conception of the virtuous agent does not admit of her acting thus—if they think such coin-tossing would be irresponsible, or light-minded, or indeed simply insane—then they have no need to ask the question. *My* question was, 'Would the virtuous agent toss a coin?'; they agree that of course she would not. Why not? Because it would be irresponsible, or light-minded, or the height of folly.

The acceptance of the possibility of irresolvable dilemmas within virtue ethics (by those of us who do accept it) should not be seen in itself as conceding much to 'pluralism'. If I say that I can imagine a case in which two virtuous agents are faced with a dilemma, and one does A while the other does B, I am not saying that I am imagining a case in which the two virtuous agents each think that what the other does is wrong (vicious, contrary to virtue) because they have radically different views about what is required by a certain virtue, or about whether a certain character trait is a vice, or about whether something is to be greatly valued or of little importance. I am imagining a case in which my two virtuous agents have the same 'moral views' about everything, up to and including the view that, in this particular case, neither decision is *the* right one, and hence neither is wrong. Each recognizes the propriety of the other's reason for doing what she did—say, 'To avoid *that* evil', 'To secure *this* good'—for her recognition of the fact that this is as good a moral reason as her own (say, 'To avoid *this* evil', 'To secure *that* good') is what forced each to accept the idea that the dilemma was irresolvable in the first place. Though each can give such a reason for what they did (A in one case, B in the other), neither attempts to give 'the moral reason' why they did one *rather than* the other. The 'reason' for or explanation of *that* would be, if available at all, in terms of psychological autobiography ('I decided to sleep on it, and when I woke up I just found myself thinking in terms of doing A', or 'I just felt terrified at the thought of doing A: I'm sure this was totally irrational, but I did, so I did B').[24]

The topic of this chapter has been the view that virtue ethics cannot be a normative rival to utilitarianism and deontology because 'it cannot tell us what we should do'. In defending the existence of normative virtue ethics I have not attempted to argue that it can 'tell us what we should do' in such a way that the difficult business of acting well is made easy for us. I have not only admitted but welcomed the fact that, in some cases, moral wisdom is required if the v-rules are to be applied correctly and apparent dilemmas thereby resolved (or indeed identified, since a choice that may seem quite straightforward to the foolish or wicked may rightly appear difficult, calling for much thought, to the wise). Nor have I attempted to show that virtue ethics is guaranteed to be able to resolve every dilemma. It seems bizarre to insist that a normative ethics must be able to do this prior to forming a reasonable belief that there cannot be irresolvable dilemmas, but those who have formed such a belief may share a normative ethics with those who have different views concerning realism, or the existence of God. A normative ethics, I suggested, should be able to accommodate both views on this question, as virtue ethics does, not model itself mindlessly on scientific theory.[25]

---

[24] It must be remembered that, *ex hypothesi*, these are things said by virtuous agents about what they did when confronted with an irresolvable dilemma. Of course they would be very irresponsible accounts of why one had done A rather than B in a resolvable case.

[25] At the request of the editor, I have repeated here several points I have made in two other papers, 'Virtue Theory and Abortion', *Philosophy and Public Affairs* 20 (1991), 223–46, and 'Applying Virtue Ethics', in *Virtues and Reasons: Philippa Foot and Moral Theory*, ed. R. Hursthouse, G. Lawrence, and W. S. Quinn (Oxford, 1995), 57–75.

3

The Virtues: Theory and Common
Sense in Greek Philosophy

T. H. IRWIN

---

1. COMMON SENSE

'Can you tell me, Socrates, whether virtue is taught? Or is it not taught, but acquired by practice? Or is it neither acquired by practice nor learnt, but does it arise in people by nature or in some other way?' (*Meno* 70^{a}1–4). This is Meno's first question to Socrates in Plato's *Meno*. Meno's question suggests that he is familiar with virtue and is interested in acquiring it. The investigation of virtue is not a philosopher's question whose point has to be explained to non-philosophers. On the contrary, Greek common sense already recognizes the virtues as appropriate and important topics of moral reflection.

Meno implies that he not only is interested in virtue, but also has a firm view about what the virtues are. He describes the virtue of a man as 'being well-equipped for doing the city's business, and in doing so to treat his friends well and to treat his enemies badly, while taking care to suffer no bad treatment himself' (71^{e}3–5; see 91^{a}1–6). He describes the virtue of a woman with equal confidence, and claims that it is equally easy to describe the virtues of children, old men, males, females, free people, and slaves; each action and period of life has its own virtue in relation to its own proper function (72^{a}1–5). Once again there is nothing eccentric in Meno's views about the division and articulation of the virtues. Since there are many different social roles, there are also many virtues, and Meno accepts quite a long list of them (74^{a}4–6).

Meno's views about virtue are summed up in Aristotle's account of the common-sense view of virtue as 'a capacity to provide and protect goods' and 'a capacity for conferring many and great benefits, and all sorts of benefits on all occasions' (*Rhetoric* 1366^{a}36–^{b}1). The different virtues (or 'parts' of virtue, 1366^{b}1) are distinguished by the different sorts of benefits and good results to be expected from each of them.

This description confirms a suggestion of Meno's remarks, that virtues are directed towards specific practical results. We have some conception of the sorts of actions that we expect from people in different social roles, and the virtues are the tendencies that reliably produce such actions. If this is how we conceive the virtues, our conception of them need not demand any particular pattern of beliefs or motives in the agent, as long as the actions are appropriate. Later in the *Meno*, indeed, Anytus suggests that if we want to acquire the virtues, we need only imitate the behaviour of people who are recognized as virtuous already (91^{a}6–93^{a}4).

Aristotle also insists that a virtue must be fine, and therefore praiseworthy (*Rhet.* 1366^{a}33–6). It becomes fine and praiseworthy by being directed to the benefit of others; and so if virtue is a capacity for conferring benefits, the greatest virtues must be those that are most useful to others (*Rhet.* 1366^{b}3–4). Aristotle's appeal to this description of virtue shows that he takes 'conferring benefits' to mean 'conferring benefits on others'. Aristotle takes this other-directed aspect of virtue to be part of the ordinary conception of virtue. It is not so prominent in Meno's remarks. Still, Meno recognizes the other-directed aspect of virtue. After some discussion he admits that justice and temperance seem to be common features of the different sorts of virtuous people that he has described (73^{a}6–^{c}5). He does not explain how the (apparently) self-regarding aspects of 'the virtue of a man', as he initially described it, conform to the demand for justice and temperance.

The other-directed virtues raise the question whether it will always be in the agent's interest to do what the virtues require. Some of Plato's contemporaries answer 'No.' When Neoptolemus in Sophocles' *Philoctetes* faces the choice between following Odysseus' advice and remaining loyal to Philoctetes, he allows that Odysseus' advice suggests the wiser course of action, but insists that this course of action would also be 'shameful' (*aischron*, opposite of 'fine', *kalon*), and therefore must be rejected; and so he concludes that if an action is just, that is better than being wise (*Ph.* 1234, 1245–6). This attitude to virtue and self-interest is summed up by Polus in Plato's *Gorgias*, who claims that it is finer to be just than to be unjust, even if one has to suffer other people's injustice, but it is more beneficial to be unjust, if one has the chance to commit injustice on others for one's own benefit (*Gorgias* 474^{c}4–^{d}2). If we agree with Polus, it is natural to say that it is not always in my interest to be virtuous. On the other hand, Thrasymachus in Plato's

Republic assumes that if justice is not beneficial to the just agent, it follows that it is not a virtue (*Rep.* 348^{b}8–349^{a}3).

We have now said enough about common-sense views of virtue to show where the philosophers start from and what they try to do. Common-sense views characteristically include these beliefs about the virtues:

1. The virtues are directed towards action; their point is to cause the agent to do the actions that we count (for whatever reason) as desirable.
2. There are different virtues for different people, corresponding to their different circumstances and social roles.
3. The virtues are separable; if we have one of them, it does not follow that we have all the others.
4. They are fine, and hence the agent is praiseworthy for them.
5. They are not necessarily good for the agent, since they require disadvantageous actions.
6. They do not require knowledge or intellectual understanding; they require the right intuitive responses to particular situations, and moral training should aim at producing these responses.

Plato's dialogues suggest that these claims about the virtues would elicit widespread agreement; and Aristotle's remarks do not suggest a radically different picture of common-sense views. Moreover, these views are not unfamiliar or unintelligible to us. Most of us would not immediately reject them if they were said to apply to a morally good or admirable person.

The main tendency of Greek moral philosophy is to reject all these common-sense claims except for the fourth; indeed, philosophers tend to argue that if we retain the fourth claim, we must reject the other five. In arguing against common sense on these five points, Greek philosophers develop versions of a philosophical theory of the virtues. In this essay I will focus primarily on Socrates, Plato, Aristotle, and the Stoics. The views of these philosophers differ sharply on many issues about the virtues, and I will mention some of the main differences; on the whole, however, I will focus especially on points of similarity.

2. THE SUPERORDINATE STATUS OF VIRTUE

In Aristotle's view, 'the virtues arise in us neither by nature nor contrary to nature; we are naturally receptive of them, but we are completed through habit' (*Nicomachean Ethics* (*NE*) 1103ᵃ23–6). Aristotle assumes that by having the virtues we are 'completed' (or 'perfected'), and that therefore any condition that fails to complete us cannot count as a virtue of character.

It is easy to see how some of the recognized virtues might be included in a list of valuable 'assets' or 'resources' that we would like to have at our disposal in living our lives. Socrates mentions, among other things, wealth, health, advantages of birth, abilities, and honour (*Euthydemus* 279a–b). Among resources we can also include some traits or tendencies of mind or character. Some control of fear, some ability to resist the temptations of pleasure, and some ability to think of means to ends are all benefits in any person's life.

The Greek moralists, however, believe that if we simply list the virtues among assets or resources, we have not captured the distinctive feature of the virtues that 'completes' or 'perfects' us. Completion requires the right use of resources, but mere possession of resources does not guarantee their right use (*Euthd.* 280d–e). Aristotle, indeed, suggests that liability to misuse is 'a common feature of all goods, except virtue' (*Rhet.* 1355ᵇ4–5). The Stoics rely on the same point in order to explain their use of 'good': 'What can be used both well or badly is not good; but wealth and health can be used both well and badly; hence wealth and health are not goods' (Diogenes Laertius 7. 103). Only the virtuous person knows the correct use of these assets, and that is why 'the good person is the one for whom the natural goods are good' (Aristotle, *Eudemian Ethics* (= *EE*) 1248ᵇ26–7); only the good person uses assets correctly. As long as we describe abilities or states of character that can be used either well or badly, we are not describing virtues; once we find some state of character that needs nothing else to ensure its correct use, we have found a virtue. Let us call this claim about virtues the 'supremacy thesis'.

3. VIRTUE AND HAPPINESS

If we can recognize goods that are assets and resources, and we can also see why they need to be used well, we must also have some conception of the goal in the light of which they are to be co-ordinated and used well. Greek moralists agree that the relevant goal is the agent's happiness (*eudaimonia*). They believe this because they accept a version of eudaemonism—that if *S* is a rational agent, the ultimate end that

S has reason to pursue in all of *S*'s actions is *S*'s own happiness. Aristotle believes that a rational agent must organize his life around a conception of happiness, because happiness is something 'complete' and 'self-sufficient', including every good that deserves pursuit (*NE* 1097^{b}6–21).[1] To organize our lives around a complete end is to introduce some structure into our lives and our ends.[2] If we refused to look at our lives in this way, we would be failing to see the implications of some facts about our ends and our attitudes to them. (1) We do not in fact think of our ends as simply a list; we have some view about whether we prefer A to B and A to C, and whether we prefer A to the combination of B and C. (2) We must admit that we face questions about the relative weight of different ends. If we decide these questions on particular occasions without reference to a conception of our lives as a whole, we may be making decisions we shall regret, because our decision on one occasion will not refer to all the ends that (we agree on reflection) ought to be considered in deciding between these options.

Aristotle claims, then, that, given what we care about and have reason to care about in our lives, it would be foolish not to organize them around some conception of our lives as wholes (*EE* 1214^{b}6–14), a conception that expresses our considered views about the relative importance of different ends and of how they ought to fit together, restrain each other, or enhance each other. This conception of an all-embracing plan for organizing one's life explains why the Stoics identify happiness with 'living coherently' (*homologoumenōs zēn*, Diogenes Laertius 7. 85–9). They are expressing the point that Aristotle expresses in claiming that happiness should be something whole and complete, so that our life is not just a series of unco-ordinated pursuits of different ends. When we live 'coherently', we have found a conception of our lives that makes our different ends fit together in some rational structure.

4. EUDAEMONISM AND THE VIRTUES

If we accept both the eudaemonist claim and the supremacy thesis about the virtues, then we must conclude that the virtues are the best states for promoting the agent's happiness. For if the eudaemonist claim

---

[1] The interpretation of 'self-sufficient' is disputed. See, e.g., R. Kraut, *Aristotle on the Human Good* (Princeton, NJ, 1989), ch. 5.

[2] See T. H. Irwin, *Aristotle's First Principles* (Oxford, 1988), § 192.

is correct, but the virtues are not the best states for promoting the agent's happiness, then a rational agent must regulate virtue by reference to some superordinate principle, to make sure that her virtue does not interfere with her happiness; in that case the supremacy thesis must be false. Since the supremacy thesis implies that no principle is superordinate to virtue, a eudaemonist must regard virtue as the best state for promoting the agent's happiness.

The virtues might satisfy this constraint in different ways. Socrates and the Stoics believe that virtue is actually sufficient for happiness; Plato and Aristotle maintain the more moderate claim that the virtuous person is in all circumstances happier than anyone else. But all these moralists agree in insisting that virtuous people must improve their degree of happiness by being virtuous, and that no one can improve their degree of happiness as much by any other course of action. Let us say that they agree on a 'eudaemonist constraint' on virtue.

This eudaemonist constraint may seem unwarranted and unduly optimistic; worse still, it may seem to conflict with the attitude characteristic of a morally virtuous person. We are inclined to object—with some support from Greek common sense—that not every virtue always satisfies the eudaemonist constraint; the other-regarding virtues seem to violate it rather conspicuously. When a virtue violates the eudaemonist constraint, we might suppose that we expect virtuous people to set aside their own happiness, and to follow the virtuous course of action even at severe cost to themselves.

If we think of the virtues this way, we may infer that eudaemonism is actually inconsistent with the supremacy thesis; the eudaemonist constraint tries to fit the supremacy thesis into a eudaemonist framework, but (we might suppose) misinterprets the supremacy thesis. The supremacy thesis expresses quite widespread assumptions about the overriding status of morality in relation to other aims. We may well suppose that the supremacy thesis implies the superiority of virtue over the demands of the agent's happiness, and that therefore the Greek moralists really reject the supremacy thesis in accepting the eudaemonist constraint.

The Greek moralists do not take seriously the possibility of rejecting the eudaemonist constraint. If they rejected it, they would be admitting that virtue does not determine the character of the all-embracing plan of virtuous agents for organizing their lives; and then it would be difficult to see how virtue could reasonably determine a rational person's aims. For this reason Greek moralists assume that we cannot defend the supremacy of virtue without accepting the eudaemonist constraint.

5. THE RELATION OF VIRTUE TO HAPPINESS

If we accept the eudaemonist constraint, however, we still have not said how exactly the virtues contribute to the agent's happiness. Socrates might be taken to suggest that virtue is a superordinate productive craft (*technē*), regulating the use of the other crafts so as to achieve happiness.[3] On this view, virtue has an instrumental function just as the other crafts have; and if it is to fulfil this instrumental function, it must rely on some fairly definite conception of happiness that is settled independently of the choices of the virtuous person. A craft that regulates the manufacture of cars will not succeed if it has to make up a conception of a well-made car as it goes along; it must presuppose a conception of the end it is aiming at.

This Socratic conception of virtue as a superordinate craft is accepted by Epicurus, who recognizes that it implies a strictly instrumental status for the virtues.[4] It is rejected, however, by other moralists, who believe that it misrepresents the relation of virtuous action to happiness. If we treat virtue as simply a superordinate craft, then we imply that virtuous actions are to be chosen simply for their consequences, and that if we could gain the same consequences without virtuous action, we would have lost nothing of intrinsic value. Virtue, however, cannot (according to critics of the instrumental view) have purely instrumental status; we should not suppose that virtuous people have to take some independent conception of happiness as the starting-point of their deliberations and that their deliberations are purely instrumental.

Aristotle expresses this objection to a purely instrumental conception of virtue by distinguishing 'production' (*poiēsis*) from 'action' (*praxis*). Production is strictly instrumental, in so far as its end is related to it purely causally, so that the end is something external to the productive process itself. Action, however, is not aimed exclusively at an end outside the action itself; 'for good action itself is the end' (*NE* 1140^{b}6–7). For this reason Aristotle rejects the identification of a virtue with a craft. In his view, happiness is partly constituted by virtuous action, and should not be regarded as an external end to which virtue is purely instrumental.

---

[3] There is room for dispute about whether Socrates actually believes that virtue is a sort of craft, or simply accepts the analogy within limits.

[4] This view is suggested in Plutarch, *Non posse suaviter vivi* 1091b (see H. Usener, *Epicurea* (Leipzig, 1887), § 423); *Adversus Colotem* 1108c (Usener, § 512).

These views about the relation of virtue to happiness underlie both Plato's and Aristotle's demand that the virtuous person should choose virtue and virtuous action for its own sake, and not simply for its consequences; the distinction between virtuous action and instrumental production explains why this demand on the virtuous person is consistent with the eudaemonist constraint. In Plato's *Republic*, Glaucon and Adeimantus demand a defence of justice as a good to be chosen for its own sake, and not simply for the sake of its consequences (*Rep.* 357ᵃ1–358ᵃ3, 366ᵈ7–367ᵉ5).[5] Aristotle expresses the same demand when he insists that it is characteristic of the virtuous person to decide on the virtuous action for its own sake (*NE* 1105ᵃ32).

The Stoics accept this Platonic and Aristotelian demand, while identifying virtue with a 'craft concerned with the whole of life'.[6] Every virtuous action is also an 'appropriate action' (*kathēkon*),[7] and appropriate actions are reasonable efforts to achieve objectives that are distinct from virtue; the Stoics call these objectives 'the primary things according to nature', which are 'preferred indifferents'. To this extent it is reasonable to identify virtue with a craft. On the other hand, the characteristic action of a virtuous person is not merely an appropriate action, but a 'successful action' (*katorthōma*). This is a 'complete' appropriate action;[8] it differs from an incomplete appropriate action in being performed in the right way, so that, for instance, if returning a deposit is an appropriate action, returning it justly is a successful action (Cicero, *De Finibus* 3. 59). The relevant success is not success in reaching the preferred external results (Sextus, *Against the Mathematicians* 11. 200). The virtuous person's doing the appropriate actions for the right reason, because of their appropriateness, constitutes the distinguishing feature of virtue, and therefore constitutes the success proper to successful action. Hence happiness and virtue are constituted by 'acting reasonably in the selection of things according to nature' and by 'living completing all the appropriate actions' (Diogenes Laertius 7. 88).

By defining virtuous action in this way the Stoics try to accommodate two of its essential features: (1) It is essentially aimed at some nonmoral advantage, and to that extent has an instrumental role. If it did

---

[5] On the interpretation of *Republic* ii I mostly agree with C. Kirwan, 'Glaucon's challenge', *Phronesis* 10 (1965), 162–73. Contrast N. White, 'The Classification of Goods in Plato's *Republic*', *Journal of the History of Philosophy* 22 (1984), 393–421.

[6] Stobaeus, *Eclogae* 2. 67. 1, ed. C. Wachsmuth (Berlin, 1884). See A. A. Long and D. N. Sedley, *The Hellenistic Philosophers*, 2 vols. (Cambridge, 1987; cited hereafter as 'LS'), § 61G.   [7] On appropriate actions see LS § 59.

[8] See Stobaeus, *Eclogae* 2. 93. 14–16 = LS 59K.

not have this role, we could not understand why virtuous people want to reduce other people's undeserved and unnecessary suffering rather than add to it, or why they want wealth and honour to be distributed to those who deserve it instead of remaining with one person. Virtuous people have these concerns because they believe it is reasonable (in appropriate circumstances) to seek to avoid suffering and to achieve wealth and honour; if they did not take this attitude to non-moral advantages and disadvantages, their virtuous actions would not be directed at the promotion of the advantages and the prevention or reduction of the disadvantages. (2) Virtuous action is also to be valued for its own sake, as an exercise of practical reason aiming at these non-moral advantages; that is why happiness cannot be completely external to virtuous action.[9]

6. VIRTUES, ACTIONS, AND MOTIVES

The conception of virtue that emerges from the supremacy thesis and the eudaemonist constraint already departs some way from common sense. Common sense connects virtues with actions; philosophical theories, on the other hand, emphasize knowledge, motives, intentions, and desires—features of the virtuous agent that need not make a direct difference to action. What explains this shift away from the common sense focus on action?

One reason becomes clear when we notice the difficulty of giving an account of the actions that we expect from each virtue. The Socratic dialogues suggest that it is difficult to give an account of virtuous action in purely behavioural terms. If we start out by suggesting that the brave person is the one who stands firm in battle (Plato, *Laches* 190^e4–6), never retreats, and is never afraid in the face of danger, we must admit that it is sometimes reasonable to retreat and sometimes reasonable to be afraid, and that moreover we would expect the brave person to see that these things are reasonable. Someone who was so anxious to avoid seeming cowardly that he would hazard the life of his companions and the prospects of success for their cause rather than retreat would simply be a danger to himself and others; and someone who was so fearless

---

[9] The Stoics actually identify virtue with happiness. I have explored some of their reasons in 'Stoic and Aristotelian Conceptions of Happiness', in M. Schofield and G. Striker (eds.), *The Norms of Nature* (Cambridge, 1986), ch. 8.

that he refused to take reasonable precautions and faced danger even when there was nothing to be gained by it would be merely foolish (see Aristotle, *NE* 1115^{b}24–32). In both cases we would expect the brave person to recognize the considerations that tell in favour of retreat or precautions; for he should be especially good at telling the difference between genuine bravery and the foolish and dangerous attitudes that are easily confused with it. And so we must give up the simple behavioural account of bravery.

If we add qualifications and say that the brave person stands firm unless it is better to retreat, or that he is unafraid except when fear is appropriate, we are giving up any attempt to define the virtue by appeal to behavioural rules that can be applied without the further exercise of moral judgement. In some cases it will take a brave person to weigh the relevant considerations and to decide what the brave action is; in such cases we will have to say, as Aristotle says, that the virtuous action is the one that the virtuous person would do (*NE* 1105^{b}5–7). In these cases we will have to abandon any attempt to say what the virtuous person does by appeal to rules whose content can be specified independently of the virtuous person's judgement; 'these matters fall among particulars, and the judgement depends on perception' (*NE* 1109^{b}22–3).

This difficulty in defining virtue in purely behavioural terms helps to explain why the philosophers turn from actions to states of character. The supremacy thesis requires virtue to regulate the use of other goods. But if we cannot regulate the use of other goods appropriately by simply acquiring a tendency to behave in accordance with rules that can be specified in purely behavioural terms, then a virtue cannot be identified with such a tendency. It must be identified with the state of virtuous agents that equips them to supplement the behavioural rules in the ways that are required by the right regulation of other goods.

This objection to purely behavioural accounts of the virtues should not be exaggerated. The philosophers do not deny that we can form a reasonable, though non-exhaustive, view about the actions to be expected of a virtuous person; judgements about virtuous actions are not wholly dependent on the virtuous person's judgement. If the actions of a supposedly just person aim at harming other people for his own benefit, then he is not a just person. We do not depend on the virtuous person's judgement for the identification of virtuous actions or virtuous people; in fact, Aristotle's descriptions of the different virtues of character imply that he thinks we can form reasonable judgements about what is to be expected of a virtuous person who forms the right attitude to danger, bodily pleasure, wealth, honour, anger, and so on.

Nor does an emphasis on character imply that action is unimportant, or that the results secured by the action are unimportant. The Stoics describe virtue, and therefore happiness, as doing all we can to secure non-moral goods.[10] In describing virtue in these terms, the Stoics insist that the virtuous person must care about the preferred indifferents—the non-moral goods that, in the Stoic view, are neither parts of nor means to happiness. They agree with common sense in believing that health and security are preferable to their opposites, and that this fact explains why we expect the virtuous person to promote these results rather than their opposites. The character of virtuous action should not be unintelligible to us if we have reasonable views about what results deserve to be promoted or prevented.

These reasons for identifying a virtue with a state of character rather than a purely behavioural tendency are consistent with a purely instrumental conception of the relation of virtue to happiness. If, however, we reject the instrumental conception, we have a further reason for emphasis on character rather than action; for we may claim that we care about virtuous character for its own sake, apart from its behavioural results. This is not our only reason for caring about character. A genuinely kind person is preferable to someone who simply does the kind action in order to look good, because the kind person will keep on doing the kind action in cases where other people benefit just as much but the kindness will not be as conspicuous to others. To this extent the virtue is a more reliable producer of virtuous actions than a substitute for the virtue would be. But this is not the whole story. Plato and Aristotle assume that even in cases where there is no behavioural difference we still value the person who chooses the virtuous action for its own sake over the person who chooses it for its consequences (see *NE* 1144ᵃ1–3, 11–20).

This claim about the intrinsic value of virtuous character rests on the plausible assumption that we care about what people—ourselves or others—are like, and not simply about what they do. We care about how other people think of us—not simply about how we predict they will act towards us; and in deciding what to think of other people we care about how they look at questions of value, not simply about what they do about them.

---

[10] See Stobaeus, *Eclogae* 2. 76. 11–15 (Wachsmuth) = LS § 58K. The Stoics do not regard external goods (as Aristotle describes them) as strictly good.

For some purposes, admittedly, questions about what other people are like are unimportant in comparison with questions about what they will do. But not all moral relations with other people are like this. In some cases I care about another person's outlook; and to the extent that I care about it, it is reasonable to focus on character independently of the actions that are likely to result from it.

This attitude to character is reasonable if we accept the supremacy thesis and the eudaemonist constraint. Virtue contributes to the agent's happiness because it is the appropriate ordering of the agent's rational and non-rational desires and aims. In so far as we have reason to want our desires and aims to be regulated in this way, we have reason to want the virtues of character. The virtuous person cares about being virtuous primarily because this is the appropriate exercise of practical reason; this is the aspect of virtue that makes it part of a rational agent's good.

7. VIRTUE AND KNOWLEDGE

If a virtue is to be identified primarily with a state of character, what sort of state is relevant? The Greek moralists disagree about the relative importance of rational and non-rational aspects of character. When Socrates identifies virtue with a superordinate craft, he suggests that it is knowledge of instrumental means to happiness; we have seen how most of his successors reject that suggestion. He also implies that knowledge is sufficient for virtue, that our account of what distinguishes a virtuous from a vicious person does not need to mention any essential difference in desire except the differences that are explained by degrees of knowledge or ignorance. In Socrates' view, the fault in vicious people is not that their desires are turned in the wrong direction, but that they are ignorant of how to achieve their own good; knowledge of the appropriate instrumental means would make them virtuous.

Part of this view must be rejected if we reject an instrumental conception of the relation of virtue to happiness. If virtuous and vicious people have a different view of the components of their happiness, vicious people cannot be converted simply by acquiring different beliefs about instrumental means; they must come to a different view about the nature and character of their own good, and this difference in outlook requires a basic reconsideration of their aims in life. A change in moral outlook cannot simply be a change in strategy, and the development of a virtue cannot simply be the mastery of a particular strategy for securing goods that everyone recognizes as good.[11]

But even if we disagree with Socrates on this point, we might still suppose that virtue is simply the result of rational deliberation about one's own good, and that when we accept the right conclusions from our deliberation, we will have become virtuous. Socrates recognizes that most people suppose there is more to virtue than knowledge of one's own good; even if we know what is best, they say, it is still possible to fail to do it, if we are overcome by non-rational desires. Anger, laziness, sexual appetite, hunger, thirst, and so on, seem to provide clear examples of desires that can persist and be effective even when we realize that it would be bad for us on a particular occasion to be guided by them (Plato, *Protagoras* 352b–c). Action on such desires displays 'incontinence' (*akrasia*, Aristotle, *NE* 1145^{b}12–14) or 'weakness of will'. Socrates believes that when we appear to act on these non-rational motives, we are really acting on sheer ignorance about our good. Plato argues against him (*Rep.* 436b–441c) that some desires do, and some do not, respond to reasoning about the good, and those that do not can cause an agent to act incontinently.[12]

If we agree with Plato in recognizing non-rational as well as rational desires, we cannot agree with the Socratic view that acquiring a virtue consists simply in grasping and mastering a body of knowledge. Both Plato and Aristotle insist on the importance of non-rational desires in moral education. Aristotle argues that the virtues must be a result of 'habituation' (*ethismos*), training in the right sorts of pleasure and pain connected with the right sorts of action (*NE* 1103^{b}23–5). The appropriate sort of elementary habituation is needed to ensure the right harmony between rational and non-rational desires.

Aristotle is concerned to secure harmony in a virtuous person's desires, not simply because he wants to ensure the dominance of rational desires, but because he wants to avoid conflict. People who succeed in following their rational choices against their non-rational inclinations are 'continent' or self-controlled; but Aristotle does not take continence to be sufficient for virtue (*NE* 1102^{b}26–8, 1151^{b}34–1152^{a}6). In distinguishing continence from virtue, Aristotle shows that he does not think virtues are

---

[11] Epicurus may be an exception to this generalization, for the reason suggested by n. 4 above.

[12] The relation of Plato's argument to Socrates is discussed by J. Cooper, 'Plato's Theory of Human Motivation', *History of Philosophy Quarterly* 1 (1984), 3–21; M. Woods, 'Plato's Division of the Soul', *Proceedings of the British Academy* 73 (1987), 23–48.

to be defined simply by the virtuous actions they produce. For all he says, a continent person might succeed in doing the very same actions that a virtuous person does; but because the continent person suffers conflict in choosing to do the right actions, continence does not suffice for virtue. Virtue requires the appropriate attitude to the virtuous action, and the continent person has not formed this attitude.

What mistake do continent people make, in Aristotle's view? In deciding whether or not to do the virtuous action, continent people have to consider whether or not they should overcome their reluctance about doing it. But this is not the sort of thing that a virtuous person ought to be considering; and so they do not look at the action as a virtuous person should. A virtuous person is not reluctant to give up the goods that have to be given up in order to act virtuously. He is not, however, entirely single-minded in his desires; he cannot be, if he recognizes the genuine value in the things he has to give up. None the less, he is whole-hearted in his acceptance of the virtuous course of action. This attitude of being whole-hearted without being fanatically or unrealistically single-minded distinguishes the virtuous person both from the continent person, who is not whole-hearted, and from the 'insensitive' person, who has the vice of deficient feeling, and therefore is too single-minded.[13] Aristotle insists that the virtuous person must form the right sort of attachment to the virtuous action, and that this attachment cannot consist simply in a reliable tendency to follow one's correct rational judgment about what is best; the appropriate sort of attachment must involve the agent's desires as a whole.

8. THE FINE AND THE GOOD

In the light of the supremacy thesis and the eudaemonist constraint, we can understand why Greek moralists characteristically regard the virtues as states of character that in themselves partly constitute the agent's happiness. But we may wonder whether this conception of the virtues leads us too far away from the common-sense view that connects the virtues with actions, and specifically with other-regarding actions. Common sense agrees that virtuous action is characteristically fine and

---

[13] I have said a little more on the difference between continence and virtue in 'Some Rational Aspects of Incontinence', *Southern Journal of Philosophy* 27, Supp. (1988), 49–88, pp. 78–81. A different view is taken by J. McDowell, 'Virtue and Reason', *Monist* 62 (1979), 331–50.

praiseworthy, and that characteristically fine and praiseworthy actions are those that benefit other people, even at the expense of the agent. We might suppose that moralists who accept both the supremacy thesis and the eudaemonist constraint cannot also accept this commonly recognized connection between the virtues and the fine. For the eudaemonist constraint seems to imply that the virtues will be supreme only if they aim at the agent's own happiness; and in that case how can they also be reliably concerned with the good of others?

Aristotle shows that he does not intend to reject the common-sense view. For he insists that the virtuous person must choose virtuous action for its own sake and for the sake of the fine (*NE* 1122^{b}6–7). Since virtuous people choose virtuous action for its own sake because it is a part of their happiness, they must also believe that fine action is a part of their happiness precisely because it is fine. They can justifiably believe this if they can show that their own happiness is so closely connected with the happiness of others that they can reasonably aim at the good of others in pursuing their own good.

To show that the happiness of the virtuous agent is appropriately connected with the happiness of others, Aristotle appeals to his account of friendship. He argues that it is reasonable for virtuous people to have the same sort of concern for the good of others that they have for their own (self-confined) good, and that this concern is appropriately extended both to individual friends and to the good of a larger community. Once the appropriate connection of interests is understood, we can see why the virtuous person is concerned with the fine and with the good of others in the way that common sense expects.

This attempt to connect the agent's good with the good of others is characteristic of all the Greek moral theories that try to reconcile the non-instrumental status of virtue, the supremacy thesis, and the eudaemonist constraint with the other-regarding character of some of the virtues. On this view, we have good reason to pursue the moral virtues, not because we have some immediate reason to fulfil the obligations they prescribe, but because we can see that they promote the good of others and we have good reason to count this as part of our own good.

The fact that the virtues are connected with the agent's happiness, in so far as the good of others is part of his own happiness, does not mean that virtuous people must always be considering their own happiness. Aristotle contrasts concern for the fine with concern for the expedient (*NE* 1169^{a}3–6), and argues that virtuous people act for the sake of the fine; even though they recognize that being brave or just promotes their own happiness, their concern in deciding what to do is to identify the brave or just action, not to reflect (directly) on their own happiness. If virtue consists primarily in a state of character and secondarily in the actions resulting from it, the eudaemonist constraint itself may seem more reasonable. It would seem unreasonable if it required us to consider whether every single virtuous action promotes our happiness; for we might well argue that this sort of calculation is alien to the character of the virtuous person. It is more plausible to assume that questions about happiness ought to affect the choice of whether or not to acquire a state of character; for since a state of character affects the rest of our character, and hence affects the overriding aims we pursue in our lives, it is reasonable to form or maintain a state of character in the light of beliefs about the most desirable overall shape of our lives.

9. THE UNITY AND RECIPROCITY OF THE VIRTUES

If virtues must embody concern for the fine, and at the same time must conform to the supremacy thesis and the eudaemonist constraint, how many virtues will there be, and how will they be connected? Meno begins his discussion with Socrates by recognizing many virtues, corresponding to different social roles and different aspects of life. It may well seem obvious that each of the virtues is separable from the others; bravery does not seem to guarantee justice or temperance, and these do not seem to guarantee bravery. The separability of the virtues is more apparent if we recognize different virtues corresponding to different social roles; if an agent's virtues derive their point and justification from the role that the agent occupies, it is not only possible but even desirable to have one virtue without the others. We might think it is a good thing if police officers and judges are fair and scrupulous without being prone to compassion or kindness, and if our friends are kind and considerate without being sticklers for justice; for in these cases we may think the development of one virtue actually impedes another.

Despite these apparent facts, Greek moralists characteristically deny that the virtues are separable. Aristotle recognizes that it seems plausible to separate the virtues; but he believes that it seems plausible only if we confuse 'natural virtue' with 'full virtue'. Natural tendencies and abilities may make it easier for us to acquire, say, bravery rather than temperance or justice; indeed, these different natural abilities may actually work against each other if they are not properly trained. But when we have acquired the genuine virtues, this sort of tension has disappeared; we have to admit that each of these virtues requires the other. Aristotle claims that each genuine virtue requires wisdom (*phronēsis*); and since wisdom implies all the virtues, each of the virtues implies all the others (*NE* 1144^{b}32–1145^{a}2).

If the reciprocity thesis is right, then we show bravery in circumstances other than those that involve fear and endurance, temperance in circumstances other than those that involve control of appetites, and so on. Part of the argument for this claim can be gathered from the implications of some of Socrates' remarks about bravery. He argues that bravery cannot be identified with endurance, because brave action must always be fine, whereas endurance may lead us to act badly, in cases where it is foolish endurance (*La.* 192c–d). The brave person is expected to know the dangers that do and do not deserve to be faced. Worthwhile dangers do not include those that we face in robbing a bank or in carrying out some prank, and the brave person is expected to realize this. The virtues cannot, then, be distributed to different and non-overlapping spheres of action; for in this case justice is needed to show why it is reasonable to face danger in one sort of situation but not in another.

The argument for the reciprocity of the virtues becomes still stronger if we remember that we are concerned with the virtues not simply in so far as they reliably produce virtuous actions, but in so far as they include understanding of the point of virtuous action. Brave people, on this view, are not those who simply select the right actions; their selection of them must be guided by appreciation of the considerations that are relevant to their selection. If they must appreciate the relevant considerations, then they need the virtues in the light of which the genuinely relevant considerations appear relevant.

We might resist this line of argument; we might insist that it is intolerably counter-intuitive to deny that bank robbers or Don Giovanni can display bravery. But if we try this line of resistance to the reciprocity thesis, we tend to degrade each virtue to an asset that can be used either well or badly (see *Meno* 88^{b}3); and the more we treat the virtues as mere assets, the less they seem to qualify as virtues. Bravery becomes parallel to stubbornness or optimism or caution—the sort of thing that can be modified and organized to be a component of a virtue or ancillary to a virtue. But in reducing the virtues to mere assets, we fail to recognize their superordinate status. Once we accept the supremacy thesis, it is difficult to deny the reciprocity of the virtues. And so we should be less surprised that Greek moralists accept the reciprocity of the virtues; to deny it they would have to reject their basic claims about the sort of thing that a virtue has to be.

10. VIRTUES AND THE WILL

Meno begins by assuming that the virtues correspond to different patterns of action in different social roles. The philosophical reconstruction and modification of common sense leads to a different conception of the virtues, tending to identify them with states of the agent's will.[14] Success in action is neither necessary nor sufficient for virtue; for successful action does not imply the appropriate attitude, and the appropriate attitude does not guarantee success in achieving the external results that the agent seeks to achieve. When Plato seeks to prove that justice, no matter how unsuccessful in external results, is still superior to injustice, he focuses attention on the agent's outlook, and away from the results that may or may not be achieved. Aristotle expresses the same point in identifying virtue with a state that involves rational choice or decision (*prohairesis*, *NE* 1106^{b}36) rather than with a tendency to act. He does not mean that virtuous people ought not to act on their decisions; on the contrary, he insists that the expression of a virtuous state in action is preferable to simply having the state. But he does not take external success to be necessary for the virtue; he insists that virtuous agents retain their virtue even in adverse external circumstances (*NE* 1100^{b}30–5).

The Stoics emphasize this aspect of virtue especially strongly, though they are not the only ones who recognize it. In identifying virtue with what is fine and praiseworthy, we distinguish it from the external successes and failures that do not appropriately enter into praise and blame of the agent. The virtuous person chooses to do appropriate actions precisely because they are appropriate and reasonable; and an appropriate action is one that can be reasonably defended as a way to secure a nonmoral good. In saying that it can be reasonably defended, the Stoics do not mean that it must actually secure the external result it seeks to secure, but that it must be defensible in the light of what the agent knew and

---

[14] I have tried to defend this claim more fully in 'Who Discovered the Will?', *Philosophical Perspectives* 6 (1992), 453–73. For a different view see C. Kahn, 'Discovering the Will: From Aristotle to Augustine', in J. Dillon and A. Long (eds.), *The Question of 'Eclecticism'* (Berkeley, Calif., 1988), 234–59.

believed before doing the action. And so when the Stoics describe the action characteristic of the virtuous person as a 'success' (*katorthōma*), they deliberately contrast the ordinary sort of success (in achieving the preferred external result) with the different sort of success that can reasonably be demanded of the virtuous person.

In putting forward this account of virtue, the Stoics are only developing the common-sense assumption that a virtue must be a perfection of the virtuous person. They argue that if this is what we are looking for, we should identify the virtue with the perfections of persons themselves, as rational agents capable of rational decision between alternatives; we should not identify it through some reference to external success that is irrelevant to the perfection of the agents themselves. Though the conception of virtue as good use of free choice would no doubt have seemed strange and unfamiliar to Meno and his contemporaries, it can be defended as a reasonable expression of plausible and intuitive demands that are implicitly imposed on any acceptable account of a genuine virtue.

4

Partiality and the Virtues

JOHN COTTINGHAM

Much of philosophical ethics suffers from being overly impersonal. Utilitarianism, on one strongly advocated interpretation, urges on us a life of rigorous impartiality, enjoining us to push our own children to the back of the queue when there are stronger utility-claimants in line.[1] Even the 'indirect' or 'rule' versions of utility theory seem to allow us our partialities and personal ties only grudgingly: the seal of approval depends on our solemnly demonstrating (if we can) that the general institution of such preferential commitments helps maximize global utility.[2] Consequentialism's chief rival, deontological ethics, also seems to locate morality in a place well apart from our ordinary impulses of partiality. Notwithstanding the scholarship and eloquence of its defenders,[3] Kant's insistence that moral worth is reserved for the austerely motivated act of pure duty, 'uninfluenced by any sensible interest',[4] seems to bleach out the moral worth from much of our lives—conditioned as they are by the ties of partiality, the 'sensible warm motions' of the human heart.

[1] See P. Singer, *Practical Ethics* (Cambridge, 1979), 172.
[2] I have argued elsewhere, first, that such derivative justifications of partiality may not work (because they offer too many hostages to empirical calculations about the most effective means of securing global welfare), and secondly, that in any case the derivative route fails fully to accommodate fundamental intuitions we have about the individual's autonomous right to determine the shape of his or her own life. See J. Cottingham, 'The Ethics of Self-Concern', *Ethics* 101 (1991), 798–817, pp. 803–5. For an interesting account of the most plausible strategy open to the rule-consequentialist, see B. Hooker, 'Rule-consequentialism and Demandingness: a Reply to Carson', *Mind* 100 (1991), 269–76.
[3] See especially O. O'Neill, 'Kant's Virtues', Chap. 5 in this volume.
[4] Man has a higher purpose for which he possesses reason, 'namely ... to take into consideration what is good or evil in itself, about which only pure reason, uninfluenced by any sensible interest, can judge' (*Critique of Practical Reason* (1788), tr. T. K. Abbott (London, 1873), 153; cited in M. Klein, 'Morality and Justice in Kant', *Ratio* NS 3 (1990), 1–20, p. 8).

The result of this depersonalizing tendency in what are still the two leading branches of modern ethical theory is that much of the work done by philosophers of ethics has little relation to the way nearly all of us live. This is not to beat the soggy drum of 'relevance', nor has it anything much to do with the question of whether there should be more 'practical' ethics. The point, rather, is that many ethical writers, whether working at an abstract level or on concrete problems, are officially subscribing to accounts of rightness and goodness which simply do not impinge on, or make contact with, the partialistic commitments and preferential ties that deeply and pervasively inform their own lives. Such a schism between word and deed generates a problem not merely about the application of philosophical ethics, but about its very coherence; for there is a serious instability in any moral theory which urges on us attitudes that we could not in honesty conceive of incorporating into our ordinary blueprint for daily living. Such theories are always at risk, if nothing else, of violating basic rules about the meaning of normative and deontic language.[5]

Does virtue ethics fare any better?[6] In this paper I shall argue (in Part One) that the ethical excellences unfolded in the classical Aristotelian conception of the virtuous life presuppose, for the most part, a pre-existing network of preferences and partialities. Turning from exposition to evaluation (in Part Two), I shall suggest that the presupposition of such networks is the basis of that rootedness in the real world which gives virtue theory a decisive edge over its competitors; the 'autocentric' perspective, as I shall call it, can be seen as one of the hallmarks that confer worth and authenticity on virtue theory as against its impersonally oriented rivals. I shall also argue that if it is properly formulated, the theory can largely be rescued from the accusation of complacency or bland social conservatism with which it is sometimes charged. Finally, in the third section of the paper, I shall move the focus from Aristotle down to the early modern period. The seventeenth century, here, as in so many other areas of philosophy, is a watershed. On

---

[5] See further Cottingham, 'The Ethics of Self-Concern', 800–1.

[6] I am presupposing for the moment (though supporting considerations will emerge in the course of the paper) that virtue ethics offers a vision of the good life which is radically distinct from that put forward in standard versions of either consequentialist or deontological ethics. What I do not address is the question whether a (suitably qualified) consequentialism might turn out to be at least extensionally equivalent to virtue ethics, in the sense of yielding the same recommendations for how we should set about organizing our lives. Compare Roger Crisp's argument that the life of virtue is one which is, on a certain interpretation, recommended by utilitarianism, in 'Utilitarianism and the Life of Virtue', *Philosophical Quarterly* 167 (1992), 139–60.

the one hand, we see the particularist ethics of excellence still alive and well; ethics is designed for actual human beings already involved in partialistic structures of personal and social preference. On the other hand, the traditional conception is already under heavy attack from a quite distinct vision of ethics, which is, paradoxically, both more abstract and universalist in its scope, and, at the same time, more introverted in its focus. The resulting tensions, I shall suggest, are particularly discernible in the development of Cartesian ethics; by analysing them we can come to appreciate how and why virtue ethics began that long decline from which it is only just beginning to recover.

1. ARISTOTELIAN PARTIALITY

The Aristotelian blueprint for ethical excellence implicitly presupposes, from the outset, a world in which people are already deeply involved in civic and personal networks of partiality. The first in Aristotle's long catalogue of virtues (and one of the 'cardinal virtues' in the medieval and renaissance tradition largely inspired by him) is courage; but not, notice, some impartially motivated inner strength—the Kantian *fortitudo moralis* or zeal in the performance of impersonally oriented moral duty— but rather a disposition whose merit is determined by its appropriate social directedness. Courage *par excellence* is facing danger 'in the right way and at the right time'; further, 'each thing is defined by its end'.[7] It follows that, in its 'strictest sense', courage is the prerogative of the brave champion, facing death 'when the danger is greatest and most glorious, as is borne out by the honours paid to the fallen in city-states and in the courts of monarchs'.[8] One ought not to be brave under compulsion but because it is a fine thing (*kalon*), and hence civic courage (the first and most important in the list of states analogous to courage) is grounded in a proper sense of shame, and a 'desire for something noble . . . , and avoidance of reproach, which is a disgrace'.[9] In a way which is perhaps hard fully to appreciate for those influenced by the later Christian tradition of humility and self-denial, Aristotelian courage is linked to *kudos*, the Homeric conception of self-esteem, the desire to display prowess, to win applause, to avoid the ultimate shame of losing face before one's fellows. And this in turn entails that the ethical worth of the relevant virtue is determined not by the demands

---

[7] *Nicomachean Ethics* (= *NE*) 1115^{b}17–22.   [8] *NE* 1115^{a}30–5.
[9] *NE* 1116^{a}28–9.

of welfare maximization (though it may contingently bring such benefits), nor by the austere requirements of impersonal duty, but by its role
in enhancing the personal prestige of the holder, and by its value within
the interconnected networks of honour and mutual respect which bind
the citizens of a community. The (later Horatian) maxim *dulce et de-
corum est pro patria mori* (whatever our modern reservations may
be at the end of a century of global war) puts supreme value on patriotism, civic loyalty, and personal honour; and all these virtues are
inescapably partialistic. Value is not determined from the standpoint
of an impartial spectator or universal God of all mankind; the acts of
courage are what my own honour and reputation require, and what is
demanded by the specific expectations of those to whom I am in honour
bound.[10]

Aristotle's second chief virtue, that of inner balance or temperance,
sōphrosunē, is partialistic in an even more direct and self-evident way,
being concerned with individual flourishing at the level of those phy-
siologically based desires and appetites that are part of our specific
biological inheritance. 'Such pleasures as conduce to health and bodily
fitness', says Aristotle, 'the temperate person will desire in moderation
and in the right way';[11] but notice that the moderation which is central
to this, as to all the virtues, is not concerned with restrictions derived
from any impartial distributive weighting. A preferential, self-oriented
weighting is *already in operation*: the 'right reason' which the temperate
person employs is entirely directed to the calculation of what balance
of appetites generates, within the individual life, an inner glow of psychic
harmony. The individual who has trained the habits of bodily desire in
such a way as to produce a graceful, untroubled, and healthy personal
life, has already implicitly assigned a heavy priority, in his or her conception of the good life, to his or her own personal flourishing. This is not
to repeat the ancient canard that Aristotelian ethics is crassly egoistic;
in Aristotle's blueprint for human fulfilment, there is a good measure
of genuine concern for others.[12] The point, rather, is about the perspective from which ethics is approached, which turns out to be autocentric, in the sense of being constructed, as it were, from the inside
outwards. The opening question for ethics is: how should I—this particular, biologically-based creature—live? And the answer—nobly,
harmoniously, with rewarding personal relationships, with graceful and
well-ordered habits of desire—makes my own life special and precious

---

[10] For more on this theme, see J. Casey, *Pagan Virtue* (Oxford, 1990), 52.
[11] *NE* 1119ª16–17.   [12] See Cottingham, 'The Ethics of Self-Concern', 813.

in a way which (as I have argued elsewhere) impersonalist systems of morality cannot properly accommodate.[13] Thus, in the case of temperance, the harmonious regulation of my appetites is a task which requires a preferential assignment of time and resources to determining the conditions of fulfilment for a particular individual—myself. To see this more clearly, one only has to reflect on how far the life of the Aristotelian *sōphrōn*, or temperate person, will diverge from the life of abstinence and self-denial enjoined by systems of ethics which reject as worldly, and even sinful, the operation of the bodily passions.[14]

At a fairly deep level, the virtue theorist accepts, and builds upon, the structural constraints of our human nature. Value is supervenient (in part) on the biological ties and pulls located within us; it is not determined, *ab extra*, from the demands of some higher law, or based on some vision of transcendent blessedness. The point is reinforced by the familiar contrast between Aristotelian harmony and Kantian duty. *Enkrateia*, or self-control, that subordination of appetite to the moral will, which is for Kant the highest expression of a moral nature, is for Aristotle a mere *pis aller*: the very moral struggle which arises when our human passions pull against the demands of right action is, to the Aristotelian way of thinking, already a sign that all is not as it should be. Far from earning extra points on the scale of goodness, self-control is a second-best virtue, rescuing (but in no sense transfiguring or validating) the life of the individual whose emotional and behavioural habits have not been properly and harmoniously laid down. The cardinal virtue of temperance, in short, is inherently partialistic, first in the sense that it presupposes a preferential assignment of value by each individual to the task of determining the conditions for his or her own personal psychic balance, and secondly in the sense that it accords value to lives not in so far as they conform to an abstract and timeless conception of right action, but in so far as they display the natural growth and flowering of creatures whose commitments and goals are already largely determined by specific biological and social ties.[15]

[13] Ibid. 802–5. As is made clear in the paper referred to, the 'preciousness' and 'specialness' involved does not imply the megalomaniacal claim that my own life is somehow intrinsically more valuable, from a cosmic perspective, than anyone else's.

[14] *NE* III. 10, esp. 1118ᵃ23–ᵇ8.

[15] With respect to the 'biological ties' referred to here, I would go along with Philippa Foot's persuasively argued thesis that it is important to draw a connection between the goodness of an individual and considerations about the way of life of the species of which that individual is a member (see P. Foot, 'Does Moral Subjectivism Rest on a Mistake?', *Oxford Journal of Legal Studies* 15 (1995), 1–14, pp. 7–9). This leaves room for disagreement about how derivative the account of individual goodness is from such

It would be tedious to unravel the way in which this sort of partialism manifests itself throughout the Aristotelian catalogue of virtues.
But it should be fairly clear that the excellences of liberality, of magnificence, of magnanimity, of proper ambition, and of social fluency or
wittiness all presuppose an agent who is in no sense either a global
utility-maximizer or an impartial seeker after Kantian moral worth.
The blueprint for civic and individual excellence assigns value in a way
which is heavily dependent on a decent upbringing, a tolerably secure
position in society, solid endowments of wealth and income, a modicum
of health and personal charm—in short, the requirements not just for a
worthy life (in the inner Kantian sense), but for outward success and
flourishing. Recent work on what we now call 'moral luck' brings this
aspect of virtue ethics into particularly sharp relief. To take the central
case of *megalopsychia*—magnanimity or 'great-souledness', for example,
there seems no escaping the fact that this Aristotelian excellence presupposes a whole network of strongly partialistic ties and commitments,
whose operation depends in large part on the contingencies of fortune.
Aristotle's noble or great-souled man is born into a high culture, healthy,
intelligent, affluent and calmly confident of his entitlement to honour
and esteem. From a post-Christian perspective on morality (as John
Casey has pointed out), the presumptions behind this paradigm of excellence may seem simply 'odious'.[16] How can we stomach the thought
that Pericles, in building the Acropolis, is more to be admired than the
poor widow who casts her two mites into the Temple treasury? ('Verily
I say unto you, That this poor widow hath cast more in, than all they . . . ,
[for] she of her want did cast in all that she had.')[17]

I shall come back later to some of the issues involved here. But, for
the moment, two observations. First, and bluntly, those tempted to take
the high moral ground against Aristotle must be prepared to undergo a
good deal of honest self-examination if their position is even to stand

species-related considerations. My own inclination is to say that in the case of human
beings (unlike that of other animals, whose *telos* is more tightly determined), the role of
the individual in working out the blueprint for a worthwhile life is primary rather than
derivative. Species-related considerations will, to be sure, operate as powerful constraints
on individual life-plans by imposing inevitable costs on various ways of living; but this
will still leave open a wide range of possible patterns of life, so that the working out of
the recipe for *eudaimonia* will be very much a matter of (relatively autonomous) individual reasoning. For the notion of biological constraints as imposing 'costs', see M.
Midgley, *Beast and Man* (Brighton, 1979), 192–4; see also Cottingham, 'The Ethics of
Self-Concern', p. 815, n. 54.

[16] Casey, *Pagan Virtue*, 201.   [17] Mark 12: 43–4, AV.

a chance of emerging as a stable one. And the chances are, to say the least, not at all good. For even a minimal level of honesty is enough to reveal to most of us that in the structuring of the great part of our day-to-day lives we are indeed Aristotelians—Aristotelians *malgré nous*, perhaps, but Aristotelians for all that. We just do seek out friends who are enjoyable to be with, who share our (culturally determined and income-dependent) tastes and pursuits; we do pursue excellence in our careers, and the rewards of fulfilment in our personal relationships; we do wish for ourselves and our families lives not just of worthy striving but of growth and flourishing, of efforts crowned, of tangible achievement. To say in the face of all this that what we *really* value is the desperate self-abnegation of the poor woman, who sacrifices even the pittance she has for some impersonal cause, cannot, for most of us at least, be any more than an empty flourish—the Wittgensteinian cog that does not mesh with any other part of the machinery, a piece of hollow rhetoric unconnected with the values by which we actually live.[18]

The second point, perhaps more closely linked to the direct concerns of the present paper, requires a fuller appreciation of the pervasive strand of deep partiality that informs the life of Aristotelian excellence. The most vivid example of what is involved arises in the case of that central component in Aristotle's conception of the good life—*philia* (love or friendship), a concept that occupies nearly two whole books in the *Nicomachean Ethics*. The Aristotelian *philos*, as I have stressed elsewhere, is someone *special*, and this very fact puts a severe limit on the number of genuine *philoi* it is possible to have in a lifetime. The development of rewarding personal relationships, which is, in virtue theory, the very core of the good life, requires an emphatically preferential assignment of time and resources to a few chosen individuals— one's close friends and family. Of the more impartial and impersonal general love which Plato had advocated, and which Christian theorists were later to expand even more widely in their vision of universal *agapē* for all mankind, the Aristotelian is politely sceptical: better to be a real cousin, says Aristotle, than a son in Plato's sense.[19]

---

[18] In so far as there is a place, in the life so described, for Kantian-style evaluations of pure moral worth, it may be (as Martha Klein has suggested in a perceptive recent paper) that these function as little more than consolation prizes, rather like (though this is not her simile) the patronizing 'A for effort' sometimes awarded to the irredeemable D-grade student. See article cited at n. 4 above.

[19] See Plato, *Republic* 462b; Aristotle, *Politics* 1262ᵃ13–14.

But even without the scepticism (and with our modern vision of a fragile planet of interdependent communities, we have good reason to take seriously the call for a 'widening circle' of moral concern), the fact remains that requirements of restricted, preferential affection command, for most of us, a vastly larger place in the assignment of our priorities in life than could be justified from a more impersonal perspective. The virtue theorist (to come back to my earlier rejection of the charge of crass egoism) can plausibly find a place for the good use of surplus time and resources in works of general charity and benevolence. But that assignment will operate only after the central ingredients of human flourishing are in place; and the securing of those ingredients requires—honest self-examination is again recommended for those who doubt it—the existence of strong and stable networks of unashamed partiality and preference. This autocentric perspective is even more clearly apparent in Aristotelian *philautia*—self-concern or self-esteem: so far from being intrinsically suspect (as it is in some versions of the Christian canons of morality), self-concern is, for the Aristotelian, a perfectly proper and legitimate ingredient of the good life, to be condemned only when it slides into *pleonexia* (the vice of excess which involves trying to grab more than one's fair share), or, equally important, when it slips into the vice of deficiency which allows an undue degree of self-abasement and self-sacrifice.[20]

In large part, then, the virtue theorist's vision of the good for humankind is one in which individuals are securely established in a graceful life of health, honour, mutual self-respect, and personal commitment. It is the life wished on the young couple in Shakespeare's *Tempest*: 'Honour, riches, marriage-blessing, Long continuance and increasing . . . Spring come to you at the farthest, in the very end of harvest.'[21] These are not mere externals, the contingent blessings without which a moral life can still retain the inner lustre of righteousness (Kant); rather, they are the very stuff of the good life for humankind, not just in the sense of prerequisites for virtue (though some of them are that), but in the sense of constituting an ideal pattern for the flowering of our human nature. The ethic of the virtue theorist is an ethic for particular individuals, in a particular social setting, whose lives are informed from the outset by an autocentrically determined network of preferential commitments.

[20] For these themes, see Cottingham, 'The Ethics of Self-Concern', 810–13. For the contrast between the *philautos* and the *pleonektēs*, see *NE* IX. 8.

[21] *Tempest*, IV. i; some of these lines are cited in Casey, *Pagan Virtue*, 78.

2. THE ETHICAL CREDENTIALS OF VIRTUE THEORY

It is now time to address the complaint that a partialistic ethic, constructed on the premisses so far outlined, simply fails to meet central
intuitions we have about how moral evaluation ought to operate. I have
already indicated that an extreme charge of rank egoism will not stick,
and also that the critics of virtue theory's partialistic orientation may
find it hard, when examining their own lives, to articulate a rival theory
that amounts to anything more than an exercise in pious self-delusion
or outright hypocrisy. But for all that, doubts may remain. It is hard to
read much of what Aristotle says about *megaloprepeia* (magnificence),
for example, without catching a whiff of aristocratic complacency. Those
who have this virtue deserve praise, Aristotle tells us, for their lavish
expenditure on armaments or civic banquets; 'such expenditure befits
those who have appropriate resources, acquired either by themselves or
from ancestors or connections, and persons of noble birth or great reputation or other such qualities, because such conditions involve grand-
eur and distinction.'[22] Although he makes it clear that the magnificent
man is not just a vulgar show-off (this would be a lapse into the vice
of excess), to the egalitarian modern ear there is nonetheless a harsh
ring to Aristotle's whole-hearted endorsement of the claims of the
fortunate few.

Perhaps we could stomach Aristotle's attitude better if it were restricted
to a rather special kind of high civic virtue; but in the remainder of his
list of excellences there is much that strikes a similarly discordant note.
The *megalopsychos*, or great-souled man, who merits the crown of virtue because his accomplishments and deserts are the greatest,[23] also
appears to be one of fortune's favourites. Although Aristotle is careful
to insist that good luck is not sufficient for the possession of this virtue, it nonetheless helps a great deal: 'people of high birth or great
power or wealth are felt to deserve honour because they are in a position of superiority, and anything that is superior in something good is
held in greater honour.'[24] A certain bland complacency of outlook also
seems to infect the account of many of the other, less public virtues: the
exercise of proper ambition, the development of the social graces like
eutrapelia (wittiness), the securing of the benefits of *philia*, all seem to

---

[22] *NE* 1122^{b}29–33.   [23] *NE* IV. 3, esp. 1124^{a}1–4.
[24] *NE* 1124^{a}21–3. Aristotle adds that 'in truth only the good man ought to be hon-
oured, but the possessor of both goodness and these other advantages is more readily felt
to deserve honour'.

presuppose political and social arrangements which exclude a very large number of people from the attainment of true *eudaimonia*. Because Aristotle frequently insists that the virtues are interlinked, it would be unfair to lumber him with promoting the ethics of the bourgeois dinner-table; the possession of virtues like patience, truthfulness, and modesty rescues Aristotle's virtuous man from the charge of being a blinkered port-quaffer on the high table of life.[25] Nevertheless, it seems no accident that Aristotle seems to have acquiesced, without many qualms, in social arrangements which allowed few if any opportunities for women, for slaves, for foreigners to participate in the life of virtue at its highest level.[26]

I think that there is some defence for the virtue theorist against this type of worry, but that it is best to acknowledge that it can only be a limited one. A certain meritocratic, or at least achievement-oriented, conception of value is built into the very foundations of the theory—it is, after all, a theory of *excellence* in the strict etymological sense of that in respect of which a person stands out (*excellere*) above the crowd of lesser achievers; the etymological link is preserved, in a different way, in Greek as well, where the very word for virtue, *aretē*, has comparative, or rather superlative, associations—being connected with the term *aristos*, 'best'.[27] The stakes are high, the contribution of fortune considerable, and not all will be capable, whether for reasons of birth or background, or because of the blows of chance, to succeed. I do not want here to rehearse the debates, familiar from the recent literature, about moral luck, or about the extent to which Aristotelian virtue may still offer some hope that even those stricken with the misfortunes of Priam may salvage something from the wreckage.[28] For on any reading of Aristotle it remains unavoidable, surely, that the achievement of true *eudaimonia*, in its fullest and most flourishing form, is simply, and sadly, beyond the power of the autonomous will to achieve unaided.

Here maybe it is best for the virtue theorist simply to bite the bullet

[25] For the three virtues mentioned, see *NE* II. 7. It should be added, however, that the virtue of truthfulness seems to be defined in a fairly autocentric way by Aristotle, being concerned largely with giving an appropriate estimate of one's own attainments (the vice of excess is 'boastfulness'). Modesty is characterized as not strictly a virtue, though it is brought under Aristotle's general triadic pattern, being an intermediate disposition (between shyness and shamelessness) which is 'deserving of praise'.   [26] *NE* VIII. 11.

[27] Both terms seem to have been used originally in connection with prowess or pre-eminence on the battlefield (the same root being present in 'Ares', the god of war).

[28] See M. Nussbaum, *The Fragility of Goodness* (Cambridge, 1986), ch. 11. See also the discussion of Priam in *Nicomachean Ethics* I. 10.

and admit the result (perhaps not all that surprising upon reflection) that
the achievement of Aristotelian ethical excellence, like other forms of
human excellence—technical, intellectual, social, political, artistic—
will be contingent on more than mere inner worth. Indeed, I would suggest that it is a central feature of the conception of ethics put forward by
virtue theory that ethical appraisal is seen as continuous with, and of the
same fundamental type as, other kinds of human appraisal.[29] For those
who find it monstrous that the unfairness inherent in all these other
forms of human endeavour should infuse even the ethical sphere, there
can be no ultimately satisfying answer. But is this really a problem for
virtue theory, or is it not rather its opponents who are pursuing an *ignis
fatuus*? For notice that even the Kantian manoeuvre of shrinking the
domain of the moral to that of the autonomous will of the rational agent
does not guarantee complete immunity to luck, since what Bernard
Williams and Thomas Nagel have called 'constitutive luck' will inevitably play a part in determining the degree of inner moral fortitude each
of us possesses.[30] The upshot is that if *complete* immunity from all
contingency is sought in the domain of the moral, it seems that this
could be provided (though I have no space to argue the point here) only
by invoking some transcendent authority who has the power to make all
things good, to redeem even the most blighted life by responding to the
mere fact of our humanity. Such a move, in its most extreme form (and
it is not clear that even the morality of the Gospels goes this far), carries a great price: the removal of ethics from the sphere of what we can
intelligibly understand as appraisal.

These considerations aside, there remains one important respect in
which virtue theory can perfectly well defend itself against the cruder
charge canvassed above, that of a blinkered and complacent social conservatism. Although the Aristotelian virtues presuppose a partialist and
particularistic conception of how life should be lived, there is nothing in
the theory that inherently restricts the good life to one particular small
group. Aristotelian ethics is the pursuit of *to anthrōpinon agathon*—the
good for humankind—and the resulting blueprint is perfectly capable of

[29] The idea that 'good' is a systematically ambiguous term, or at any rate that 'moral'
goodness is a *sui generis* concept whose operation obeys wholly different rules from those
which govern other attributions of goodness, has always struck me as one of the more
outlandish aspects of much twentieth-century work on ethics; I believe (though there is
no space to argue the point here) that it is a notable virtue of virtue theory that it
implicitly rejects the notion of a special 'language of morals'.

[30] Cf. T. Nagel, 'Moral Luck', in *Mortal Questions* (Cambridge, 1979), 24–38, and B.
Williams, 'Moral Luck', in *Moral Luck* (Cambridge, 1981), 20–39.

being generalized to cover a wide variety of historical and social set-
tings. To say that the good life involves striving for excellence does
indeed suppose (as noted above) that not all will succeed equally well;
but this is quite different from the arbitrary exclusion of entire classes
of human beings from the chance even to embark on the quest for excellence. Aristotelian *eudaimonia* represents the maximal flourishing of
our specially human capacities for personal growth and interpersonal
commitment, and in this sense it is an ideal applicable to all human
beings who are capable of entering into the relevant personal and social
relationships.[31] The fact that Aristotle, for reasons we now see to be
inadequate, acquiesced in economic and social conditions that restricted
full membership of the ethical realm to a privileged minority is no
reason to tar all virtue theorists with the same brush. One striking
reason for the early success of Christianity over its pagan rivals seems
to have been precisely its universalist insistence that the kingdom of
heaven was, as St Paul put it, open to all—gentile or Jew, bond or
free.[32] Interpreted transcendentally, in a way which attempts to put
ethics wholly beyond the reach of contingency, this seems to generate
(as I suggested a moment ago) an unstable conception of morality; but
a secular analogue of the Pauline maxim—one which urges us to promote
global conditions in which as many people as possible can enjoy the
opportunity to strive for excellence and develop their human capacities
to the full—is one which the virtue theorist can readily take on board.

Let me end this section with a brief word about justice. If what I
have been saying about the partialism inherent in classical virtue theory
is correct, then justice emerges as very much the odd man out in the
catalogue of cardinal virtues. Crude Polemarchan justice—helping one's
friends and harming one's enemies—might fit in easily enough, but
justice as fairness and equity seems by its very nature impartialistic.[33]
Moreover, its place in the overall blueprint for individual flourishing

---

[31] Cf. Aristotle's own comment at *NE* I. 9: 'Fulfilment will be something widely available [*polukoinon*]; for by dint of some learning and diligence it is capable of being achieved
by all for whom the road to excellence is not closed by incapacity' (1099^{b}18–20).

[32] See Colossians 3: 11.

[33] This point may well also underlie the wide gap which, on the conventional reading
of Kant, separates his theory of justice from his account of the virtues. Although Onora
O'Neill has persuasively argued that a correct reading of the *Tugendlehre* undermines the
supposed strong antithesis between Kantian justice and Kantian virtue, the contrast which
she examines between the types of duty requiring, respectively, 'external' and 'internal'
legislation nonetheless generates (as O'Neill herself makes clear) a fairly striking contrast between the demands of *jus* and the demands of *ethica*. See further O'Neill, 'Kant's
Virtues', Ch. 5 in this volume.

remains obscure; and it is no accident, surely, that Aristotle's triadic account of virtues, each flanked by a vice of excess and of deficiency, hopelessly breaks down when we come to Book Five of the *Nicomachean Ethics*. In the case of justice there simply is no regular pattern of action and desire with respect to the distribution of goods which, when excessively or deficiently exercised, yields the desired pattern of flanking vices.[34]

Add to this the following point: that failures in liberality, say, or the development of friendships, generate immediate and tangible costs in the *eudaimonia* of the individuals concerned; but it is perfectly possible to conceive (we have examples today very near home) of an affluent community of privileged practitioners of virtue, enjoying rich and rewarding relationships, developing their human capacities to the full, yet blandly negligent of the extent to which their agreeable lives depend on hogging the planet's scarce resources. One might try to argue that such callousness to the demands of justice in the wider world might eventually blight the fruits of private and civic virtue, but that would be an unpromising route to take: the virtuous patricians of the Roman empire flourished perfectly well for three hundred years without any striking setbacks of this kind. Indeed, the model of partialistic virtue, untroubled by wider concerns of equity, was still alive and well in Montaigne's time:

[M]an in his highest estate . . . [is one of] that small number of excellent and select men who, having been endowed with fine and particular natural ability, have further strengthened and sharpened it by care, by study and by art, and have raised it to the highest pitch of wisdom . . . They have fashioned their soul to all directions and all angles, supported and propped it with all the outside assistance that was fit for it, and enriched and adorned it with all they could borrow, for its advantage, from the inside and the outside of the world; it is in them that the utmost height of human nature is to be found.[35]

Even if we could demonstrate to such Montaignesque gentlemen that prudence in preserving their estates required a wider concern for justice (the 'I want to be able to walk home from the opera without being mugged' argument), this would still make the demands of justice altogether too secondary and derivative to accord with our strong intuitions about its

---

[34] See *NE* 1133^{b}30–1134^{a}13, and see H. Kelsen, 'Aristotle's Doctrine of Justice', in J. Walsh and H. Shapiro (eds.), *Aristotle's Ethics* (Belmont, Calif., 1967), 102–19.

[35] Michel de Montaigne, *Apology for Raymond Sebond* (1580), tr. D. Frame; quoted in J. B. Schneewind (ed.), *Moral Philosophy from Montaigne to Kant* (Cambridge, 1990), vol. i, pp. 38–9.

place on the ethical map. I said a moment ago that the universal demand
to extend to everyone the widest opportunities for human flourishing
was one the virtue theorist could 'readily take on board'. This remains
true; but it has to be said that the driving force for such equitable extension of resources must come from some other source than the autocentric
perspective from which virtue theory is constructed.[36]

3. THE AUTOCENTRIC PERSPECTIVE

In the brief final section of this paper, I want to move us down to the
early modern era, in order to glimpse some of the pressures which
shaped the way in which virtue theory is perceived today. We have
already seen how the central vision of the virtue theorists was vividly
alive in the thinking of Renaissance writers like Montaigne. And it is
perhaps not surprising to see that vision strongly present in the ethics
of René Descartes, whose thought, despite the familiar accolade of
'father of modern philosophy', was still pervasively structured by the presuppositions of (Aristotelian-inspired) Renaissance scholasticism. The
question which dominated the thoughts of the young Descartes in his
night of troubled dreams on 10 November 1619 was Ausonius' old question, *Quod vitae sectabor iter?*—'What road in life shall I follow?'[37] The
question is a strikingly autocentric one. To begin with, the very fact that it
is framed directly in the first person (like so many fundamental Cartesian
questions) makes us initially predisposed to see it as generating a search
not for some impersonally-defined good, but for the key to fulfilment
for an individual life. Closer inspection confirms this impression, for
the fundamental question is not one about right conduct, or about de-
vising some decision procedure for particular acts, but about the individual's choice of an entire pattern of life—about the discovery of a
complete personal pathway. This calls to mind the Aristotelian dictum

[36] Cf. J. Griffin, *Well-Being* (Oxford, 1986), 63–4. It is worth noting that earlier concepts of justice were by no means always so universalist as those we are accustomed to
today. Aquinas gives as the first species of justice *pietas*, dutiful respect, which is perhaps
the most partialistic virtue one could think of. Compare Casey, *Pagan Virtue*, 194–8.

[37] Recorded by Descartes in an early notebook, some of whose contents have sur-
vived: see AT X 206; CSM I 14. (In this paper the following standard abbreviations are
used to refer to editions of Descartes: AT: C. Adam and P. Tannery (eds.), *Œuvres de
Descartes*, rev. edn., 12 vols. (Paris, 1964–76); CSM: J. Cottingham, R. Stoothoff and D.
Murdoch (eds.), *The Philosophical Writings of Descartes*, 2 vols. (Cambridge, 1984–5);
CSMK: Volume three of the preceding, by the same translators and A. Kenny (Cambridge, 1991).)

that *eudaimonia* is something predicated of a *teleios bios*—the complete life of a single individual.[38] For Descartes, as for Aristotle, moral philosophy is about the construction of an individual life-plan: 'not to have one's life planned with a view to some end is a sign of great folly', says Aristotle;[39] Descartes speaks of moral philosophy as the crowning project of a rationally planned programme (*un dessein*) for the acquisition of knowledge and the conduct of life.[40] There are many other points of contact: to take but one notable example, the Aristotelian insistence that virtue is a matter of permanent dispositions of character is echoed in Descartes's thesis that 'what we commonly call "virtues" are ingrained habits or dispositions (*habitudes*) in the soul.'[41]

In Descartes's conception of the good life, developed in his last work, the *Passions of the Soul*, the traditional catalogue of cardinal virtues is boiled down to just one, which he calls '*la générosité*'. This is the crowning virtue—the 'key to all the other virtues and a general remedy for every disorder of the passions'.[42] The translation of the French term is a difficult matter. The English transliteration 'generosity' is almost unavoidable, and is not entirely misleading (it would have been perfectly natural, even in seventeenth-century French, to apply the term *générosité* to acts which we should nowadays call acts of generosity); but for Descartes the term had powerful resonances which are largely absent in our modern usage. As a fluent Latinist, Descartes was of course acutely aware of the connotations of the cognate Latin adjective '*generosus*', of which the primary meaning is 'noble' or 'well-born' (being derived from the Latin noun '*genus*', whose basic meaning is 'race' or 'family'). By a simple shift, '*generosus*' then came to mean 'noble-minded' or 'magnanimous' (and was used by some Latin writers to indicate the possession of Aristotle's overarching virtue of great-souledness). Descartes himself compares his own notion of generosity to the scholastic concept of magnanimity in article 161 of the *Passions*.

At first sight, then, the Cartesian virtue of *générosité*, or nobility of

[38] *NE* 1098ª18. See also I. 10. Compare Bernard Williams's apt comment on the Ausonian line recalled by Descartes: 'it is important that the word is *iter*, not *via*: there is a journey to be made' ('Descartes and Historiography', in J. Cottingham (ed.), *Reason, Will and Sensation: Studies in Cartesian Metaphysics* (Oxford, 1994), 220.

[39] *Eudemian Ethics* 1214ᵇ10–11.

[40] *Principles of Philosophy*, Preface to French Edition (1647), AT IXB 17; CSM I 188. For the application of the Cartesian plan (*dessein*) to moral philosophy, see the introduction by G. Rodis-Lewis in Descartes, *The Passions of the Soul*, ed. and tr. S. Voss (Indianapolis, 1989), xv–xxv, p. xxii.

[41] *Passions of the Soul* (1649), art. 161: AT XI 453; CSM I 387.

[42] Ibid: AT XI 454; CSM I 388.

spirit, plugs straight into the aristocratic or excellence-centred presuppositions of traditional virtue theory. The connection Descartes makes is that the virtue of noble-mindedness, as traditionally conceived, implied a certain dignity and legitimate self-esteem, and this will precisely be true of the person of *générosité*: it 'causes a person's self-esteem to be as great as it may legitimately be'.[43] But on closer inspection, a decisive shift from the *aretē* tradition can be discerned. Descartes's moral education, at the hands of the Jesuits at La Flèche, had been dominated by the presuppositions not just of pagan humanism (though these did play a large role) but also, inevitably, of Christian morality. And what this meant, above all, was a commitment to the central notion of the kingdom of heaven as open to all. '*Le chemin [au ciel]*', Descartes writes in the *Discourse*, '*n'en est pas moins ouvert aux plus ignorants qu'aux plus doctes*'; the road to heaven does not depend on the vicissitudes of birth or education.[44] There is, incidentally, a strong epistemic analogue of this universalism in the Cartesian account of knowledge. Good sense, the innate natural light of reason, is equally present in all men, and as Descartes explains in his dramatic dialogue the *Search for Truth*, the untutored Polyander ('Everyman') has as good, if not a better, chance of achieving enlightenment than Epistemon ('Mr Knowledgeable'), whose inner intuitions are clouded by the sophistications of technical philosophy.[45] In the ethical sphere, this comes out as an insistence that the good life, like the achievement of reliable knowledge, should in principle be available to all who set about the task of achieving it in the right way.

Now clearly *générosité*, in the traditional genetic sense of 'nobility', depends very largely on accidents of birth and natural endowment. 'It is easy to believe,' Descartes observes, 'that the souls which God puts into our bodies are not all equally noble and strong'; and while 'good upbringing is a great help in correcting defects of birth', this too will presumably depend largely on factors outside the agent's control.[46] But Descartes's Christianized vision of ethics leads him to construe the crowning virtue of *générosité* in a radically different way from Aristotelian nobility—as a virtue whose achievement must at all costs be immune to the vicissitudes of fortune, and (in a striking anticipation of

[43] *Passions of the Soul*, art. 153: AT XI 445–6; CSM I 384.

[44] *Discourse on the Method* (1637), part I: AT VI 8; CSM I 114.

[45] *Search for Truth*: AT X 500–3; CSM II 402–3. See also the opening of the *Discourse on the Method*: AT VI 1; CSM I 111.

[46] *Passions of the Soul*, art. 161: AT XI 453; CSM I 388.

Kant) will depend on inner rectitude alone. *True* generosity, Descartes proclaims (and the epithet should warn us that some spectacular high redefinition is going on), is a matter not of outward achievement but of the inner exercise of our will. '[N]othing truly belongs to [us] but [the] freedom to dispose [our] volitions, and [we] ought to be praised or blamed for no other reason than [for] using this freedom well or badly.'[47] We now have a striking turn-around; for the calm self-esteem of the Aristotelian *megalopsyches* is retained, not as the satisfaction of one whose outward achievements match his natural endowments and civic status, but rather as the '*feeling within* [*ourselves* of] a firm and con-stant resolution to use [our freedom] well—that is, never to lack the will to undertake and carry out what [we judge] to be best'.[48] True *générosité*, then, involves, like its pagan original, justified self-esteem, but quite unlike the pagan model, it is self-esteem for the resolute and well-directed use of free will, which is (allegedly) within the power of all. The Cartesian ethical sphere, in contrast to the Aristotelian, is a sphere which is largely sealed off from the effects of moral luck. Those possessed of *générosité*, says Descartes,

do not consider themselves much inferior to those who have greater wealth or honour, or even to those who have more intelligence, knowledge, or beauty, or generally to those who surpass them in some other perfections; [but] equally they do not have much more esteem for themselves than for those whom they surpass. For all these things seem to them to be very unimportant by contrast with *the virtuous will for which alone they esteem themselves*, and which they suppose also to be present, or at least capable of being present, in every other person.[49]

In a few brief sentences, the decisive transition has been made from the particularist ethics of excellence and achievement to the universalist morality of the kingdom of ends.

The philosophical importance of Descartes's theory of *générosité* lies in the fact that his ideas here, as in so many other areas of his philosophy, form a kind of bridge between the ancient and modern worlds. His thinking is sufficiently rooted in the robust naturalism of traditional virtue theory for him to acknowledge, in many places, the importance of good upbringing and above all training and habituation

---

[47] Ibid. art. 153: AT XI 446; CSM I 384.   [48] Ibid. (emphasis supplied).

[49] Ibid. art. 154: AT XI 446–7; CSM I 384 (emphasis supplied). For further discussion of Descartes's account of the virtue of *générosité* (in a rather different context). see C. Taylor, *Sources of the Self* (Cambridge, 1989), ch. 8.

for the development of a worthwhile human life.[50] But the primacy which his account gives to the autonomous power of the will as the only true basis for moral appraisal clearly looks forward to a conception of ethics in which the ultimate bearer of moral worth is excellence of a peculiarly private and spiritual kind.

Where does all this leave the issues of partiality and self-preference? There is no simple answer to this, but I will conclude with some rather schematic observations on the results of the Cartesian inward turn. First, though, a short summary of some of the salient features of virtue theory which I hope have emerged, directly or indirectly, in this paper:

(1) The dominant feature of virtue theory is, I have been suggesting, its autocentric orientation, in the sense which should by now be clear (though I shall return to it briefly in a moment);

(2) in addition to this, virtue theory is characteristically 'aretic', or excellence-centred;[51]

(3) (closely connected with the second point) it presupposes the existence of a strong continuum between ethical and other types of human appraisal (and rejects the notion of an insulated, *sui generis* domain of 'moral' goodness);

(4) it construes the 'unit of appraisal' not as the particular action or class of actions (whether deontologically or consequentially assessed) but as the complete life of an individual;

(5) it tends to resist the post-Kantian notion (prefigured in Descartes) of the supremacy and autonomy of the will in ethics, accepting instead that the possibilities for individual *eudaimonia* are constrained (though not uniquely determined) by the inescapable social and biological context of our human existence.

The autocentricity which I have been stressing as a principal hall-mark of traditional virtue theory gives us a strong point of contact between

---

[50] *Passions of the Soul*, art. 50: AT XI 368–70; CSM I 348.

[51] A possible worry is that there may be a tension between the first and second features referred to here: may not the requirements of excellence be in conflict with the partialities and preferences which characterise the autocentric perspective? Thus, talk of 'networks of partiality' may seem to license nepotism, of which the outcome is often counter-aretic: the best candidate does not get the job. (I am grateful to Ingmar Persson for raising this point in discussion.) The Aristotelian may reply to this that *philia* involves more than just arbitrarily favouring someone because you like them, or are related to them. True *philia* involves a reciprocal relationship of justified self-esteem, where the *philoi* are valued both for their own sake and for the genuine excellences of character they possess. See *NE* 1156^{b}6–32. For the ethical status of various types of partiality, see J. Cottingham, 'Ethics and Impartiality', *Philosophical Studies* 43 (1983), 83–9, and 'Partiality, Favouritism and Morality', *Philosophical Quarterly* 36 (1986), 357–73.

Aristotelian and Cartesian ethics: each of us must construct the blueprint for fulfilment from the inside outwards, by using our reason to
reflect on the best pattern for a worthwhile life. But in Descartes, the
turn inwards involves (for reasons which go beyond this paper) a much
more dramatic introversion, a bizarre narrowing of focus to the single
point of pure consciousness. The dualistic splitting off of the mind or
soul from the prison house of the body means that the subject of ethical
deliberation turns out to be not an *anthrōpos*, a biological creature of
flesh and blood, but rather a pure *res cogitans*. The danger inherent in
this narrowed conception of the self is that ethical excellence will be
exiled from its sphere of operation. Instead of being robustly rooted in
the biological and social networks that define our human lives, instead of
realistically embracing the partialities and commitments that provide
the context in which real humans grow and flourish, the ethical project
becomes an austere and abstract affair—that of the exercise of a pure
good will towards what reason directs. None the less, as the passages just
cited from Descartes make clear, this turn inwards offers a spectacular
prize: a universal and egalitarian vision of goodness which promises
to rescue value from the dominance of fortune. And the attractions of
this model (illusory or not, as the case may be) have exercised such a
powerful pull on our moral imagination that traditional virtue theory, in
the centuries following Descartes, has progressively lost its power to
command our allegiance.

Three problems emerge from this, which seem to define the predicament in which modern ethics finds itself. The first is the need to get
back to an ethics which is rooted in the realities of the human condition; signs of this need are apparent even in Descartes, who, notwithstanding his official dualism, gradually came to see almost in spite of
himself that ethics requires for its development an account of the human
being as a 'substantial union of mind and body', embracing the entire
network of physiological and emotional constraints which determine
our real lives.[52] The second problem is the puzzle of moral luck—the
need to face the fact that the partialistically-rooted and worldly values
of aretic ethics must necessarily offer hostages to fortune, and hence
deny the powerful pull of our Christian inheritance calling for universal
salvation (or some secular analogue thereof). And the third problem is

[52] See *Passions of the Soul, passim*, esp. articles 31–6, 45–50, 147, and 211. For the
'substantial union', see Descartes's letters to Elizabeth of 21 May 1643 (AT III 665;
CSMK 218) and 28 June 1643 (AT III 691; CSMK 227). See also J. Cottingham, *Descartes*
(Oxford, 1986), 127–33 and 152–6.

John Cottingham

that of justice, the need to respond to the demands of fairness and equity which appear to go way beyond what can be generated from the autocentric perspective of ethical eudaimonism. The prospects for success in any of these areas are not easy to assess. But the revival of virtue theory has already achieved the valuable result of placing all three issues firmly on the ethical agenda.[53]

[53] I am most grateful to Harley Cahen and Roger Crisp for helpful comments on an earlier draft of this paper.

5

Kant's Virtues

ONORA O'NEILL

Most proponents of virtue ethics in recent years find little to admire in Kantian ethics, which they depict as rigidly rule-governed, unable to take account of differences between persons and cases, based on unconvincing accounts of self, freedom, and action, burdened with an excessive individualism, fixated on rights, and specifically unable to give an adequate account of the virtues.[1] Some, if not all, of these and kindred accusations may be true of those recent liberal theories of justice which are conventionally labelled 'Kantian', many of which indeed say nothing about the virtues. However, it is less obvious whether or how far they apply to Kant's ethics. In particular, Kant thought that his conception of practical reasoning could be used to develop an account of virtue as well as one of justice. He presents this account in some detail in the second part of the *Metaphysic of Morals*[2] and frequently alludes to and elaborates it in other works. Of course, what Kant offers under the heading of a 'Doctrine of Virtue' (*Tugendlehre*) may have all the inadequacies commonly attributed to Kantian ethics. Or it may not.

---

[1] The accusations are to be found in a wide range of works, and have been particularly prominent in communitarian writings and discussions of virtue ethics during the last decade. See, for example, A. MacIntyre, *After Virtue: A Study in Moral Theory* (London, 1981); M. Sandel, *Liberalism and the Limits of Justice* (Cambridge, 1982); L. W. Blum, *Friendship, Altruism and Morality* (London, 1980).

[2] The assumed tension between theories of justice and accounts of the virtues is foreshadowed in the history of Kant's *Metaphysik der Sitten*. Its two parts, the *Metaphysische Anfangsgründe der Rechtslehre* (usually: *Rechtslehre*) and the *Tugendlehre*, did not appear in a single volume in Kant's lifetime, and appeared in a single volume in English only recently (*The Metaphysics of Morals*, tr. M. Gregor (Cambridge, 1991)). A recent critical edition of the *Rechtslehre* argues that the original printing—and all subsequent editions—muddled the sequence of Kant's text, and seeks to reconstruct a more perspicuous version; see *Metaphysische Anfangsgründe der Rechtslehre* ed. B. Ludwig (Hamburg, 1986). This reconstruction is important for the *Tugendlehre* too, since the most substantial alternations proposed are in the introduction to the entire work.

Concern for universal standards of justice and for lives of virtues are now often depicted as antithetical. If they are, there must be deep flaws in the work of those classical, medieval, and early modern writers who purportedly combine accounts of the two, as well as in Kant's purported integration of *Rechtslehre* and *Tugendlehre*.[3] Yet it is hard to see just what the obstacle to any integrated account of justice and the virtues is supposed to be. It is sometimes said that the main flaw in those contemporary theories of justice that are labelled 'Kantian' which debars them from giving an account of the virtues is that they do not establish the requisite objective and universal account of the human good. On Rawls's views, for example, there is no objective good, but our various subjective conceptions of the good have enough in common to establish an account of justice which can command agreement (at least among those who conceive of themselves as the citizens of liberal democratic polities).[4] Most other contemporary work on justice is also viewed— both by proponents and by critics—as continuing the social contract tradition, in that it relies on the thinnest of accounts of human nature, and offers no fuller account of the Good for Man on which an objective ethics might be based.

However, even a cursory look at the variety of contemporary virtue ethics suggests that the decisive objection its proponents have to theories of justice cannot be that they lack an objective account of the Good for Man. Few contemporary advocates of virtue ethics are moral realists of any sort; few argue for a definitive account of the human good or of human flourishing. Many are historicists or other sorts of relativist. They see the virtues not as components of the objective good, but as the established practices and patterns of ethical response of a certain society or culture at a given time, which display and articulate that society's conception of the good. Even some writers who invoke Aristotle's authority endow him with a genteel historicism.[5] An account of the virtues is not to be derived from a knowledge of the Good, or even of the Good for Man, or from a theory of human nature, or of the nature of rational beings as such. Rather, it is to be read out of the identities

---

[3] On the relation between justice and virtues in early modern writers, see J. Schneewind, 'The Misfortunes of Virtue', *Ethics* 101 (1991), 42–63, and 'Natural Law, Skepticism and Methods of Ethics', *Journal of the History of Ideas* 52 (1991), 289–308.

[4] J. Rawls, *A Theory of Justice* (Cambridge, Mass., 1971); 'Justice as Fairness: Political not Metaphysical', *Philosophy and Public Affairs* 14 (1985), 223–51.

[5] See, for example, MacIntyre, *After Virtue*; N. Sherman, *The Fabric of Character* (Oxford, 1989); M. Nussbaum, *The Fragility of Goodness: Luck and Ethics in Greek Tragedy and Philosophy* (Cambridge, 1986), esp. 245–63.

achieved by and available to men and women at determinate times and places, that is, out of socially determinate but historically variable conceptions of the good and the practices which embody this conception.

So it seems that contemporary theorists of justice disagree with those of their critics who view virtue as primary not over the plausibility of moral realism, but over a linked set of considerations about the respective moral weight of appeals to actual practices and identities and to more abstract universal principles. Both groups would probably agree in diagnosing the flaw in pre-modern and early modern works that link justice and the virtues as an uncritical reliance on realist (often theological) premisses. They might also then agree that the integrated accounts of justice and of virtue offered by those earlier, realist writers show nothing about what can be done if we cannot establish moral realism.

Kant's account of the virtues is a more direct challenge to contemporary assumptions that justice and the virtues are antithetical, because he proposes an account of universal standards both of justice and of virtue, but claims not to rely on any objective account of the Good for Man, or any other form of moral realism. Nor, of course, does Kant's argument invoke historically achieved practices and identities. We cannot say of Kant, as we might of ancient, medieval, and early modern writers, that he manages to combine accounts of justice and of virtue only by relying on a moral realism which he does not substantiate. In his rejection of moral realism Kant is our contemporary, yet more challenging than most actual contemporaries since he claims to combine more than they think can be combined.

1. GENERAL SKETCH: SOME REMINDERS FROM KANT'S *GRUNDLEGUNG*

Kant's central arguments on action, reason, and morality may, of course, be quite inadequate; I shall neither rehearse nor examine them here. I shall not discuss the considerations by which he aimed to show that the Categorical Imperative, through which principles of duty are to be identified, is (a version of) the supreme principle of reason.[6] Nor shall I discuss the adequacy of the arguments by which he vindicates specific

---

[6] I have tried to do so in *Constructions of Reason: Explorations of Kant's Practical Philosophy* (Cambridge, 1989), part i, and in 'Vindicating Reason', in P. Guyer (ed.), *A Companion to Kant* (Cambridge, 1992), 280–308.

maxims of duty, or of other arguments that might be developed on Kantian lines to identify further such maxims. Rather, I shall consider whether *if* these parts of Kant's ethics are sustainable, his claims about the virtues could also be made intelligible, and perhaps convincing. So I shall focus on a group of specific queries and puzzles about the position of the virtues in Kant's account of duties, and in particular on the problematic sense in which his duties of virtue are inward. The stage can be set for these specific queries by outlining some of Kant's basic claims about duty, which are familiar from the *Grundlegung* and other works, and by sketching his classification of virtues.

Kant's conception of duties, and so of duties of virtue, cannot be detached from his account of action. The pivotal, and perhaps the most difficult, part of that account is Kant's notion of the maxim, or practical principle which informs an action.[7] Maxims are subjective practical principles, that is principles of action which inform the action of an agent—a subject—at some time (*GMS* IV, 421 n.).[8] The sense in which maxims are subjective is not, then, that their content must be subjective as opposed to objective: in dutiful action the content of an agent's

[7] On Kant's theory of action see R. Bittner, 'Maximen', in G. Funke (ed.), *Akten des 4. Internationalen Kant-Kongresses*, 2/2 (Berlin, 1975), 485–98, and 'How to Act on Principle', unpublished; O'Neill, *Constructions of Reason*, part ii. I am particularly indebted to Bittner's recent work for challenging and sharpening my understanding of Kant's theory of action.

[8] References to and quotations from Kant's works are given parenthetically in the text, using the following abbreviations and translations:

GMS for *Grundlegung zur Metaphysik der Sitten* (*Groundwork of the Metaphysic of Morals*, 1785), tr. H. J. Paton, under the title '*The Moral Law*' (London, 1948).

MS for *Metaphysik der Sitten* (*Metaphysics of Morals*, 1797): see n. 2 for information on text and translation.

R for *Religion innerhalb der Grenzen der Blossen Vernunft* (*Religion within the Limits of Reason Alone*, 1793), trs. T. M. Greene and H. H. Hudson (Chicago, 1934).

TP for *Über den Gemeinspruch: 'Das mag in der Theorie richtig sein, taugt aber nicht für die Praxis'* (*On the Common Saying: 'This may be True in Theory, but it does not Apply in Practice'*, 1793), tr. H. B. Nisbet, in H. Reiss (ed.), *Kant's Political Writings*, 2nd edn. (Cambridge, 1991).

SF for *Streit der Fakultäten* (*The Conflict of the Faculties*, 1798). A complete translation is available by Mary Gregor, but page references in the text are to the far more readily available extract translated by H. B. Nisbet in *Kant's Political Writings*.

ZEF for *Zum Ewigen Frieden* (*Perpetual Peace*, 1795), tr. H. B. Nisbet, in *Kant's Political Writings*.

The volume and page numbers refer to those of the Prussian Academy Edition; the same page numbers are included in most English translations; where they are not, the page numbers of the translation cited are included in parentheses after the Academy Edition page number. Quotations from translations have all been checked against the original; where a passage in English appeared cumbersome or misleading, I have offered my own translation.

maxim would be objective. Maxims are termed 'subjective' to indicate that here we are talking about the role of a principle (a principle-token) in the life and action of some subject at or through some time.

Since Kant rejects the preference-based theories of action characteristic of modern liberalism (and relied on even by those contemporary writers who are thought most Kantian), he cannot view the rationality of action in terms of maximizing preference-satisfaction, whether individual or social. The way in which reason can bear on action must be wholly different. The Categorical Imperative—the 'supreme principle of practical reason'—is only the demand to act on maxims on which all *could* act.[9] There is no reference here either to principles to which all consent, or to principles to which they would consent under certain (supposedly ideal) hypothetical conditions. Since Kant does not start with the assumption that the preferences of agents constitute data for ethics, he would not see the pursuit of the objects of actual or of hypothetical preference (whether individual or social) as intrinsically rational, but at most as conditionally, i.e. instrumentally, rational. Kant's conception of practical reason differs from that characteristic of preference-based theories of action in that it is not (merely) instrumental but modal: put intuitively, his view is just that reasoned thought and action should be informed by principles that can be followed by others. Instrumental rationality is not, however, rejected in this conception of practical reason, but rather *aufgehoben*, or picked up and incorporated within it: anything that even approximated to a rejection of means-ends rationality would guarantee that other supposed principles of action could not be interpreted, let alone followed, by others, hence would count as unreasoned. Since the modal constraint that reasoning requires is that we rely on principles that can be followed (understood, acted on, according to context) by others, in acting we must reject those principles that cannot be acted on by all; and so we must rely on principles that have the capacity to be universal laws, i.e. that are lawlike (*gesetzmäßig*—not, as translations often suggest, *lawful*, which hints at some further unexplained source of normative force).

There are various ways in which a principle of action may fail to be lawlike, and Kant says rather too little about the differing types of failure. The most straightforward failure of universalizability is exemplified by principles of damaging, destroying or bypassing capacities to

---

[9] Kant's criterion neither refers to the ways in which agents would act—that would introduce notions of preference or disposition—nor draws on a conception of how they should act—that would be circular.

act in at least some others, including therefore their capacities to act on those (as well as other) principles. Here the proposed principle 'cannot even be conceived as a universal law' (*GMS* IV, 424). The demand that maxims be universalizable therefore evidently rules out maxims whose universal enactment destroys or undermines even some others' capacities to act (e.g. maxims of violence or coercion or destruction).[10] However, the demand that principles be conceivable as universal laws also rules out maxims which destroy agency more indirectly, for example, by dominating or controlling others' capacities to act through institutional structures and practices, or through the misuse of these capacities (e.g. maxims of privilege, of subordination, of deception). Kant classifies the duties that are defined by the contradiction in conception test as *perfect duties*.

Kant's scheme also allows for *imperfect duties*. These duties are defined by the requirement of avoiding principles which, even if they can be 'conceived as a universal law', still cannot be 'willed as a universal law'. This second part of Kant's account of duty depends on the premiss that human beings are purposive, finite rational agents, who pursue sundry ends, which they will not always be able to achieve. Given this view of their situation, they would act irrationally if they willed a principle of universal unhelpfulness or of universal refusal to develop new and needed abilities. Kant observes that a society could exist even if everybody lets their talents rust (supposedly likely the South Sea Islanders) (*GMS* IV, 423) or refuses to help others (there is no contradiction in conception here), and 'yet it is impossible to *will* that such a principle should hold everywhere as a law of nature' (ibid.). This sort of impossibility—the contradiction in the will—arises because mere instrumental rationality commits purposive finite beings to willing that their individual incapacities to achieve their goals be made good from some source or another. Yet willing universal unhelpfulness or universal unconcern for the development of one's own abilities amounts to willing away indispensable ways for such deficits to be made up. Such maxims generate 'contradictions in the will' of those who try to universalize them. Kant concludes that it is a duty not to make a principle of indifference to others (of unhelpfulness) or of failure to develop

---

[10] It is irrelevant to point out that coercion, violence, and the like are not always effective, so that intended victims may sometimes be able to act. A maxim is permissible only in case it can be acted on by all. A hypothetical social world in which everybody supposedly acts to destroy or damage others, but none succeeds, is a world in which we would deny the universal ascription of maxims of destruction or damage.

one's abilities, but that these are imperfect or incomplete duties. In the *Grundlegung* it appears that this imperfection is just a matter of greater indeterminacy in the requirements of duty, that principles of imperfect duty do not specify how, when, or (in the case of imperfect duties to others) for whom the maxim should be enacted.

In Part II of the *Grundlegung* Kant illustrates this classification of duty using four stock examples. His grid lists duties *to self* and *to others* under the respective headings of *perfect* and *imperfect* duties.[11] The illustration of perfect duties to others—the duty not to promise falsely—is a prototype for the duties of justice which are later elaborated in the *Rechtslehre*. The action such duties demand (in this case not making false promises) is relatively well-defined and is owed to specifiable others; it can be legally enforced, for example, by giving those who are defrauded by false promisers rights of redress which can be pursued in the courts. This is not, of course, to say that the maxim not to promise falsely is an algorithm that fully guides action, let alone that it demands uniformity of conduct of those who conform to the rule. What one has to do evidently depends on the relation between what one is tempted to promise and what one is minded to deliver. (The fantasy that rules whose scope is universal must be rules that prescribe uniform action for all who fall within that scope is not one that Kant shares—however often it is ascribed to him.) The other three types of duty listed in the *Grundlegung* are all of them apparently unfit to be legal duties. All are examples of types of duties dealt with not in the *Rechtslehre* but in the *Tugendlehre*.

2. KANT'S CLASSIFICATION OF DUTIES IN THE *TUGENDLEHRE*

In the opening paragraph of the *Tugendlehre* Kant notes that while the ancients used the term *ethica* to signify the whole of moral philosophy, it has now become customary to distinguish between the two sorts of duties that constitute *ius* and *ethica*. He does not infer that *ethica* has been superseded by *ius*, but only that we must understand the difference. The duties which form the subject matter of *Rechtslehre* can be

---

[11] See T. Campbell, 'Perfect and Imperfect Obligations', *The Modern Schoolman* 52 (1975), 285–94, for an account of the varied uses of the distinction between perfect and imperfect duties. As we shall see, there is more to Kant's use of this ancient distinction than an awareness that imperfect duties are less determinate than perfect duties.

imposed by 'outer' legislation. Other duties, which cannot be matters for 'outer' legislation, constitute the domain of ethics in its modern, narrower sense. Since nobody can be compelled by others to perform duties which are not capable of outer legislation, these duties are classified as needing 'inner' legislation.

This contrast between duties needing 'outer' and 'inner' legislation allows Kant ready—perhaps too ready—access to the thought that if there are some duties which cannot be externally enforced, they must by default be self-imposed, so that fulfilling them will always need effort or courage,[12] which can be equated with *virtus* or *fortitudo moralis*, and consequently that an account of these duties will constitute a 'Doctrine of Virtue'.[13] The duties that constitute ethics in the modern sense are duties of virtue not only because this term is ancient, available, and respectable, but also to mark an important contrast with *ius*: whatever else these duties that are not part of justice demand, they demand strength of will or self-mastery. Neither *apatheia* or mere passive habit is ever enough. Courage is needed for all the variously directed virtues that constitute *ethica* (*MS* VI, 406–9). For Kant the moral life is a matter of struggle rather than of harmony, and the regulative virtue is neither prudence, nor justice, nor temperance, but courage: 'moral strength, as courage (*fortitudo moralis*) is . . . also called true or practical wisdom' (*MS* VI, 405).[14]

---

[12] *Tapferkeit*; later Kant makes the point using other idioms. At several points he speaks of 'moral strength of will' (*eine moralische Stärke des Willens*) (*MS* VI, 405), and at one explicit passage he speaks of the need '*seiner selbst in einem gegebenen fall Meister (animus sui compos) und über sich selbst Herr zu sein (imperium in semetipsum), d.i. seine Affecten zu zähmen und seine Leidenschaften zu beherrschen*' (*MS* VI, 407). In the *Religion* he again stresses the close etymological link between virtue and courage, and the claim of courage to have an organizing role for all virtue (*R* VI, 67 (50)). These thoughts also explain why Kant holds that only finite beings can have virtues: Holy Wills would not have to struggle or be courageous to be good, so we do not call their goodness 'virtue' (*MS* VI, 383 and 404).

[13] '*Also ist die allgemeine Pflichtenlehre in dem Theil, der nicht die äußere Freiheit, sondern die innere unter Gesetze bringte, eine Tugendlehre*' (*MS* VI, 380).

[14] In this Kant differs sharply from the Stoic writers he admires. The source of the difference lies in his accounts of freedom and of evil. Although Kant does not think that our nature or our natural desires are bad (*R* VI, 69 (51)), he does hold that the moral life may require overcoming rather than harmonizing with nature: 'Those valiant men [the Stoics] mistook their enemy: for he is not to be sought in the merely undisciplined natural inclinations which present themselves so openly to everyone's consciousness; rather is he, as it were, an invisible foe . . . They called out wisdom against folly instead of summoning her against wickedness.' (*R* VI, 68 (50)). On Kant's account, virtue is 'a capacity of becoming able to master the greatest obstacles in ourselves' (*R* VI, 283 (171)) and 'the true courage of virtue consists in . . . facing the evil principle within ourselves' (*ZEF* VI, 379 (124)).

This reconstruction of what virtue is may seem to be achieved at the cost of making it an individual, inward, and private affair. By driving the virtues into the self, and specifically into the will, Kant may open himself to one of the criticisms often made of his ethics as a whole, namely that he rests too much upon the fragile structure of the voluntary, and specifically of introspection.[15]

Contemporary virtue ethicists differ in how much they are willing to rest on this fragile structure, but many of them—and in particular communitarians—insist that the locus of virtue is not the inner self but rather the shared practices, traditions, and ways of life of a community. These writers in their turn come under fire for identifying virtue too closely with social practices, with what has actually been established and accepted. Construed in this way, the alternatives both look uncomfortable. Either virtue is identified too intimately with solitary moral effort, inwardness, and introspection, and so with an excessive individualism, or it is to be assimilated too closely to established, and no doubt often to establishment, practices. This uncomfortable dilemma provides reason for looking more carefully at Kant's claim that duties of virtue are 'inner'.

3. INNER AND OUTER LEGISLATION

The distinction which Kant draws between inner and outer aspects of duty is a distinction between the sorts of 'legislation' or constraint by which they can be imposed or required. A 'legal' duty can be externally imposed; a duty of virtue must be self-imposed (*MS* VI, 379). While many would agree that certain duties which we think are not matters of justice ought not to be imposed, it is far from obvious that or why they cannot be imposed. Many debates about the limits of the State, the boundaries between public and private, and the enforcement of morals would surely be redundant if morals—virtue—could not be enforced by law. Further, we may suspect, much that is not legally enforced is (as virtue ethicists emphasize) socially enforced by other practices and disciplines. Yet Kant's claim is unequivocally that the duties with which the *Tugendlehre* deals cannot be enforced, rather than that they should not be enforced.

There appear to be two distinct reasons why Kant holds that certain

[15] See B. Williams, *Ethics and the Limits of Philosophy* (London, 1985), 194.

duties cannot be enforced, and so need 'inner legislation'. Some duties cannot be enforced because they are duties to oneself, others because they are structurally unsuited to enforcement, while a third group of duties is unenforceable for both reasons. The *Tugendlehre* takes these three groups of duties in turn.

Book I of the *Tugendlehre* concerns 'Perfect Duties to Oneself' (*MS* VI, 421–44). These are duties to refrain from fairly well-specified acts which would destroy or severely damage agents' own natural or moral capacities. Kant's examples of perfect duties not to destroy the natural basis of one's own action include refraining from suicide out of self-love (the *Grundlegung* example), or from damaging one's body, for example by self-mutilation or self-stupefaction. His examples of perfect duties not to undercut the moral basis of one's own action include duties to refrain from lying or insincerity, from self-denial (which he classifies as misdirected avarice), and from servility. Although Kant may be wrong in thinking that none of these 'perfect duties to self' can be externally enforced—after all, attempted suicide has been, and drug abuse remains, a crime in many jurisdictions—it is evidently hard to police self-regarding acts.

Kant hesitates over whether the 'perfect duties to self' that he discusses in the first part of the *Tugendlehre* should count as full duties of virtue (see *MS* VI, 409, 418). Duties of virtue in the full sense are unenforceable not because they are self-directed but because they are *imperfect*, which makes them structurally unsuited to enforcement, even when owed to others. The structural feature that distinguishes these imperfect duties is that they are duties to adopt certain ends. External legislation and compulsion must fail for such duties as well, but for quite different reasons. We can be forced to do acts but not to adopt ends or purposes (*MS* VI, 381). External compulsion could at most secure an outward show of virtue, by enforcing action that can be read as expressive of a certain maxim of ends. In the *Grundlegung* Kant does not make it fully clear that the source of the greater indeterminacy and consequent unenforceability of imperfect duties lies in this structural difference. However, in the *Metaphysik der Sitten* he frames his account of the greater indeterminacy of duties of virtue in an answer to the question 'how an end that is also a duty is possible' (*MS* VI, 381–2), which provides the basis for the accounts of imperfect duties to self (*MS* VI, 444–7) and to others (*MS* VI, 448–73) which form Book II of the *Tugendlehre*.

Evidently Kant's account of duty could not be subordinated to that of a subjective end without giving up everything that is central to his position. If Kant argues for duties to pursue ends, he will have to argue for objective ends. He does so by pointing out that since human action is intrinsically purposive—undertaken for certain ends, which are usually but not necessarily subjective—the maxims on which we act will refer to ends, so that the restraints of the Categorical Imperative can apply as readily to maxims that mention ends as to other maxims. Accordingly, the first principle of the doctrine of virtue is: 'act according to a *maxim of ends* that it can be a universal law for everyone to have' (*MS* VI, 395). This idea might be glossed by saying that while justice requires only that practical principles that specify certain sorts of outward performance be adoptable by all, virtue demands that the wider strategies and policies on which purposive beings base their lives also be adoptable by all.

This line of thought clarifies one negative sense in which duties of virtue must be inward: since they are duties whose principle cannot be tied down to specified acts, they are duties which cannot be enforced by external sanctions, for such action could, contrary to hypothesis, be externally enforced.[16] A principle of action that cannot be tied down to specific acts must, of course, still have some content, but this content may be given by constraining the end of action rather than by more specific prohibitions or prescriptions. Principles of virtue will be maxims of ends, rather than of action; their enactment will be revealed in action in highly varied ways.

Kant organizes his classification of imperfect duties—of virtue proper—on the assumption that two ranges of objective ends are particularly important. Our wider strategies and principles may aim either at natural or at moral ends. Happiness and perfection constitute the most general description of the objective ends under each of these headings. (Principles of refusing either end generate contradictions in the will.) However, the relation of these two ends to duty is asymmetric in our own case and in others'. Our own happiness can hardly be a matter of duty, since it is something to which natural beings are by definition committed—although often wildly mistaken about what would make them happy or how to achieve it. Kant also holds that others' perfection can

---

[16] In fact many aspects of the imperfect duties discussed in the *Tugendlehre* are relatively determinate, hence enforceable, although their justification works by way of arguments to establish obligatory maxims of ends. They are, so to speak, among the indispensable elements of acting on policies, most of whose enactments will vary with circumstances. The duties cannot be reduced to requirements to act in specific ways.

hardly be a matter of duty, since it is something which we cannot provide for others.[17] It follows that the ends which we have a duty to adopt reduce to others' happiness and our own perfection (*fremde Glückseligkeit, eigene Vollkommenheit*)—so returning us to the illustrations of imperfect duty of the *Grundlegung*. In each case these ends greatly underdetermine action: evidently we cannot do all that is needed to achieve either end, what we can do will vary with circumstances, and in nearly all circumstances there will be many ways of meeting the demands of imperfect duty.

In spite of this openness of duties of virtue, they will have many implications for what we ought to do in particular circumstances. If lives are not to be based on indifference either to others' happiness or to our own perfection, a lot may be demanded. In a less Kantian vocabulary, what is required is that lives be informed both by the social virtues which sustain others' happiness and by commitment to one's own self-improvement, and that each commitment be expressed appropriately in action.

Against this background we can raise again the question whether Kant adopts too psychological and inward an account of virtue. Does his insistence that virtue is a matter of adopting certain ends, which are variously expressible, which cannot be enforced, and whose pursuit needs moral strength of will, require him to see virtue as inner orientation to be ascertained by introspection, or to deny the connection between virtue and actual practices and institutions? This reading of Kant's account of virtue is the very one that draws the criticism of contemporary virtue ethicists. Yet there are striking textual reasons not to attribute it to Kant: for how can Kant view the virtues as a matter of inner, introspectible states, given that he has deep doubts about the reliability of introspection? The great obstacle to reading Kant's account of virtue as a matter of psychological inwardness is his view of self-knowledge, or rather of our lack of self-knowledge, and his conviction that we often do not and perhaps never can know with certainty what our maxims are.

---

[17] See *MS* VI, 386. This contention is surprising. In the *Tugendlehre*, Kant divides the duty to seek our own perfection into duties to seek our moral and our natural perfection. It is clear enough that the former is a task that we must largely undertake for ourselves, although Kant also holds that educators have a role here. (See the remarks on 'ethical didactic' in *MS* VI, 478–84; and in later works Kant speaks of shared ethical duties: see n. 14 and p. 97 below.) But it is false that we cannot improve others' natural talents. Perhaps the thought should rather be that we cannot have a duty to do so, since we have a prior duty to respect others, which means that we may at most help to develop talents that they want developed. In that case the development of their natural talents would fall under Kant's conception of the duty to help others, which he construes as a duty not to refuse others all help in the pursuit of permissible ends (*MS* VI, 388).

4. MISANTHROPY, OPACITY, AND SELF-KNOWLEDGE

From the beginning of the *Grundlegung* Kant insists that we do not know clearly what our maxims are on a given occasion. It is one thing to identify what the maxims of duty are—that the Categorical Imperative can achieve. It is quite another to ascertain what a particular agent's maxim, even our own maxim, was on a particular occasion. Kant's insistence on the opacity of the human mind and the limits of self-knowledge are extraordinarily strong. In the *Grundlegung* we are reminded that it is difficult to tell whether a grocer gives honest change out of honesty or out of liking for his customer (*GMS* IV, 397); that we 'can never, even by the most strenuous self-examination, get to the bottom of our secret impulsions' (*GMS* IV, 407); that we 'become doubtful whether there is any genuine virtue to be encountered in the world' (*GMS* IV, 407); that indeed 'up to now there may have existed no loyal friend' (*GMS* IV, 408).

It has been commonplace, since Schiller satirically suggested that Kantian duty must be done with grim distaste,[18] to read these passages as exemplifying Kant's supposed misanthropy. Yet this charge is hard to sustain in the light of the later works, which stress the opacity of the human mind or heart to an even greater extent, but explicitly reject misanthropy.[19] The heightened stress on the opacity of the self in the later writings shows clearly in passages such as these: 'The depths of the human heart are unfathomable. Who knows himself well enough to say whether his motive for fulfilling his duty proceeds entirely from the thought of the law or whether there are not many other impulses . . .

[18] The theme recurs constantly in contemporary work, mostly in discussions of Kant's supposedly inadequate account of the role of the emotions in moral life. See B. Williams, 'Morality and the Emotions', in *The Problems of the Self* (Cambridge, 1973), 207–29, and 'Persons, Character and Morality', in *Moral Luck* (Cambridge, 1981), 1–19. For textually more detailed discussions see M. Baron, 'Was Effi Briest a Victim of Kantian Morality?', *Philosophy and Literature* 12 (1988), 95–113; L. Hinman, 'On the Purity of our Moral Motives: a Critique of Kant's Account of the Emotions and Acting for the Sake of Duty', *The Monist* 66 (1983), 251–67; B. Herman, 'Agency, Attachment and Difference', *Ethics* 101 (1991), 775–97.

[19] Some difficulties in extending the charge of misanthropy to the later works include the importance Kant attaches to progress and to hope, as well as passages in which he explicitly rejects claims that human desires and inclinations are morally bad. Within the *Tugendlehre* and other later works he places great emphasis on the social virtues, depicts the pursuit of happiness as an indirect duty, and attacks the 'monkish' virtues, including self-abasement, moroseness, and the like.

self-knowledge is never adequate to show us whether we possess the sum-total of virtues' (*MS* VI, 446–7), and 'maxims cannot be observed, not even in oneself' (*R* VI, 20 (16)).

This suggests to me that the stress on limits of self-knowledge may have a more systematic role in Kant's practical philosophy than it is usually given, and one that has little to do with the issue of misanthropy. By way of background, it may be worth remembering Kant's highly critical view of the doctrine of the soul of the rationalist philosophers, and in particular his clear dismissal, in the Deductions and Paralogisms of the *Critique of Pure Reason*, of the thought that we are transparent to ourselves. If we have only empirical, hence fallible, self-insight, then we cannot guarantee what our maxim is on any given occasion. Our maxims are not available for privileged inspection; they may not be directly accessible to consciousness. Others' maxims are equally hidden from us, a matter of fallible inference from their acts and avowals.

If we read Kant's practical philosophy in the way that those who accuse him of excessive individualism and too much stress on the fragile structure of the voluntary do, it would be hard to make sense of these passages. For then we must see Kant both as holding that morality, and certainly that part of morality which is not *Rechtslehre*, is a matter of getting one's maxims right, and as saying that our maxims are systematically elusive. And yet Kant is known for his robust insistence that 'I need no far-reaching ingenuity to find out what I have to do in order to possess a good will' (*GMS* IV, 403). Even if the Categorical Imperative can be used to discriminate maxims of duty, the results seem practically useless if we are then unable to tell who, if anyone, ever acts on any given maxim. I believe that the only way in which Kant's practical philosophy can be rescued from this impasse is to distinguish carefully between the requirements for acting and for judging action. More generally we must distinguish the significant contribution maxims can make to practice—to guiding action—from their meagre contribution to theoretical explanation.[20]

Consider what difference it makes if maxims are systematically

[20] Models of choice that are based on a purely instrumental conception of reason integrate the practical and the theoretical. One and the same constellation of beliefs and desires is supposed to explain acts and guide agents. However, Kant's accounts of theory and practice constitute two mutually irreducible yet jointly necessary standpoints. See the Deductions and Paralogisms of the *Critique of Pure Reason*, and also *GMS*, part iii; for attempted articulations of these issues see H. Allison, *Kant's Theory of Freedom* (Cambridge, 1990) and O'Neill, *Constructions*, chs. 3 and 4.

elusive. In the case of duties of justice it seems to make little enough difference. Here we know with some specificity what conformity to a given maxim of duty will demand, and what non-conformity would be. Moreover, here it is *conformity* to duty that most interests us. We care more whether the shopkeeper gives the right change than we care about the principle which lies behind his action. Even if we can never tell when agents act 'out of duty', so that there are some aspects of just action that systematically elude us, still it will be significant if standards to which people ought in justice to conform and can be required to conform have been identified. Nor does this gap in our knowledge matter when we seek to act justly: even if I am unsure whether I act justly 'out of duty', and indeed even if I know that I have less respectable but congruent desires, still I can do it. Just action need only be action that conforms very scrupulously to what an agent with just principles would do in those circumstances. From the point of view of justice it does not matter if our underlying principle is less pure than we aspired to make it.

But with imperfect duties matters are quite different. First, it seems that from the point of view of virtue it must matter what our principles actually are. Secondly, and yet more damagingly, it seems that the idea of mere conformity to principles of virtue will be empty if virtuous maxims specify ends but not acts.[21] Kant's reason for holding that duties of virtue cannot be externally enforced is, after all, that they are more indeterminate. If the external requirements of virtue were fixed, then it would not matter from a practical point of view whether we could know who really held those principles: but then virtue would be enforceable, and indeed indistinguishable from *ius*, contradicting two of Kant's central claims. But if the external requirements of virtue are not fixed, as Kant insists, then it seems that the only way in which we could tell whether agents act virtuously would be by ascertaining their inner principles, which is impossible according to another of his central claims. We cannot, it seems, combine the two claims that our maxims of virtue are hidden or largely hidden, and that their expression in action is not fixed. Anyone who tried to hold both of these views would seemingly lose all grip on the picture of agents as acting on principles.[22]

---

[21] Although Kant holds that imperfect duties may have some definite and inescapable requirements, these are less than virtue requires. See nn. 16 and 17.

[22] Here see Bittner, 'How to Act on Principle', who puts the point vividly: 'If you can never find out what maxim you are acting upon, the task of acting only on a morally

5. INTROSPECTION, ASCRIPTION, AND PRESCRIPTION

These considerations seem to force an unwelcome dilemma on Kant's ethics, and most of all on his account of virtue. One possibility is that we will be driven to see virtue as inward in a quite traditional, psychological sense, in that it is an inner state of agents whose outward signs may be highly variable. If so, Kant must defend an individualistic and psychologistic moral epistemology, and rest his whole conception of virtue upon a view of the voluntary; and further, he must deny the fragility of the voluntary in order to make room for his claims about strength of will. On this reading, Kant's repeated claims about the opacity of the self, human frailty, and the unknowability of maxims must simply be disregarded. Alternatively, we can maintain Kant's view of the opacity of self and our lack of knowledge of maxims, but then we cannot also maintain that the demands of virtue are systematically indeterminate. On the contrary, if we are opaque, and introspective moral psychology is either false or unreliable, then virtue must be much more determinate, and must be identified with certain outward patterns of action—for example with certain sorts of social practice or *Sittlichkeit*. On this reading, the gap between *ius* and *ethica* must be seen as illusory.

The source of this dilemma lies in Kant's account of action, while its damaging implications lie in his ethics. The damage could only be averted if his account of action could be read differently. That account centres on the idea of acting on a principle. Principles, it seems, could be imputed to agents on either of two bases. They could be thought of as objects of introspection, as inner states of agents, with variable outward expression. In this case we must put quite a lot of weight on the reliability of introspection, which must provide the privileged evidence for judging which principles agents adopt and whether they act virtuously. This will lead us to a much-criticized conception of the philosophy of mind and of moral psychology, which credits mental acts (volitions, intentions, decisions, mental reservations) with a primary role in an agent's moral life and makes them the determinants of virtue.[23] Looked at in

worthy one becomes as desperate as that of obeying a God who is radically inaccessible to human understanding.' (25)

[23] However, it is difficult to read Kant's account of action as centred on mental acts or inner events. A Kantian practical principle is by definition a determination of the will, not a separate mental event that causes action, and not an inert mental state that can be linked to action only when supplemented by an external source of motivation such as a desire or preference.

this way, Kant's 'moral strength of will' appears as the *deus ex machina* that is to catapult those inner states into action.

Alternatively, we could reconnect principles to action in the world, by viewing action as criterial for the ascription of principles. However, if we taken an ascriptive rather than an introspective view of principles, we face other difficulties. For then we seemingly cannot hold onto the view that the connection between principles of virtue and action is wholly underdefined. Yet the ascriptive reading of maxims has a certain amount of textual support. Background evidence includes the many discussions of self-knowledge and opacity already referred to, which severely damage any introspective reading of maxims. But the main passages that point to an ascriptive rather than an introspective view of maxims are to be found in the *Religion*. There Kant states explicitly that an agent 'can form no certain and definite conception of his real disposition through an immediate consciousness thereof and can only abstract it from the way of life he has actually followed', and that 'it is from the action before him that he must infer his disposition' (*R* VI, 77 (71)).[24]

However, an ascriptive account of maxims offers cold comfort. On a *wholly* ascriptive reading of Kant's account of maxims, we must ascribe to agents whatever principles make sense of the pattern of their action, and this inference will always be underdetermined. It follows that multiple principles will always be ascribable, that we will never know that a particular maxim is or was acted on, and that we will not be able to make good sense of the notion that duties of virtue are inward in a way that duties of justice are not. If patterns of outward action are the total evidence for having a maxim, we have lost all grip on the picture of principles as distinct from their enactment; there is no sense in which virtue is distinctively inward and we may as well view virtue as *Sittlichkeit*. The view of maxims as determinations of the will would then have to be seen as no more than an epicycle in a conception of virtue as practice, as the lingering trace of an older conception of the power of introspection to discern the features of an inner realm.

If introspection and ascription were the only ways for thinking of maxims, we would have to conclude that Kant's account of duties of virtue—and perhaps his entire account of morality—is deeply flawed because it hovers between two incompatible conceptions of the relation

[24] However, these passages refer explicitly to the most fundamental maxims—dispositions (*Gesinnungen*)—that inform action; perhaps they are not decisive for our understanding of other more specific maxims, to which we may have a limited, fallible introspective access.

of principle to action, neither of which he fully accepts.[25] Kant's ethics would indeed fail because his epistemology of action and his moral psychology both fail. I believe that there are at least two further ways of looking at the matter which are worth exploring.

The first of these would argue that maxims are discoverable by a combination of introspection and ascription. Kant does not, after all, deny that empirical, fallible self-knowledge is possible—and that may be all we need to get *some* view of what agents take their maxims to be, which can be supplemented and corrected by the evidence their acts and avowals provide. This dual approach to the ascertaining of maxims is enough to give us some grip on the thought that maxims are inward, and even to make sense of Kant's claim that progress towards self-knowledge, although never fully attainable, is a duty (*MS* VI, 441–2). Above all, it does not collapse evidence for maxims into evidence for action, and so can make sense of the underlying picture of agents as holding maxims which they may translate into action with variable enthusiasm or efficacy, with variable fortitude or frailty (see *R* VI, 29–30 (24–5)).

However, it seems that this dual view of maxims as ascertainable by a combination of introspection and ascription will be quite inadequate for practical purposes. For there action, if there is to be any, lies ahead. Hence it seems that in contexts of action we would be driven back to a solely introspective view of maxims—otherwise we would have to put far too much weight on the desperate strategy of finding out what our maxim is by waiting to find out what we do. Yet maxims are defined by Kant as practical principles, whose primary relevance is for agents who seek to work out what to do.

If the practical task is primary, this suggests another way in which maxims can be important, which does not depend upon the introspective or ascriptive identification of maxims already present in an agent. In deliberation agents may ask themselves questions such as 'What must I do if I am not to be indifferent to others' happiness?', or 'In the situation in which I find myself, what could I do if I am not to neglect to develop my talents?', or 'What does kindness (or honesty or gratitude)

---

[25] Once again Bittner puts the challenge well: 'Two things are difficult to understand about the account of agency in terms of maxims. First, what it is for an individual to have a maxim and second what it is to act on a maxim. The account of agency in terms of maxims needs this concept. According to this account an agent acts as he does because he has the maxim he has. If there is no such thing as having a maxim which is intelligible separately from acting on it, this claim becomes empty, and the maxim turns into a bare *virtus dormitiva*' ('How to Act on Principle', 6–7).

require here?'[26] Seen from the practical standpoint, maxims can be identified as the prescriptions agents strive to follow, whose enactment in varying circumstances is the object of their practical deliberation and of their moral striving.

Even if maxims are not knowable by introspection, and not determinable by ascription, reference to practical principles can be indispensable for guiding action. The greater indeterminacy of principles of virtue—of principles of ends whose rejection cannot coherently be universalized—does not mean that we do not need to refer to those principles in order to act virtuously. However, virtuous action does not require us to know which principles we have successfully internalized, but only which principles we are striving to live up to. The theoretical ambitions of ascertaining what agents' maxims actually are will remain unsatisfied: even agents who deliberate well and seek to live virtuously will provide less than conclusive evidence that their action really flows from maxims of virtue. No doubt they will live lives which neglect neither the happiness of others nor the cultivation of talents, and will treat principles of virtue as defining the ideals towards which they strive (see *MS* VI, 469–74 on friendship). Yet whatever pattern of action they achieve could also reflect quite other maxims, and the evidence provided by introspection and ascription will never be decisive. However, these limitations of self- and of other-knowledge are not obstacles to the practical task of striving to live in a way that would, in the circumstances, constitute a clear enactment of virtue.

Even if we were wholly opaque to ourselves and to others, and lacked even the limited and fallible capacities for introspection Kant credits us with, we could still use practical principles to guide action. When we do so we have to identify a principle—for example a principle of virtue—and to ask what might be done if we are to strive to make that principle inform our lives and our action. This emphasis on the practical context and the task of striving to live by moral principles can, I think, shed a bit more light on the reasons why Kant, despite his great admiration for the Stoics, makes courage rather than temperance the regulative virtue. He sees virtue not as a matter of bringing our varied desires into harmony by moderating and tempering them, but as the more strenuous demand that where they conflict we subordinate self-love to morality (see *R* VI, 69–70 n., 49–50 n.). Although our natural

---

[26] Often they will not need to deliberate—appropriate action will be done without hesitation. Kant does not hold that virtuous action inevitably needs deliberation, but that it may.

inclinations, '*considered in themselves*, are *good*' (*R* VI, 69 (51)), there is no guarantee that all the desires we happen to have will harmonize with morality. When they do harmonize, Kantian morality will make no further demand for temperance; when they do not, it will demand not temperance but courage. The role of strength of will and self-mastery in lives of Kantian virtue goes beyond the demands of moderation: 'the true strength of virtue is a tranquil mind with a deliberate and firm resolution to put the law of virtue into practice' (*MS* VI, 409). Hence for Kant virtue is not so much an account of what agents ought to be, as of what they ought actively to strive towards: 'Virtue is always in progress and yet always beginning from the beginning. It is always in progress because, considered objectively, it is an ideal that is unattainable, while yet our duty is constantly to approximate it.' (ibid.)[27] The inwardness of virtue will not then be a matter of its being an object of introspection, or of inference, but of its being enactable only through a certain sort of effort which nobody else can supply for us.

However, for these very reasons we will also be faced with great ambiguities in trying to judge others' action or our own past action. Patterns of action will always be compatible with the ascription of various maxims, and if maxims cannot be known directly or with certainty, we may often be unsure which of several maxims should be ascribed to an agent. This, I suspect, is how things really are; in life, as in novels, the hermeneutics of action often leaves us unsure which principles may be ascribed to others or to ourselves, hence unsure whether they or we act virtuously. We often cannot tell whether conflicting evidence points to an aberration or bad judgement in somebody of virtuous character, or is revelatory of bad character in someone whose mask of virtue has hitherto convinced us (see 'vices still concealed under the mask of virtue', *R* VI, 33 (29)). As Kant's many striking comments on the opacity of the human heart show, he never thought the theoretical task of judging our own and others' virtue achievable:

no-one can have certain awareness of *having fulfilled* his duty completely unselfishly. For this is part of inward experience, and such awareness of one's psychological state would involve an absolutely clear conception of all the secondary notions and considerations which, through imagination, habit and.

---

[27] Further textual evidence for the regulative role of courage in the Kantian life of virtue lies in the metaphors that characterize progress towards virtue in *Religion Within the Limits of Reason Alone*, whose four books are organized under the headings of *coexistence* (*Einwohnung*; better, *juxtaposition*) of evil with good in human nature, their *conflict*, the *victory* of the good, and *service* of the good.

inclination, accompany the concept of duty. And this is too much to ask for. . . . But man is aware with the utmost clarity that he *ought to fulfil* his duty (*TP* VIII, 284 (69)).

A prescriptive reading of Kant's account of the relation of maxims to acts can also explain the ease and unconcern with which Kant shifts his attention in several later works from the virtues of individuals to the virtues of a social order—a move that would be wholly puzzling if virtues were psychological states of individuals that could only be discerned by introspection. The best-known passage where Kant does this is in his discussion of duties of social transformation and improvement in the *Religion* and elsewhere. There he claims that 'the human race', as an ethical commonwealth, has the duty to seek certain ends. Many other passages in the later works turn to the duties of virtue of societies to achieve an ethical transformation (see *R* VI, 97 (89); *SF* VII, 87 (184)). Kant is untroubled by the thought that such maxims of virtue cannot be thought of as inward psychological states, because he views their 'inwardness' as no more than the impossibility of enforcing such practical principles by external legislation.

If this picture is plausible, then while Kant's account of virtue can be read as articulating an indispensable element of an answer to the question 'How ought I, or we, to act virtuously?', it cannot answer the question 'How can we know who is virtuous?', nor even the more intimate and worrying questions, 'How can I know whether I am virtuous?' and 'How can we know that we are heading towards a virtuous society?' In the matters of virtue, Kant holds that we can go no further than to say of a life we know, or of somebody's conduct, or of the progress of some society, that it bears marks that would in those circumstances be found in lives and societies informed by principles of virtue. From a theoretical standpoint this might be less than we might want: for we might want to know who had succeeded and who had failed morally. From a practical standpoint it can be enough to know the ends of virtuous lives and societies—to know what maxims they should strive to exemplify—and to discern some ways of striving towards those ends in actual circumstances.

6

Virtue Ethics, Utilitarianism, and Symmetry

MICHAEL SLOTE

A distinctive approach to ethics needs its own distinctive ethical principle or set of principles. Whatever one says, for example, about the arguments Rawls gives in defence of his Difference Principle, the Principle itself is an ethically interesting one, and indeed it may represent the most markedly original feature of Rawls's view. (There are obvious precedents to the notion of an original position, and as Rawls himself pointed out, the device of a veil of ignorance had been employed previously. But the idea, roughly, that we should raise the floor of benefits as high as possible for our society is only very partially anticipated in the historically familiar assumption that social, political, or moral rules should be to everyone's benefit even if they benefit some more than others.)

Act-utilitarianism also, of course, is distinguished by its underlying principles or principle (assuming only that we are capable of fixing on a particular formulation of the Principle of Utility), and other well-known ethical theories, e.g. Kantianism, also rest on or employ certain individuating fundamental principles. But virtue ethics has seemed different. Its advocates have considered it an advantage in ethics to rely on ideals of character or motive rather than on injunctions or rules, and so it may seem obvious that what is most distinctive of genuine virtue ethics will be its *refusal* to promulgate itself through, and base itself on, rules, principles, or general injunctions. (On such an understanding of virtue ethics, Aristotle's doctrine of the mean presumably does not give rise to an *injunction* to act medially in all situations.)

In the present essay, however, I shall argue that a certain sort of common-sense virtue ethics is naturally, indeed essentially, associated with its own distinctive principles or general injunctions. And it will turn out that an important subset of those principles bears a strong resemblance to utilitarianism's own Principle of Utility. Both utilitarianism and the virtue ethics I wish to describe (and in some measure defend) are self-other symmetric in a way that both Kantian ethics and common-sense moral views about obligation and permissibility are not, and in what follows I shall say more about the notion of self-other symmetry. But I shall then go on to show that utilitarianism and virtue ethics are self-other symmetric *in different ways*, and getting clear about the differences will in the end enable us to formulate distinctive general principles for a virtue ethics that seeks to remain true to our intuitive understanding of what is admirable and deplorable in human character and action.

I

Self-other symmetry is a familiar feature of utilitarianism and its Principle of Utility. Act-utilitarianism and act-consequentialism more generally are agent-neutral: no person may be treated in any way fundamentally different from the way any other person is treated, and this uniformity of treatment crosses the boundary between agent/self and other as well as that between different others. In utilitarianism, if something is permissibly done or obligatory to do with respect to one individual, it is permissible or obligatory in regard to any other individual, as long as the pleasure-related causal facts behind such moral judgements remain otherwise the same. Therefore, if it is wrong for me in some way to neglect the good of another person, it is, according to utilitarianism, wrong for me to neglect myself in that way, and similarly with respect to hurting myself or hurting another. By the same token, the utilitarian or consequentialist will hold that where there is a choice between my own greater good and the lesser good of another, it will be morally worse for me to choose the latter, just as it would be morally worse to prefer *my own* lesser good to the greater good of another person.

By contrast, ordinary intuitive or common-sense morality is self-other asymmetric in the very ways we have just seen utilitarianism to be self-other symmetric. Neglecting the well-being of another person can sometimes intuitively seem wrong in a way or to a degree that it does not seem wrong—though it may be foolish or eccentric—to neglect oneself, and similar points apply, from the standpoint of common-sense, to issues of harming others vs. harming oneself. Furthermore, ordinary moral thinking would tend to regard it as morally *better* to choose the lesser good of another rather than secure one's own greater good, and it would ascribe no positive moral value to actions that simply give their agent pleasure or something she very much wants for her own uses.

Common-sense moral thinking is thus highly self-other asymmetric, and in that respect stands in marked contrast with act-utilitarianism and act-consequentialism.[1]

In related but somewhat different ways, Kantian moral views are also self-other asymmetric. For Kant there is no fundamental duty or obligation to secure one's own happiness or well-being, but such a duty or obligation toward others does exist; and it can be morally good (from duty) to seek the happiness of others and bad not to do so, but corresponding moral judgments about the agent's own happiness lack a Kantian basis.[2]

Interestingly enough, our ordinary aretic judgements about what is admirable and what is deplorable, what is a virtue and what is a vice or anti-virtue, are not self-other asymmetric in the manner of ordinary moral judgements, but resemble, rather, what we have found to be true of act-utilitarianism and act-consequentialism. Our assessment of whether a given character trait counts as a virtue or of whether a given act exemplifies a virtue is favourably affected by the consideration that it benefits people other than its possessor or agent. But it is no less favourably affected by the consideration that a given trait or act is or tends to be useful to its possessor or agent. And analogous points can be made about traits or acts that harm others and those that harm the possessor/agent.

Note, however, that talk about what is admirable, or what is or exemplifies a virtue, is not specifically moral. The kind of sagacity, prudence, and far-sightedness demonstrated, legendarily, by Bernard Baruch when he sold all his common stock right before the crash of 1929 is admired by many of us, but it would be odd to speak of the above traits as *moral* virtues or of what Baruch did as *morally* good or admirable. Rather, we think of the above traits as virtues, as admirable *tout court*, and if we admire Baruch, it is not for his moral stature or accomplishments. Our thinking about virtue status and our admiration generally are not limited to what is normally thought of as moral and/or other-regarding,[3] and indeed, our ordinary thinking about moral rightness and goodness

---

[1] The 'agent-sacrificing' self-other asymmetry we have just ascribed to ordinary moral thought is not inconsistent with the common-sense moral permissibility of *favouring* oneself over others in certain ways. On this point see my *From Morality to Virtue* (Oxford, 1992), ch. 1.

[2] For fuller discussion of Kantian asymmetries between self and other, see *From Morality to Virtue*, chs. 1, 2, 3, and 6.

[3] When we speak of virtue in the singular and without the indefinite article, we are typically speaking of moral virtue, but our talk of what counts as *a* virtue and of (the) virtues is not limited in this way, and I am understanding the idea of an ethics of virtue in this broader sense.

is self-other asymmetric in a way that we have just seen our thought about the virtues and about what is admirable not to be.

However, that now leaves both utilitarianism and our common-sense understanding of what is admirable or a virtue counting as self-other symmetric. And we might well at this point wonder whether the latter view must therefore coincide with utilitarianism in its ultimate principles and judgements. But if neither disregards or plays down the self-regarding in the manner of common-sense morality and (to a lesser extent) of Kantian ethics, still, utilitarianism and common-virtue ethics have different ways of relating the self-regarding and the other-regarding. Both can be said to be self-other symmetric, but they espouse differing, indeed incompatible, ideals of self-other symmetry. Utilitarianism's symmetry derives in a familiar fashion from its agent-neutrality, but the self-other symmetry I believe we can find in our ordinary views about the admirable in human character and action—what I shall henceforth call 'common-sense virtue ethics'—is far less philosophically familiar, and it is time for us to say more about it.

II

When we look at the whole range of traits commonly regarded as virtues and actions we admire, we observe a fair or rough balance between other-regarding and self-regarding considerations. Justice, kindness, probity, and generosity are chiefly admired for what they lead those who possess them to do in their relations with other people; but prudence, sagacity, circumspection, discretion, and fortitude are esteemed primarily under their self-regarding aspect; and still other traits—notably, self-control, courage, and, perhaps, wisdom in practical matters—are in substantial measure admired both for what they do for their exemplifiers and for what they lead their exemplifiers to do in regard to other people.

Nor do traits (or for that matter acts) admired for other-regarding reasons have any sort of general precedence over predominantly self-regarding virtues (or acts) that might be taken to entail a self-other asymmetry of the sort I mentioned in connection with common-sense *morality*. The other-regarding traits mentioned above lack any (commonsensically) recognized status as greater or more important virtues than the self-regarding traits also mentioned above, and neither does a 'mixed' virtue like courage, self-control, or wisdom seem inferior to, or less of a virtue than, such predominantly other-regarding virtues as justice and kindness. Moreover, in regard to a mixed virtue such as courage, the importance we place on its other-regarding aspects is not obviously greater than that placed on its self-regarding aspects. It seems just as important a fact about courage that people need it for their own well-being as that it enables its possessors to serve the needs of others. And similar points can be made about other mixed virtues like patience and self-control.

However, even if the self-regarding and other-regarding aspects of the virtues are equally significant and valuable, it does not automatically follow that we as individuals *should balance* those two types of considerations or factors in our actions. Perhaps common-sense virtue ethics will allow for specialization in (the) virtue(s), regarding it, for example, as no less admirable for one exclusively to cultivate and exhibit self-regarding virtues than for one to be concerned with and act on both self-regarding and other-regarding considerations. This does not, however, appear to be possible. There are plenty of self-regarding virtues, but selfishness itself is ordinarily regarded as deplorable, criticizable, and not admirable, and that is just another way of saying that common-sense virtue ethics recommends against an exclusive cultivation and ex-emplification of self-regarding concerns.

But if selfishness is no virtue, then neither, to contemporary ways of thinking, is selflessness. The Victorians admired pure or total selflessness, but nowadays—perhaps because we are less priggish and high-minded, perhaps because we think we know more about human psychology and are less willing to take things at face value—selflessness is a practically automatic object of suspicion. The person who not only shows a great concern for others, but who, in addition, seems to deprecate or ignore his own needs whenever there is the slightest good he can do for others, would typically be thought to have something wrong with him and be suspected of masochism, of being burdened by inordinate and mis-directed guilt. So I think we can plausibly deny that either selfishness or selflessness is a virtue, and taken together with what we have already said about the relatively equal intuitive importance of other-regarding and self-regarding virtues and forms of admirability, this implies that common-sense virtue ethics espouses an ideal of (some degree of) bal-ance between self-regarding and other-regarding concerns: one is not admirable and is open to criticism if one does not have and act upon both self-regarding and other-regarding concerns, if one is not concerned both with oneself and with others.

Nothing in the above entails, however, that one should have and act from—that one is not admirable unless one has and acts from—an equal concern for every single individual. Someone whose self-regarding and other-regarding concerns are in some kind of (rough) balance may be more concerned with some other people than with others, and a common-sense ethics of virtue will presumably consider it *less* than admirable if one is no more concerned with particular friends or family members than with given individuals one hardly knows. So if common-sense virtue ethics advocates a kind of self-other symmetry, it is clearly not the kind of self-other symmetry that arises out of the agent-neutrality of act-utilitarianism and act-consequentialism. According to these latter conceptions of morality, the welfare or preferences of every individual are given equal weight in the reckoning of the goodness of results that constitutes the basis for its claims about moral obligation and moral rightness—and this equality of weight and concern cuts across the difference between self and other, as well as that between different others, in regard to the evaluation of any given agent's activities. So intuitive or common-sense virtue ethics allows for—is not committed to criticizing—the giving of different weights to (certain) different individuals, whereas agent-neutral, impersonal utilitarianism and consequentialism precisely rule this out. And clearly, in insisting that every single individual count equally for a given agent/trait-possessor, utilitarianism and consequentialism are committed to (*inter alia*) an obvious form of self-other symmetry. The problem then is to see in what sense or in what way common-sense thinking about the admirable can also embody a form of symmetry with respect to the categories of self and other.

But common-sense virtue ethics does in fact embody or advocate a distinctive and important form of self-other symmetry. For it effectively holds that every agent/trait-possessor should exemplify a balance of concern between herself and others *treated as a class or category to which everyone other than the agent/trait-possessor belongs*. In that case, we can clarify the difference between the symmetries involved in virtue ethics and in utilitarianism by saying that whereas our ordinary understanding of what is admirable and counts as a virtue embodies roughly balanced, equal, or symmetrical concern for self and others, where 'others' is to be understood *in sensu composito*, i.e. as applying to other people as a class, utilitarianism, by contrast, advocates balance or symmetry of concern for self and others in a sense which understands 'others' *in sensu diviso*, i.e. as applying to each and every other individual as compared with the agent/trait-possessor herself. And this means, among other things, that utilitarianism and common-sense virtue ethics differ as regards the importance and evaluation of purely self-regarding traits and actions.

Utilitarian evaluation reflects an equality of concern for the self and for every other single individual, and where enough other people can be affected by a trait or activity, concern for the given self/agent/trait-possessor may be practically insignificant by comparison with the sum of concern for other people that is mandated by the situation. Since over long periods most or many of us can affect thousands or even millions of other people, the self is likely to be submerged in the sea of concern for others that gives rise to utilitarian ethical judgements and to be required to sacrifice her own deepest commitments and projects in the name of overall utility or the optimific outcome. And these points are frequently and familiarly urged as criticisms of act-utilitarian and act-consequentialistic ethics.

By contrast, our ordinary thinking about the virtues—though it may not rule out the possibility of self-sacrifice, even enormous self-sacrifice, as a condition of human admirability or non-deplorability in certain circumstances—seems less committed to evaluations and recommendations that take such little account of the agent/trait-possessor's self-regarding concerns. (I shall have more to say shortly about the particular content of such concerns.) If the common-sense ideal of admirable character, desire, and action involves a balance of some sort between the self as a category, on the one hand, and other people taken as a category, rather than individually, on the other, then the self/agent/trait-possessor weighs in far more heavily against particular others and the whole class of others than is allowed under utilitarianism or consequentialism, and there is far more room for self-concern than can typically be accommodated by the latter. The choice between utilitarianism and intuitive virtue ethics involves, among other things, therefore, a choice between two distinctive kinds of self-other symmetry (neither kind being characteristic either of common-sense or of Kantian moral thinking), and as we have just been seeing, there may be an advantage in accepting ordinary virtue ethics' *in sensu composito* ideal of symmetry between the self and other people rather than the utilitarian/consequentialist *in sensu diviso* ideal of self-other symmetry.

III

At this point, I think it would be useful if I were to say a bit more about the nature and ethical commitments of common-sense virtue ethics. We need to see more clearly how such ethics differs from common-sense and other forms of moral thinking, and once we have done so, some important issues will arise about how virtue ethics is best embodied in ethical principles or rules.

Perhaps the greatest unclarity of our exposition to this point has been about whether common-sense virtue ethics is meant to replace or merely to supplement common-sense morality. Given the latter alternative, the comparison with utilitarianism or consequentialism as a total view of ethics will have been somewhat misleading and otiose, and if what I have been calling 'common-sense virtue ethics' is merely a fragment of a total common-sensism that includes self-other asymmetric common-sense morality, then it is misleading even to call it 'virtue ethics'. Many ethical views speak of what is admirable or a virtue while—more typically after—speaking of right and wrong conduct, but so-called 'virtue ethics' is generally conceived as a distinctive approach to ethics in which deontic notions like rightness, wrongness, and obligation are played down or treated as derivative or dispensed with altogether. So if the present essay is properly to be regarded as concerned with virtue ethics, it must treat our ordinary views about what is admirable or a virtue as (the basis for) a total ethics, rather than as a supplement to or conjunct of common-sense morality, and that is indeed how I am proposing to proceed.

But this raises some very difficult questions. For it seems as if I am espousing a virtue ethics that does away with or refuses to make the deontic judgements of common-sense morality, and I have thus far said nothing that seems to justify such a radical move. To be sure, common-sense moral judgements—not just deontic judgements, but also aretic judgements of *moral* goodness and *moral* admirability—embody self-other asymmetry of a kind pointed to above, but unless symmetry considerations are somehow to be regarded as pre-eminent for ethics, it hardly follows that we should get rid of common-sense morality or its deontic judgements. Why, then, do I advocate abandoning common-sense morality for an ethics that bases everything on intuitive judgements of admirability *tout court*?

Largely, I am afraid, for reasons that have been given elsewhere and that cannot be entirely summarized here.[4] But let me try to say something. There are a number of deep problems with common-sense morality that do not touch common-sense virtue ethics, and these may give us some

---

[4] See *From Morality to Virtue*, esp. chs. 1, 2, 3, and 6.

reason and motive for dropping the former if it can also be shown that the latter fulfils the essential functions of an overall ethical view.

Chief among the difficulties of common-sense morality is the by-now familiar problem of moral luck. Our intuitive judgements about the blameworthiness, moral goodness, and (degree of) wrongness of particular actions depend on factors of luck or accident that, in our moments of larger intuitive reflection, we say should not affect the making of such judgements, and I think it can therefore be shown, indeed already has been shown, that our intuitive judgements in this area are at odds with one another, are mutually contradictory. At least some moral intuitions, some intuitive moral judgements, must be abandoned if we are to avoid inconsistency and paradox in our ethical thinking; but no similar problem arises in connection with our judgements about what is admirable or deplorable *tout court* (as opposed to what is morally admirable or deplorable). We can admire people for what we regard as outside their (total) control and subject to luck: e.g. their looks, their genius, their calm or easy-going temperament; and we can deplore someone's stupidity or their hot temper even while regarding these things as somewhat outside the control of given individuals. The idea that what is admirable or criticizable about people is subject to luck or accident is not offensive in the way that the idea of specifically *moral* luck is offensive to us, because admiration and criticism of the sorts just mentioned do not commit us to specifically moral judgements. We can thus avoid the problems of moral luck if we drop common-sense morality and base our entire ethics on our ideas about what is admirable or deplorable about human beings and their actions. The ethics we end up with allows us to criticize various deep human character traits and motivations without committing us to regarding them, or their possessors, as (morally) blameworthy or reprehensible, and such a morally neutral 'no-fault' approach to ethics is clearly reminiscent of Spinoza.

There are, however, other reasons for discarding common-sense moral thinking having to do in part with the self-other asymmetry of such thinking: it can be argued in particular that if we conjoin or combine self-other asymmetry with certain other features of common-sense morality, we get very odd, and even in some sense incoherent, results, and it turns out that somewhat similar arguments can also be deployed against Kantian ethics. But rather than try to say more, I would rather, in the space allotted, say something about whether, in the absence of all specifically moral judgements, an intuitive virtue ethics can cover all the ground that we expect a large-scale or overall ethical view or theory to cover.

For example, we are now committed to basing everything we say on judgements concerning the admirability of certain traits, actions, or ways of living, and it may easily be wondered at this point whether any such ethics can accommodate the kinds of imperatives and 'ought'-judgements that are generally regarded as endemic to any recognizable form of ethical thinking. To be sure, I have attributed to common-sense virtue ethics certain general views about what one should or should not do. But the notion of 'should' or 'ought' is deontic, even if it is not specifically or irrecusably a moral notion, and one might well therefore wonder how an ethics based in non-moral but aretic notions like the admirable and the deplorable could ever generate the kinds of 'should'-judgements, whether particular or general, that we have come to expect from ethics. We might then also wonder whether an ethics of virtue can make room for grammatical imperatives that can be used to advise or guide either others or oneself.

But the above worries assume that it is difficult to tie 'should's and grammatical imperatives to aretic judgements in the way they seem so naturally to be tied to deontic claims of rightness, wrongness, and obligation, and it is not at all clear that 'should's and imperatives do not naturally arise out of (or derive from) aretic judgements in or outside ethics. If doing a given dance-step in a given way is aesthetically better than doing it in some different way, isn't it reasonable to conclude that the first way is the way the step *should* be done, and won't that conclusion understandably give rise to appropriate instructions or recommendations to dancers or dance students in the form of grammatical imperatives? Similarly, if we deplore a certain way of treating oneself or others, can't we readily say that one should not treat oneself or others that way and tell ourselves in the imperative mood not to treat ourselves or others in that way (again or any more)? If all this shows that the distinction between the aretic and the deontic is less extreme than we thought, so that virtue ethics ends up seeming less extreme or *outré* than is often imagined, so be it! For it at least allows us to fill out an ethics of virtue with 'should'- and 'ought'-judgements that help to make good its claim to being a total view or theory of ethical value, one that can take its place among and stand critical comparison with the currently dominant large-scale approaches to ethics and ethical theory: utilitarianism, intuitionism or commonsensism, Kantian ethics, and contract theory. Certainly, I have not attempted in this brief compass to criticize all these views or to give all my reasons for preferring the present sort of virtue-ethical approach, but I perhaps have given the reader some sense of where such a virtue ethics lies on the landscape of current ethical theory. And by way of concluding this sketch and expanding somewhat on the theme of symmetry that has been so helpful in locating common-sense virtue ethics, I would like at this point to say something briefly about how such ethics differs from Kantian ethics in regard to the treatment of ourselves and other people.

For Kant, there are both perfect and imperfect duties both to oneself and to others, but I shall simplify by focusing only on the imperfect duties. In a nutshell, Kant's view (e.g. in the *Doctrine of Virtue*) is that we have a duty to seek the happiness of other people and a duty of moral self-perfection (as well as a duty to develop our own talents). These duties are said to be imperfect duties because they do not require us *at every moment* to act in accordance with them (by contrast, we have a *perfect* duty not to kill because we are at every moment supposed to act in accordance with that requirement). Kant argues that we have no fundamental duty to seek our own happiness and no duty to seek the moral perfection of others, and I think those arguments get into difficulties that there is no time to enter into here. What I do, however, want to point out is the asymmetry in what Kant says we imperfectly owe to others and to ourselves. We have a duty to seek the happiness of others and a duty to perfect ourselves morally (as well as to develop our own talents) but no duty to seek our own happiness or to seek the moral perfection of others. This self-other asymmetry as regards the contents of our duties or obligations stands in marked contrast with what I take to be the inevitable development, or at least one *natural*, development, of a common-sense ethics of virtue. (For simplicity's sake, I shall ignore common-sense virtue ethics' analogues of Kantian perfect duties.)

When I spoke earlier of an ideal of balance between one's actions or concern for others and one's actions or concern for oneself, I made it clear that one's own happiness or well-being was a proper goal of one's actions or concern for oneself. And although our common-sense virtue ethics avoids specifically moral concepts, I see no reason why it should not hold that the non-moral *admirability* of others is, on intuitive grounds, a proper goal of one's concern for other people. (Think of how we regard students and children.) So it seems not at all implausible to regard common-sense virtue ethics as holding that we should both seek our own well-being and admirability and seek the well-being and admirability of others.[5] Given our avoidance of the moral, this general claim or injunction does not articulate any imperfect duties in Kant's sense, but it does express the aretic non-moral equivalent of such duties, since, for one thing, it is clearly not telling us we should at every moment act on behalf of others or on our own behalf. And more importantly in terms of the ethical commitments or content of common-sense virtue ethics, the above general injunction is self-other symmetric regarding the goals of ethical action in the way Kant's views are not. But clearly, I have only just sketched a possible view, and more is and has to be said elsewhere.[6]

[5] In speaking of seeking our own admirability, I mean only that we should seek achievements and traits that would be admirable of or in us, not that we should (self-consciously) be cultivating our own admirability as such. Similar points apply to the injunction to seek the admirability of others.

[6] Some radical forms of virtue ethics claim that act-evaluation is always derivative from the evaluation of character traits, motives, or overall character, but Aristotle fairly clearly does allow for an independent ethical evaluation of single actions, and I have been assuming here that common-sense virtue ethics also makes room for such act-evaluations. For a discussion of how present-day common-sense virtue ethics relates to Aristotle's, as well as to more radical forms of, virtue ethics, see *From Morality to Virtue*, chs. 1 and 5.

7

The Virtues and Human Nature

JULIA DRIVER

'Human Nature' has traditionally entered into virtue theory at two planes. The first is psychological: What are human beings like? What actions and feelings are they capable of? How are people typically motivated? After all, virtue will not prescribe what cannot be performed or felt by human beings. Even though I am endorsing the importance of psychology for virtue theory (since understanding human virtue will involve understanding our flaws and motives), my view is that within the virtue theory tradition the importance of psychology has been both underestimated and overestimated. Its importance has been underestimated in that some ethical disputes turn out to be disputes about human psychology. Its importance has been overestimated in that some writers have elevated one kind of psychology by making it definitional of virtue; thus subjective elements take on an exaggerated importance. I will argue that it is a mistake to *define* virtue in terms of particular types of intentional psychological states. My contention is that the behavioural aspects of virtue are more important than its phenomenology, because virtue is best defined along consequentialist lines.[1]

The second plane is a strange mixture of breadth and narrowness. Human nature is important in understanding the good to which virtuous agents aspire because an understanding of human nature will provide the basis for an understanding of 'human flourishing'. The intuition is that virtue promotes *human* good. The differences amongst theorists lie in how the connection is to be spelled out, and what exactly is to count as 'human flourishing' and whose flourishing—the agent's or others'— is taken to be relevant. Views of virtues—what they are and how they

---

[1] Virtue ethics is the project of basing ethics on virtue evaluation. I reject this approach. This is an essay in virtue theory, since what I am trying to do is give an account of what virtues *are*.

function—can vary dramatically in content, then, depending on what views of human nature are adopted. The problem of specifying the good for humans has been almost intractable, and some writers fear that this is the area where virtue ethics, and virtue theory more generally, will have the most difficulty.[2] I will have little to say about *particular* conceptions of human flourishing. The focus of this paper is on the first plane. With respect to the second, my concern is the modest one of arguing that while an account of flourishing is important to a complete understanding of virtue as a normative concept, one can still develop an independent theory of virtue.

1. THE VIRTUES AS CORRECTIVES

One popular view of the virtues is that they work to 'correct' for the baser human impulses and motives. The idea is that humans are naturally self-interested, motivated by desires to promote their own good, and by aversions to whatever constitutes something bad for themselves. Virtues are solutions to design flaws in human beings. This type of view is articulated by Philippa Foot in 'Virtues and Vices':

> there is, for instance, a virtue of industriousness only because idleness is a temptation; . . . With virtues such as justice and charity it is a little different, because they correspond not to any particular desire or tendency that has to be kept in check but rather to a deficiency of motivation; and it is this that they must make good. If people were as much attached to the good of others as they are to their own good there would no more be a general virtue of benevolence than there is a general virtue of self-love.[3]

The intuition that Foot appeals to with this model of the virtues is attractive, because we tend to think that humans are, thankfully, prudent creatures, but that this prudence overshoots into selfishness that undermines co-operation.

One problem with this view of virtue is that the corrective may itself overshoot the mark. The overly generous give all of their money away, for example. Here Foot would say that the trait is not operating as a virtue. But a further difficulty is that the virtues also correct for a lack

---

[2] See, for example, G. E. M. Anscombe, 'Modern Moral Philosophy', *Philosophy* 33 (1958), 1–19; and S. Conly, 'Flourishing and the Failure of the Ethics of Virtue', in P. French, T. Uehling, and H. Wettstein (eds.), *Ethical Theory: Character and Virtue, Midwest Studies in Philosophy XIII* (Notre Dame, Ind., 1988), 83–96. Brad Hooker takes up the issue of human flourishing in his essay in the present volume.

[3] P. Foot, 'Virtues and Vices', in *Virtues and Vices* (Oxford, 1978), 1–18, p. 9.

of prudence. Cases of this will be quite common: a woman may realize that she should exercise in order to stay fit and prolong her life, yet also know that unless she makes a commitment to meet someone at the gym at a certain time she will become distracted by the desire to help others. If she has *promised* to meet Sue at the gym at six, however, it will be her duty to do that. She will feel that conscientiousness demands of her that she keep her promises. The virtue serves her legitimate interests— but her interests nevertheless. She is using her concern to be moral in order to make sure that she exercises.

Foot could argue that even though the virtues occasionally serve this function, that is not what *makes* them virtues. A pen may occasionally be used to prop open a door, but that is not what makes it a pen. But to test this response we simply need to ask ourselves to suppose that Foot's view of human nature is false; suppose that humans do not even tend to be motivated by base desires and self-interest. We must imagine that Hobbes is entirely wrong, and instead people are motivated by a desire to help others that needs to be kept in check to keep people from miserably trying to help each other all the time. Here the basic altruism may be a virtue, though in this case *not* because it corrects for selfishness.

Further, the prudential gain from morality may be as systematic as the moral gain from prudence that egoists like to point out. Indeed, self-help programmes try to get people to behave more prudently by having them make promises to themselves—thus harnessing their moral impulses. Here it is prudence which corrects for the flaws of the moral sense.

2. DUBIOUS VIRTUE PSYCHOLOGY

The view that virtues are correctives rests on a particular view of human nature. While it is true that many virtues do function as correctives, I have argued that this account is not general enough. Other accounts of virtue in the tradition have similarly rested upon certain views of human nature; these too I shall argue are too narrow. The correct account of virtue will not rest upon identifying certain psychological states as necessary for virtue. On my view, a moral virtue is a character trait which produces good consequences for others.[4] Psychological states are important only

---

[4] I say good consequences 'for others' in order to distinguish moral from prudential virtues. I do not mean to say that moral virtues may *not* produce good for the agent as well. Unfortunately a discussion of this distinction is beyond the scope of this paper.

in so far as they facilitate the production of those consequences. Thus, an account of moral virtue will rest on few assumptions about human nature, though understanding how the virtues function for human beings will require an account of human flourishing which will itself depend upon an understanding of human nature.

In the virtue theory tradition there is a great split between Aristotle and Kant on what psychological states are necessary for virtue.[5] For Aristotle, virtue consisted in cultivated inclination—thus, pleasure was the proper accompaniment to virtuous activity, since satisfying an inclination will usually lead to pleasure: 'Actions which conform to virtue are naturally pleasant, and, as a result, such actions are not, only pleasant for those who love the noble, but also pleasant in themselves.'[6] Kant, on the other hand, believed that any inclination without the support of principle is bound to falter:

virtue is not to be defined and valued merely as an *aptitude* and ... a long-standing *habit* of morally good actions acquired by practice. For unless this aptitude results from considered, firm ... principles, then, like any other mechanism of technically practical reason, it is neither armed for all situations nor adequately secured against the changes that new temptations could bring about.[7]

The virtue cannot be grounded in inclination, *unless* the inclination is backed by something unchanging—a sense of moral duty or 'fortitude'.[8] A stable sense of duty, the ability to master oneself, was for Kant crucial to virtue.[9] For Kant, as human beings we are beings who inevitably experience base inclinations. But for Aristotle, as human beings our excellence is best realized in a harmonious, well-ordered character. This

---

[5] Some of the following material is drawn from my doctoral dissertation, *The Virtues of Ignorance* (Johns Hopkins University, 1990).

[6] See *Nicomachean Ethics* (= *NE*) 1099^{a}13–15, tr. M. Ostwald (Indianapolis, 1962). However, this is not invariably the case, since Aristotle notes that courageous activity is accompanied by pain. Yet, the agent will still get pleasure, or at least satisfaction, from accomplishing the courageous end: 'it would seem that the end which courage aims at is pleasant, obscured though it is by the attendant circumstances ... Accordingly, only in so far as it attains its end is it true to say of every virtue that it is pleasant when practiced' (*NE* 1117^{b}1–2, 15–16).

[7] Immanuel Kant, *The Doctrine of Virtue*, tr. M. Gregor (Cambridge, 1991), 189 (Prussian Academy Edn., vol. vi, pp. 383–4).

[8] Kant believes that inclination *may* be involved. Moral worth is certainly compatible with good inclination. The point is simply that a sense of duty must be present as the primary motivation. See B. Herman, 'On the Value of Acting from the Motive of Duty', *Philosophical Review* 90 (1981), 359–82, for an interesting discussion of this issue.

[9] In *The Doctrine of Virtue* Kant provides his developed theory of virtue. For a further discussion of Kant on the issue of virtue see Onora O'Neill's 'Kant's Virtues', in the present volume.

is the core of the difference between the two perspectives on virtue. However, both Aristotle and Kant believed that the conditions they placed on true virtue were warranted because the conditions made the trait more reliable. Whether or not the view sketched above is an accurate representation of Kant's theory, it has influenced other writers on virtue,[10] as has Aristotle's theory. The reason that some writers focus on something like fortitude as necessary for virtue lies in the belief that when someone decides to act well in spite of her inclinations, she will act well no matter what—and that is far better than the person whose motives may be clouded by pleasure. Even though a person *may* get pleasure in acting well, the motive is still a motive of duty—and thus virtue does not *require* pleasure.[11]

One problem for virtue theory has been to decide between conceiving of a virtue as a trait the exercise of which is accompanied by pleasure, and conceiving of it as a trait the exercise of which may not be. A good deal can be said to support both Aristotle and Kant. If one conceives of virtue as an excellence of character, then it seems plausible that the virtuous agent would enjoy doing the activity associated with the virtue.[12] If I have to put a lot of effort into acting sympathetically to people, that does seem to be an indication that I lack sympathy. Nevertheless, we have an inclination to value achievements more highly when they are difficult. On Aristotle's view acting well seems so easy, once you have the virtue, since you are then eager to do what the virtue demands. But isn't a person better when, as with Kant's unhappy agent in the *Groundwork*, in order to act well she must overcome the inclination she had to do something quite different? This benevolence is a clear case of virtue, since it is not accompanied by pleasure. The uncomfortable virtue of the unhappy agent is diagnostic of both temptation (insofar as it is uncomfortable) and self-control (in so far as the temptation is overcome).

[10] See, for example, K. Baier, 'Moral Value and Moral Worth', *The Monist* 54 (1970), 18–30. Baier claims that Kant believed that an action's 'genuine moral worth is the greater the greater the effort needed to overcome opposing natural inclinations' (24). Further, he considers this view correct, irrespective of whether or not it is actually Kant's considered view.

[11] Modern writers, such as Georg von Wright, pick up on the Kantian theme by developing a view of virtue in which self-control is necessary for being a virtuous person, because virtues will consist in the ability to control appetites and emotions; see *The Varieties of Goodness* (London, 1963). Martha Nussbaum and Gregory Trianosky, on the other hand, lean more towards an Aristotelian view in which emotional responses—properly cultivated, of course—form a crucial element in the virtuous agent's life. See Nussbaum, *Love's Knowledge* (New York, 1990), and Trianosky, 'Rightly Ordered Appetites: How to Live Morally and Live Well', *American Philosophical Quarterly* 25 (1988), 1–12.

[12] See Trianosky, ibid., for arguments in favour of the Aristotelian view.

On the other hand, the comfortable virtue of the Aristotelian character is diagnostic of good basic desires.

The mistake that is made by both Aristotle and Kant is that each focuses on one clear type of virtue. Psychological features of this type are then taken to be paradigmatic of virtue. The consequentialist can diagnose this confusion between a paradigm of virtue and a correct definition of virtue. Each writer has been impressed with the importance of good desires, or the importance of self-control, and has employed it to the neglect of the other. They are mistaken in holding one type of virtue to be the correct analysis of virtue, and not recognizing the consequentialist basis for our judgements of virtue.

Some writers have tried to do justice to good desires and self-control by maintaining that there are two types of virtue which are essentially different.[13] What these two conceptions of virtue have in common is that they both advocate a view of virtue as *necessary for successful social interaction*.[14] This much is quite true, and I believe that this suggests a strategy for developing a unified theory of virtue along consequentialist lines.

3. GOOD INTENTIONS

Regardless of one's views on whether or not pleasure, or self-control as distinct from pleasure, is crucial to virtue, it does seem plausible to maintain that, at the very *least*, the virtuous agent possesses some conception of what is good, and that he acts in accordance with this conception (i.e. he acts with 'good intentions'). Plausible though this seems, it is false.

First of all, what is a conception of what is good? This issue is itself complex, but for the purposes of this paper I would like to try to come up with a working hypothesis about conceptions of what is good. An agent has a conception of what is good when she has adopted or accepted a particular morality—that is, when she has adopted a set of rules governing moral action, and perhaps also, governing moral attitudes. In so adopting this morality, the agent accepts the prescriptions imposed by

---

[13] David Carr, in 'Two Kinds of Virtue', *Proceedings of the Aristotelian Society* 85 (1984–5), 47–61, suggests this general type of strategy for delineating two distinct types of virtue.

[14] Both Aristotle and Kant possessed a *richer* view than this. I merely intend to point out a common thread in their conceptions of virtue.

that morality. She thinks that if she acts in accordance with it, she will be doing good or right things. She may not be able to articulate what exactly these rules are. A person who speaks perfect English (and has an interest in speaking perfect English) may not be able to articulate what the English rules of grammar are, but this person is not precluded from speaking English well.

Secondly, given that we do know what a conception of the good is, is it really the case that we must act in accordance with what we believe to be good in order to be virtuous? Most writers on virtue think so. For example, Michael Stocker seems to take it for granted that, somehow, acting with good intentions is a requirement of virtuous action.[15] John Heil claims that '[o]ne who is charitable is moved, perhaps, by the plight of others, but moved as well by a certain conception of what ought to be done'.[16] If this is the case, then a person who was disposed to act well in a particular type of context, yet who did not think of his actions as good, could not be virtuous. A distinction needs to be made here between motives and intentions. Motives will cause persons to form intentions; it is intentions which more directly guide action, and which I am concerned with here. On my view, a person may be acting virtuously even when their intentions are not good ones—that is, when they themselves think that the course of action chosen is, all things considered, wrong since it will lead to a bad state of affairs. Such is the case of Huckleberry Finn.

Jonathan Bennett introduced the case because it represents a conflict between sympathy and bad morality.[17] I see it as a problem for any account of virtue that requires the agent to have good intentions. For Huck, out of sympathy, acts in a way he fully believes to be immoral. And for a person to act with good intentions, I will argue, she must *believe* that what she is doing is good.

Huckleberry Finn, the protagonist of Mark Twain's famous novel of life on the Mississippi, has adopted a bad morality—a false conception of the good. Huck, growing up in pre-Civil War Missouri, does not believe that the institution of slavery is immoral. One of his best friends, however, is a slave named Jim, and when Jim runs away from his owner Huck fails to turn him in, though he has many opportunities

[15] M. Stocker, 'Good Intentions in Greek and Modern Moral Virtue', *Australasian Journal of Philosophy* 57 (1979), 220–4.

[16] J. Heil, 'Thoughts on the Virtues,' *Journal of Value Inquiry* 19 (1985), 27–34, p. 29.

[17] J. Bennett, 'The Conscience of Huckleberry Finn', *Philosophy* 49 (1974), 123–34.

to do so. Yet Huck also believes that this failure on his part is a moral failure—that he is, in effect, a party to theft. He believes that what he is doing is dishonest and ungrateful. He expresses himself in the following way:

It hadn't ever come home to me, before, what this thing was that I was doing. But now it did; and it stayed with me, and scorched me more and more. I tried to make out to myself that *I* warn't to blame, because *I* didn't run Jim off from his rightful owner; but it warn't no use, conscience up an say, every time: 'But you knowed he was running for his freedom, and you could a paddled ashore and told somebody.' . . . Conscience says to me: 'What had poor Miss Watson done to you, that you could see her nigger go off right under your eyes and never say one single word? What did that poor old woman do to you that you could treat her so mean?'[18]

These are Huck's beliefs about what it is that he is doing, yet *we* know that, in fact, Huck acted well in not turning Jim in. Huck wants to help his friend, and see his friend happy. Yet, Jim's happiness depends on an evil. And this is what Huck baulks at.

Huck, though lacking a correct conception of the good, was still *acting in accordance with* the correct conception of the good. This was what made him, in fact, a good person. In order to be virtuous, in other words, one need not know that what one is doing is good or right. One simply has to have a disposition such that one does what is good or right. If one has this disposition, then accidents are ruled out. Huck's actions towards Jim are not accidental, because he would do the same thing over and over again.

It is Huck's *sympathy* with Jim which constitutes the virtue and conflicts with what he believes to be right. Huck may be interpreting the sympathy he feels for Jim as some sort of unwarranted favouritism. It would be the sort of favouritism condemned by morality as being incompatible with justice. Jim is his friend, but it is not morally permissible to aid one's friends in crime, in stealing property from a sweet little old lady. Huck believes that the system of which he is a part is a good system. He has nothing but contempt for the Abolitionists, who want to change things. He perceives his failure to be as good as weakness of will. Belief and feeling fail to coincide, and feeling prevails.

Huck's quandary is not unique. Indeed, I think that modern examples can be found. People occasionally experience alienation from what they believe to be good. Perhaps some people who help their terminally ill

---

[18] Bennett, 'Huckleberry Finn', 125.

relatives commit suicide experience this sort of alienation from what they think is morally good. They truly believe that assisting in suicide is always wrong. Yet their feelings when they see a loved one suffering impel them to act contrary to that belief—and to feel intense guilt afterwards.

My aim has been to refute the claim that good intentions are necessary for virtue.[19] I have claimed that when an agent acts with good intentions, he is acting according to what he thinks is the right or good thing to do (all things considered). One objection to this strategy is that I have construed 'acting with good intentions' too narrowly by requiring that the agent be concerned with *moral* good. Perhaps non-moral goods are relevant. In the case of Huckleberry Finn, the objection goes, Huck actually does have good intentions in helping Jim out, because he sees that freedom is a good for Jim, that it is what Jim wants very badly (note that on Huck's view, freedom is not a *moral* good for Jim). So Huck is concerned with helping Jim obtain *this* good; therefore he is acting with some good intention. Given this, the Huckleberry Finn case cannot be used to show that good intentions are not necessary for virtuous action.

However, my use of 'good intention' captures what is normally thought of as a good intention. That is, when we use the expression we normally do mean 'morally good intention'. It would be odd to say of someone, 'He did something he thought was wrong, but he acted with good intentions.' (NB this is not the same as the more usual utterance, 'He did something wrong, but he acted with good intentions.') After all, Huck did think that he was unjustifiably harming Miss Watson, Jim's owner. Indeed, the *traditional* conception of 'morally good intention' has been characterized by Michael Stocker in the following way: 'A's intention to do act *b* is morally good just in case A believes *b* to be overall good to do and A intends to do *b* for the sake of goodness.'[20] Clearly, Huck's intentions fail to be good ones on this plausible analysis.

But perhaps there is a very weak sense in which 'good intention' is necessary for virtue. That is, the intention of performing some good for

---

[19] I elsewhere discuss a class of virtues that do not require good intentions: see my 'The Virtues of Ignorance', *Journal of Philosophy* 86 (1989), 373–84.

[20] M. Stocker, 'Morally Good Intentions', *The Monist* 54 (1970), 124–41, p. 124. Stocker goes on to modify the analysis from that of 'good intentions' to that of 'at least partly good intentions', to some extent in order to deal with Huckleberry Finn-type cases. One change is that the agent need not believe that the object of the intention is an overall good. Even on this analysis, the most that could be said of Huckleberry is that his intention is *partly* good.

someone is necessary, even if one does not think of the good as a moral good. Because the thesis is so weak, it is difficult to think of clear counter-examples to it. This is because even if it turns out to be false, there will have to be an extremely close correlation between these good intentions and success—given human nature. Is it the case, however, that the agent cannot have *bad* intentions?

Imagine a non-human society which evolved differently from human society. The Mutors, as I call them, have adapted to their harsh environment by toughening their offspring. In particular they exploit the fact that, for them, beating one's child severely when it is exactly 5.57 years old actually increases the life expectancy of the child by 50 per cent. The child is upset by the beating, but this goes away in time. Further, the only way a Mutor could ever bring himself to treat a child thus is to develop an intense pleasure in doing so. So some Mutors have a special trait—they intensely desire to beat children who are exactly 5.57 years old. That it is good for the child is irrelevant to them. This trait is valued by others, who must bring their children to the beaters when they are the right age, since they themselves possess too much delicacy of feeling to be able to do it themselves. *It is very important to note* that the desire of these Mutors is extremely specific. They only desire to beat children at exactly that point which does the children good (though doing something good *for the children* is not their intention). Otherwise the trait would obviously do more harm than good, and could not be considered a virtue. What they are doing can be described as good, but they are not doing it because it is good. On my view this trait would be a virtue. It is an 'excellence of character' because others would value it, it actually does produce good and a significant social benefit, and the trait is specific enough so as *not* to produce *any* bad consequences. This is why this trait could not be fairly called 'viciousness'. Viciousness is not so specific. That is, a 'vicious' agent is one who enjoys inflicting pain and suffering—the exercise of the trait is not restricted to a specific practice, as the Mutors' trait is. It is our intuitions about unspecific traits (such as viciousness) which infect our intuitions about the Mutors' trait.

On the weak reading of 'good intentions', good intentions do seem necessary for human beings to possess virtue. That is because *bad* intentions or bad desires in human beings just are not that specific. This, if true, would be a matter of empirical fact about human psychology (as opposed to Mutor psychology). There is evidence to support this. Consider the happy executioner, and our suspicions of such a character. A happy executioner enjoys his job; he loves the feel of the rope slithering through his fingers as he fashions a noose, he loves to hear the snap of the neck bones breaking, etc. Most believers in capital punishment also think that it is good for people to enjoy their work. Why then the repugnance toward the happy executioner? Because they know that, given human nature, there is a distinct possibility that this chap's pleasures are not restricted to the punishment of vicious criminals. Uneasiness is caused by this realization. Thus it is with bad intentions. However, to say that human beings are so constructed as to be unable to be virtuous while acting with bad intentions is to state something contingent, something about human nature; it is not to state something definitive about virtue, unless one can argue for a chauvinistic thesis that moral virtue can obtain only for human beings, and not any other intelligent social creature. A theory of virtue should be broader than this. It must be conceptually possible to speak of the moral virtues of Mr Spock. Good intentions are necessary for virtue in so far as they are necessary for the agent's regular success.

My conclusions about good intentions can be carried over to good motives. They are not necessary to virtue, if by the necessity of 'good motives' we mean that the content of a person's desire which causes the action must be good. Good motives are important. So being motivated by the desire to see others happy usually produces good, because motives give rise to intentions to bring about happiness. But it may be that a motive of self-interest produces good for others as well, and if so, that motive may form part of a virtue. (One needs to be motivated in a certain way, perhaps, in addition to forming beliefs of a certain sort— being motivated to help others in need is useless without the ability to perceive those in need and formulate the belief that they are in need.)[21]

Despite difficulties in identifying necessary psychological conditions of virtue, one need not give up hope of a unified virtue theory. Since psychology has failed, the most promising way to develop this theory is as a consequentialist theory. The psychological states of the agent matter, but only in terms of the consequences generally produced by those states. The question of who is *really* describing virtue, Aristotle or Kant, is unimportant. Having one's inclinations in harmony with the good certainly helps virtue, as will having a strong sense of duty and acting

---

[21] Thus, what I am describing here is not a form of motive utilitarianism, as Robert Adams discusses it in 'Motive Utilitarianism', *Journal of Philosophy* 73 (1976), 467–81. First of all, I make no commitment to maximization in this account. Further, the motive which causes the agent to form various intentions to act is only part of the virtue.

from good intentions. But none can be definitive of virtue. What is definitive is this: a moral virtue is a character trait (a disposition or cluster of dispositions) which, generally speaking, produces good consequences for others. What those consequences are exactly is independent of the consequentialist nature of the theory, but a plausible suggestion is that many of these consequences involve the alleviation of problems which develop in social interaction, and thus contribute to the flourishing of individuals, which consists partly in their social relations.

4. A CONSEQUENTIALIST THEORY OF VIRTUE

Consequentialist theories of virtue have been proposed before. Hume's theory, for example, while not completely consequentialist in nature, draws a compelling connection between utility and virtue. Virtue produces pleasure, and one mechanism of that production is our appreciation of the virtues as socially useful. Benevolence, for example, gains its merit in part from 'its tendency to promote the interests of our species and bestow happiness on human society'.[22] The analysis is extended to justice—though in the case of justice 'reflections on the beneficial consequences of this virtue are the *sole* foundation of its merit'.[23] The value or merit of benevolence, on the other hand, is only partly due to its usefulness:

As a certain proof that the whole merit of benevolence is not derived from its usefulness, we may observe, that in a kind way of blame, we say, a person is *too good*; when he exceeds his part in society, and carries his attention for others beyond the proper bounds.[24]

Thus, when the benevolence becomes excessive it is no longer useful, yet it is still regarded as a virtue by Hume. The merit of benevolence must in part be derived from some natural pleasing quality it has.

But in this passage Hume did not consider another explanation for the 'kind way of blame'. The trait of benevolence can generally speaking produce good consequences, and thus be a virtue, while occasionally breaking down. Elsewhere Hume does point out that when we perceive the bad effects of a trait, we adjust our sentiments. On my

---

[22] D. Hume, *An Enquiry Concerning the Principles of Morals* (1751), ed. L. Selby-Bigge, rev. P. H. Nidditch, 3rd edn. (Oxford, 1975), 181. [23] Ibid. 183.
[24] Ibid. 258.

theory the value of all of these traits resides in their tendency to produce good consequences, not in the recognition of that tendency. Thus, I believe that it is possible for people to make mistakes about virtues and vices.[25] To be more precise, on my view, it will be possible for people to view virtue traits with displeasure—because they are mistaken about the consequences of the traits.[26] Hume may introduce the device of the judicious spectator to deal with this sort of problem. But since my account divorces virtue from an appreciation of it, no such device is needed.

Hume's account is an important step in the development of a consequentialist theory of virtue, but it does not go far enough. Jeremy Bentham developed the theory more, but Bentham was too enthralled by hedonism to identify correctly the usefulness of virtues. Bentham wrote: 'It is with disposition as with everything else: it will be good or bad according to its effects: according to the effects it has in augmenting or diminishing the happiness of the community.'[27] Bentham also does not view the goodness of a virtue to be determined by the goodness of its motive or intention. Indeed, he points out that motives are not, in themselves, ever bad. Their badness can only be determined by their effects in particular instances. Malice is not bad, unless it leads to bad consequences. Indeed, the malicious person's enjoyment of a perceived pain he is causing to others is good—as long as the pain does not, and will not, exist.[28]

On *my* account, maliciousness is a vice because, generally speaking,

[25] See Hume, *A Treatise of Human Nature* (1739–40), ed. L. Selby-Bigge (Oxford, 1888), 546–7: 'The distinction of moral good and evil is founded on the pleasure or pain, which results from the view of any sentiment, or character; and as that pleasure or pain cannot be unknown to the person who feels it, it follows, that there is just so much vice or virtue in any character, as every one places in it, and that 'tis impossible in this particular we can ever be mistaken.' Also p. 552: 'The general opinion of mankind has some authority in all cases; but in this of morals 'tis perfectly infallible.'

[26] If one accepts an ideal observer in Hume's theory, who cannot make such mistakes because he or she is rational and well informed and has corrected her perceptions against biases, then there is plenty of room for mistakes on the part of observers lacking any of these qualities. However, on this view the spectator must be in sympathy to the same degree with those affected by the putative virtue or vice. My account supposes nothing like this, and sympathy as a basis of moral judgement is not required.

[27] J. Bentham, *An Introduction to The Principles of Morals and Legislation* (1789), ed. W. Harrison (Oxford, 1948), 246.

[28] Ibid. 218. Bentham writes in a footnote: 'Let a man's motive be ill-will; call it even malice, envy, cruelty; it is still a kind of pleasure that is his motive: the pleasure he takes at the thought of the pain which he sees, or expects to see, his adversary undergo. Now even this wretched pleasure, taken by itself, is good: . . . while it lasts, and before any bad consequences arrive, it is as good as any other that is not more intense.'

it leads to bad effects. There may be a few odd situations in which it fails to do so, through accident or ill luck on the part of the agent, but by and large maliciousness in a person does show itself. Virtues are character traits which produce good effects. Under odd circumstances a virtue may also give rise to harms. But as long as the trait generally produces good, it is a virtue. Of course, a great deal more has to be said about how particular traits function as virtues, and much of this discussion is beyond the scope of this paper. But the above claim provides a starting-point for such analysis, and since it is controversial enough, it is an interesting starting-point.[29]

Now, a moral virtue is a disposition, but it is not just any 'good' disposition of a person. The fact that Anne has strong bones indicates a good disposition of Anne, i.e. her bones are likely to stand up to an unusual level of stress. A moral virtue is a character trait. It is a complex psychological disposition to feel, behave, or act well.

Virtues function in society to contribute to flourishing and happiness, often by alleviating interaction problems. The *type* of effect or consequence brought about by virtues is the type of effect conducive to the alleviation of these problems. Thus, virtue promotes social good. For example, trustworthiness and honesty make social interaction feasible, since without these traits it would be very difficult for people to co-ordinate their activities. They make interaction much more efficient. They cut security costs. Loyalty, for example, is a way of ensuring support by others. A loyal friend sticks by you, a mercenary one does not. Thus, a person need not be wary of a loyal friend. Also, if a person is trustworthy, then she needs little monitoring by others.

The reason the consequences are type-effects, rather than particular effects, is that the effects of the trait need never be actually produced in a particular instance in order for the trait to count as a virtue. The function of the virtues is to ease social interaction—and here the general sense of 'function' is used. The function of seat belts is to prevent death in car accidents, but seat belts do not always do this. Indeed, on occasion they cause death, as when a car bursts into flames immediately after being hit. The type of effect is what is referred to when the claim is made that the virtue of the seat belt is that it saves lives—even though in some cases lives are not saved.

[29] For an alternative consequentialist theory of virtue, see Thomas Hurka's excellent essay, 'Virtue as Loving the Good', in E. Paul, F. D. Miller, and J. Paul (eds.), *The Good Life and the Human Good* (Cambridge, 1992), 149–68. Hurka takes the novel approach for a consequentialist of arguing that the virtues are *intrinsically* valuable.

This is important because a person could have a virtue yet never exercise it. In a society of plenty, some people may have the disposition to help those in need, yet never exercise it because no opportunities to do so present themselves. Dispositions have a modal character. In a very repressive society, it may be the case that many people possess virtuous dispositions, yet lack the opportunity to display the requisite behaviour. For example, loyalty would have little scope in a society which discouraged friendship. Although actual good consequences may not be produced by these dispositions in a given instance, these people still have the virtues because the dispositions would produce the requisite behaviour in the appropriate contexts. Of course, the disposition must truly be present, and the only evidence we have for its presence is the action or behaviour of the agent.

5. COUNTING CONSEQUENCES

The metaphysics of virtue needs to be distinguished from the epistemology. The account of what a virtue is has been given. But there is still the epistemological problem of how to determine what consequences of the trait count. Suppose that we were all grossly mistaken about the benefits produced by generosity. Suppose that generosity produced good consequences in the short term, but the long term consequences were devastating. If generosity towards the needy in the long run produced parasites, and if generosity did this *systematically*, then it would not be a moral virtue. Long-term consequences count. For this reason, I think it entirely likely that we are mistaken in calling some traits 'virtues', precisely because we fail to see the harmful effects these traits produce. Those traits with good *foreseeable* consequences are the ones we regard as virtues—though the judgement could be mistaken. The more we know about the world, the fewer mistakes we will make. These observations provide a great deal of intuitive support for a consequentialist theory of virtue. The fact is that when we do see that we have misjudged the consequences of a trait, we change our judgement of the trait's status as a virtue.

Chastity may be an example of this. Chastity is not generally considered to be a moral virtue any more, though it certainly used to be considered one. Why the change? One popular explanation of why chastity in women is a moral virtue is sociobiological. If women were not chaste, men would have no confidence in paternity, and would not support children. The social consequences of this would be disastrous. Yet, as this picture of the social consequences of chastity becomes discredited, so does the opinion that chastity is a virtue. Another explanation of why our opinion of chastity has changed is that it is possible that, in the past, this picture of the role chastity played was correct. Adopting chastity as an ideal of behaviour *was* one strategy for avoiding social disaster. But now this strategy is obsolete. With the advent of birth control people no longer have to worry that premarital sex will inevitably result in a bastard child. Women have more control over when they get pregnant. Also, there are ways of testing children to determine paternity, if there is any serious doubt. Men can be more certain of paternity now, without the constraint of chastity's being imposed upon women. If this picture is correct, we have another explanation of why chastity is no longer considered a moral virtue. Both explanations are in terms of people's perceptions of the consequences of the trait. This is further evidence for a consequentialist virtue theory.

6. PSYCHOLOGY VERSUS MOTIVE

Still, it is one thing to provide an explanation of why a trait is a virtue, and quite another to motivate someone to adopt the trait. *Should* we even *want* to have these traits? Not necessarily. There is a vast gap between the psychology of virtues and the morality of virtues. It mirrors the gap Hare proposes between the two levels of moral thinking—the intuitive and the critical.[30]

On the critical level, when we think about these traits we can see why they are virtues or vices. I can see that loyalty is a virtue *because* loyalty binds people together in efficient social units. I can see that charity and generosity are virtues because they lead to a redistribution of goods in society from the richer to the poorer. These traits have evolved within human cultures to promote human welfare and flourishing within the cultures. That is how they function. But getting clear on the function of virtues does not enable us to get clear on whether or not accepting and inculcating these traits is good. This is because I have defined moral virtues as traits conducive to flourishing in the social context, and all along I have made the assumption that flourishing (in our case, human flourishing) is good. Without this assumption, my theory, while still

---

[30] See R. M. Hare, *Moral Thinking* (Oxford, 1981).

consequentialist, is not normative. To get the full theory we need an account of human flourishing as good, though I find that characterizing virtues as traits conducive to human flourishing is too narrow and indeed somewhat sinister, depending on how it is spelled out. While it is true that virtue must lead to human flourishing, virtue is not concerned *solely* with human flourishing. Kindness directed towards a dog is still a moral virtue, even though it contributes to human flourishing not one whit. The relevant sort of flourishing in characterizing moral virtue is the flourishing of those within the moral community. Nevertheless, some account of flourishing as good is important, since it is only after we have this that we are in a position fully to criticize a person's view of virtue.

Let me use an analogy to illustrate this point. I can understand why I use the expressions 'yuk' and 'yum' when I come into contact with various foods. 'Yuk' is an expression of disgust, and this response is elicited when I come into contact with rotten food. This response is an adaptive one, because organisms which avoid rotten food generally live long enough to pass on their genes. Likewise, 'yum' is an expression of approval and is elicited in response to wholesome food—ripe fruit, for example. Once again this is adaptive because ripe fruit as opposed to rotten fruit is good for human beings.

But knowing the history of the response need not reinforce or undermine the response. Suppose a research scientist developed a candy which tasted just like ripe sweet apples, but did not have an apple's nutritional value. My response to this candy will be 'yum' even though I know the candy is nutritionally inert, and this is quite appropriate. The only way I could argue that this response is mistaken is if I held another assumption, namely, that only natural products are good. With this assumption, the artificial substitute would be labelled 'bad' and the 'yum' response illegitimate. But, in this case, this extra assumption seems false. It is perfectly reasonable to respond approvingly to the artificial flavour.

Virtue works the same way. It roughly tracks flourishing within a group. Thus I can predict that people will approve of a trait and call it a 'virtue' when they regard it as conducive to human flourishing (just as I can predict that people will say 'yum' when presented with food that has properties we have evolved to prefer). So, the more we know, the better we deploy the word. But to use 'virtue' normatively we need the extra assumption that human flourishing is good. All plausible ethical theories grant this assumption.

Consider another example. Suppose that sociobiologists are correct in maintaining that the reason I have the emotions I do is for adapt-ive purposes. Suppose I love my cat because I was designed to produce and nurture children, but without children I take another object as the focus of my affection. It is an object which resembles an infant in relev-ant respects, because the resemblance will at the same time trigger and satisfy my maternal drive. I can accept this explanation without feeling that I should change and fulfil my function of producing and nurtur-ing children. I love my *cat*, for whatever reason. Even if some of my traits, like a disposition to show affection for small helpless things, exist because of my function of bearing children, it does not follow that I should go out and bear children to provide the affection with a 'proper' focus. Indeed, I could argue that it is better for me if I do *not* have chil-dren, since children would prevent me from pursuing other interests. The explanation provides no motivating reason for me.

At the intuitive level our view of virtue mirrors this confusion. The explanation for virtue may be consequentialist, but some of our intuitions about how we should be may be stubbornly non-consequentialist. The critical and the intuitive may fail to mesh. The case of chastity, discussed earlier, is one where they do mesh, and I believe that our critical reflec-tions do cause a change of intuitions over time.

But consider yet another example, that of romantic 'honour'. Past cul-tures have placed a great deal of emphasis on this virtue. Why? The cold voice of science would say that—for example—young men fighting duels over the love of a young woman mirrors animal behaviour that weeds out the weak, thus permitting the female to choose the stronger mate, which ensures that her children will be stronger, etc. Even if this is true, the young men fighting the duel do not fight for that reason. They fight to preserve their 'honour'. Also, even if this explana-tion of its function is true, human fighting poses a social threat because weapons have become more deadly. So, if romantic honour demands social chaos, romantic honour is not a virtue trait. At the critical level, we can see this. But at the level of intuition, many will feel the necessity of going to extraordinary lengths to preserve their honour. A consequen-tialist theory of virtue is the correct theory, but we cannot internalize it, at least with respect to some virtues and vices. There may exist an uneasy tension between our critical judgements of virtue and our reac-tions to these traits of character.

Recognizing a trait's effects will give a person reasons for adopt-ing or rejecting the trait as a virtue. But oddly, we may feel that there are other quite distinct and quite appropriate motivating reasons. One can see why a trait is valuable objectively (because it produces good consequences), yet have a different reason for valuing it (or devaluing it) subjectively.[31]

[31] An earlier version of this paper was delivered at the University of Manitoba, and I thank the members of that audience for their helpful comments. I thank Princeton University's Center for Human Values for supporting research on this paper through a Laurance S. Rockefeller fellowship. This research was also supported (in part) by two grants from The City University of New York PSC-CUNY Research Award Program, and by an NEH award allowing me to participate in Amelie Rorty's very stimulating 'Virtues and their Vicissitudes' summer seminar in 1992. Thanks are additionally owed to Jonathan Adler, Roger Crisp, Samuel Freeman, Amy Gutmann, Roy Sorensen, John Tomasi, and Susan Wolf.

8

Natural and Artificial Virtues
A Vindication of Hume's Scheme

DAVID WIGGINS

All *moral* duties may be divided into two kinds. The *first* are those to which men are impelled by a natural instinct or immediate propensity which operates on them independent of all ideas of obligation and of all views either to public or private utility. Of this nature are love of children, gratitude to benefactors, pity to the unfortunate. When we reflect on the advantage which results to society from such humane instincts, we pay them the just tribute of moral approbation and esteem. But the person actuated by them feels their power and influence antecedent to any such reflection.

The *second* kind of moral duties are such as are not supported by any original instinct of nature, but are performed entirely from a sense of obligation when we consider the necessities of human society and the impossibility of supporting it if these duties were neglected. It is thus that *justice* or a regard to the property of others, *fidelity* or the observance of promises, become obligatory, and acquire an authority over mankind. For as it is evident that every man loves himself better than any other person, he is naturally impelled to extend his acquisitions as much as possible; and nothing can restrain him in this propensity but reflection and experience, by which he learns the pernicious effects of that licence, and the total dissolution of society which must ensue from it. His original inclination, therefore, or instinct is here checked and restrained by a subsequent judgement or observation.

David Hume, 'Of the Original Contract'[1]

1. Hume's account of morality rests in the first instance upon his account of how the weak but fortifiable sentiment of benevolence and the

---

[1] D. Hume, 'Of the original contract' (1752), in *Essays Moral, Political, and Literary*, ed. E. F. Miller, rev. edn. (Indianapolis, 1987), 465–87, pp. 479–80. Punctuation here and in subsequent quotations simplified.

ever-present sentiment of self-love can issue, under the influence of imagination, reason, and sympathy (the capacity to resonate to the mental states of others), in a standard of morals which informs evaluation of characters, sustains our first understanding of the distinction of vice and virtue, and extends, reinforces, and refines our motivation to act non-egoistically. If we are party to the standard of morals that Hume describes—and in ordinary life it will be hard for the preponderance of human beings not to be carried along by the processes Hume describes and hard to struggle against the social forces that make us party to that standard—then it is to be expected that often we shall be motivated, however weakly, to act otherwise than upon self-love. Indeed, in the important class of cases from which the Humean construction starts out, the emerging standard of morals has only to recognize as a norm what is already latent within our human nature.

The social virtues of humanity and benevolence exert their influence immediately by a direct tendency or instinct, which chiefly keeps in view the simple object moving the affections and comprehends not any scheme or system nor the consequences resulting from the concurrence, imitation, or example of others. A parent flies to the relief of his child; transported by that natural sympathy which actuates him and which affords no leisure to reflect on the sentiments or conduct of the rest of mankind in like circumstances. A generous man cheerfully embraces an opportunity of serving his friend, because he then feels himself under the dominion of the beneficent affections, nor is he concerned whether any other person in the universe were ever before actuated by such noble motives, or will ever afterwards prove their influence. In all these cases the social passions have in view a single individual object, and pursue the safety or happiness alone of the person loved and esteemed. With this they are satisfied: in this they acquiesce. And as the good resulting from their benign influence is in itself complete and entire, it also excites the moral sentiment of approbation without any reflection on farther consequences and without any more enlarged views of the concurrence or imitation of the other members of society.[2]

Here Hume describes the ordinary workings of the social virtues, which are the virtues that are rooted directly in the weak sentiment of benevolence. It is in our first nature to approve them and approve their being approved. There is much more to morality than non-egoism, however, and there are many virtues beside those that exert their influence on an agent directly and without the assistance of a scheme or system requiring

---

[2] Hume, *Enquiry Concerning the Principles of Morals* (1751), ed. P. H. Nidditch, 3rd edn. (Oxford, 1975), App. iii, pp. 302–3.

'concurrence' and 'imitation' on the part of members of society distinct from the agent himself. Hume's problem is to account within his benevolence-based scheme for loyalty, honesty, veracity, allegiance, fidelity to promises, justice (respecting property and so on).

2. The first sign that there are virtues that fit imperfectly into Hume's original aetiology of morality is this. There are considerations of justice (in the strict and specific sense of the word) that we frequently allow to defeat or trump the requirements of benevolence. It is true that private benevolence and justice will sometimes call for the same act; but equally often they will not, e.g. where a poor man has wronged a less poor one. Public benevolence (the concern for the general interest as considered in advance of justice) and justice itself may sometimes call for the same act; but equally often they may not, e.g. when a dangerous and seditious bigot is deprived of his lawful inheritance or is found guilty of an offence he has not committed. Hume wants us to be free to insist that, in such a case, we ought to side with justice, not with benevolence (whether private or public). Once we appreciate the force of this insistence of Hume's, it will then be apparent (as it is apparent to Hume) that there are a significant number of virtues whose recognition as virtues appears to disrupt the pattern of explanation so far expounded. If the weak sentiment of benevolence is to be the whole theoretical origin of morality, then the aetiology of morals must find a way to explain how the force and energy of benevolence can be *redirected* so as to propel our line of conduct along altogether new channels. Sometimes the redirected force of benevolence must work against benevolence itself. It is at this point, and in order to come to terms with the virtues that do not arise directly from our benevolence, that Hume invokes the idea of a convention or a compact.

There is a theoretically cognate problem that Hume sees in the ideas of justice and kindred virtues. Hume's exposition of this problem has given his readers much difficulty. We shall expound it in his words, but shall interpose comments and make interpolations in square brackets which are designed to suggest one particular interpretation. The problem is set out at *Treatise*, Book III, Part II:

I suppose a person to have lent me a sum of money on condition that it be restored in a few days; and also suppose that, after the expiration of the term agreed on, he demands the sum. I ask, *What reason or motive have I to restore the money?* It will perhaps be said, that my regard to justice and abhorrence of villainy and knavery are sufficient reasons for me, if I have the least grain of honesty, or sense of duty and obligation. And this answer, no doubt, is just and satisfactory to man in his civilized state and when trained up according to a certain discipline and education. But in his rude and more *natural* condition [which is the place where Hume's aetiology of morals must set out from, for it is seeking to explain the emergence of the *civilized* state], if you are pleased to call such a condition natural [it is natural in this sense: it does not presuppose convention, compact or any other artifice], this answer would be rejected as perfectly unintelligible and sophistical. For one in that situation would immediately ask you *wherein consists this honesty and justice, which you find in restoring a loan and abstaining from the property of others?* It does not surely lie in the external action.[3]

Here we must break off the citation to ask why we are expected to agree that the honesty cannot consist in the external action. The answer is that, according to Hume, 'all virtuous actions derive their merit only from virtuous motives, and are considered merely as signs of those motives'.[4] For Hume the claim has the status of a would-be axiom, founded in his conception of morality as a matter of 'personal merit', that is of the virtues of individual moral agents. The passage continues,

[That wherein this honesty and justice consists] does not surely lie in the external action. It must therefore be placed in the motive from which the external action is derived. [That is the effect of the would-be axiom.] This motive [however] can never be a regard to the honesty of the action. For it is a plain fallacy to say that a virtuous motive is requisite to render an action honest, and at the same time that a regard to the honesty is the motive of the action.[5]

Hume's point is that, if the merit of the action of restoring the money is referred to the merit of the motive and the virtuous disposition associated with that motive, then the merit of that motive cannot, on pain of circularity in the explanation, be referred back to the merit of the action. Or, as Hume says,

We can never have a regard to the virtue of an action, unless the action be antecedently virtuous. No action can be virtuous, but so far as it proceeds from a virtuous motive. A virtuous motive, therefore, must precede the regard to the virtue; and it is impossible that the virtuous motive and the regard to the virtue can be the same.

It is requisite, then, to find some motive to acts of justice and honesty distinct from our regard to the honesty; and in this lies the great difficulty.[6]

---

[3] Hume, *Treatise of Human Nature* (1739), ed. L. A. Selby-Bigge, rev. P. H. Nidditch, 2nd edn. (Oxford, 1978), III. II. i. 479–80.   [4] Ibid. 478.
[5] Ibid. 480.   [6] Ibid.

Hume finds the further motive that he needs for acts of justice, honesty, fidelity to promises, and so on in the approbation that we feel for acts that conform to a useful convention. This might be a convention or compact that enjoins one to keep one's hands off what others have made, or have had assigned to them by those who have made it. Or it might be the convention that designates some promissory formula and enjoins one to take care to do what, using that formula, one has said one will do, or whatever . . .

How can conventions solve the problem Hume has proposed in Book III, Part III? Well, the conventions in question may be imagined to be conventions such that, if most people observe them, then things will be better for most people:

> [T]he benefit resulting from [justice and fidelity and so on] is not the consequence of every individual single act; but arises from the whole scheme or system concurred in by the whole, or the greater part of the society.[7]

Conventions or compacts single out practices that will bring general benefit; but then, as the practices take on life and are sustained in living, *further* value is conferred upon acts or observances that exemplify these practices. This value of any particular observance is something over and above the expected benefit of the observance itself. This newly conferred value helps to explain the motive that was called 'the regard to the honesty of the act'. For if benevolence or self-love or both will *second* some convention and *approve* it, then the convention can redirect the activity of virtuous agents into justice or fidelity.

3. At this stage, the reader may wish to reread the quotation that heads this Chapter. It is succinct and it has the virtue of confirming that Hume always persisted in his account of the natural and artificial virtues. (However inexplicit he is about this theory in the *Enquiry*, it is clear that it is there in the background.) But in our citation there are points where the reader may think that Hume does not do the best for his theory.

Contrary to what Hume suggests at one place, practices that arise from compact or convention and command our approbation need not result from any conscious or explicit agreement. At the level of discovery, they may result from accident or from our falling into certain ways of behaving that we then find ourselves encouraged to persist in. Developing further an example Hume provides, let us think of two men who find

---

[7] Hume, *Enquiry*, App. iii, p. 304.

themselves rowing a boat for the first time in their lives. Imagine that they discover after a while that they row best if they concert their efforts and pull on the oars at the same moment with a similar force, and imagine them settling down to row in that way. It does not matter how it came about that they started to row in time together. We do not need a general theory of the discovery of compacts or conventions. A theory of what sustains the corresponding practice is enough. All will be well in fact if whatever it is that encourages us to *persist* in a practice and behave as if we adhered to a compact that enjoined that persistence is something that is fully amenable to Hume's general theory. It can be self-love, which is emphasized in the *Treatise*, or it can be the concern with the general interest which is rooted in benevolence, as Hume prefers to insist in Appendix iii of the *Enquiry*; and there is nothing in Hume's theory to prevent self-love and benevolence from co-operating, each being helped out in its working by reason and imagination, no doubt.

What then does Hume mean by a convention? Sometimes he means a compact or what would have been a compact if it had been entered into *as* a compact. Sometimes he means the way of behaving in which we come together—*convenimus*—as if by a compact.

It would have been good if Hume could have said much more under these heads; and there are further complaints one may have about the account that is condensed in 'Of the Original Contract'. It would have been good if Hume had distinguished more clearly than we find him doing there (or anywhere else) between questions of the phenomenology of individual motivation and questions of aetiology and origination. For questions of aetiology and origination will usually outrun phenomenology and outrun the thoughts that individual agents can rehearse to themselves. This is a point that would become all the more evident so soon as issues of evolution were allowed to impinge upon the Humean account.

There is one more criticism one might urge of Hume's condensation of his own doctrine. It would have been helpful if here (or anywhere else) Hume had allowed himself to single out for very special attention conventions with a further property, over and above their usefulness or indispensability to us. These are conventions that all putative participants are happy to agree to (at least if they know that *some* convention must be agreed) and happy to prefer over all visible alternatives. These conventions deserve to be singled out specially because, when the aetiological examination of moral ideas leads eventually into the question of their *vindication*, this property will surely have a new and magnified importance.[8]

So much for complaints. But the general shape of Hume's explanation is clear. He can see virtues such as veracity, fidelity, loyalty, allegiance, honesty, and justice as redirections of benevolence or humanity, and he can explain how the energy to be mustered from fellow-feeling may be put at the disposal of moral preoccupations and concerns that are not only different from the concerns of humanity and self-love but potentially utterly at variance with them. It is from these redirections that Hume obtains the virtues he designates *artificial*. He calls them artificial because they are *not* virtues that arise directly from human nature without the mediation of convention or compact.

4. So far so good, but now we must ask what explains an individual person's continued adherence to useful or agreeable conventions even when such adherence runs contrary to his own interest or contrary to the general interest. How well can Hume's theory manage either of these cases? Well, the person in question may not adhere to them. So the question had better be this: where he does adhere to them, why does he do so? And is it reasonable for him to adhere to them? Hume's explanation would appear to be this:

[Men] are induced to inculcate on their children, from their earliest infancy, the principles of probity, and teach them to regard the observance of those rules by which society is maintained as worthy and honourable, and their violation as base and infamous.[9]

In this connection the reader should look also at the passage at the beginning of *Treatise*, Book III, Part II, Section ii, where Hume speaks of 'the reasons, which determine us to attribute to the observance or neglect of [the rules of justice] a moral beauty and deformity'. That is what explains our adherence—where we do adhere.

The attractive feature of this explanation is that it makes it apparent to theory how, on the inside of a practice, we can engage in it in exactly the manner in which we suppose that we can. It makes apparent to theory how we can engage in a practice in the manner that Hume himself was describing when he wrote, 'It will perhaps be said that my regard to justice and abhorrence of villainy and knavery are sufficient reasons for me, if I have the least grain of honesty, or sense of duty and obligation.'

[8] See T. M. Scanlon, 'Contractualism and Utilitarianism', in A. Sen and B. Williams (eds.), *Utilitarianism and Beyond* (Cambridge, 1982), 103–28.

[9] Hume, *Treatise*, III. II. ii, 500–1.

In the civilized state that Hume took such pains to describe and explain and mentions so approvingly here, someone's attachment to the general interest can annex the idea of moral beauty to acts that conform to certain practices, and can annex the idea of moral deformity to their non-performance. Such practices take on a life of their own in the hearts and minds of ordinary agents who are happy to live under the auspices of the civilization that Hume sees as offering them the final fulfilment of their natures as reasonable beings. These practices and the expectations that they generate are not, of course, proof against violation or abuse. But there are real safeguards (of a sort) in the ideas that we have of them—the idea of the 'beauty of an observance' and so on. Nor is there any mistake, according to Hume, in these ideas that we have internalized—unless it is a mistake that can be eliminated by piecemeal refinement and internal criticism. 'This is what we do', we might say. 'Any alternative to what we do can be considered. But what we do has itself resulted from indefinitely many reconsiderations and refinements. The requirements of honesty, fair dealing, and so on do not require us to act in this manner when we are dealing with blackguards without conscience. But they set standards that we need reason to depart from.' For Hume—as for anyone else with any sense at all of what is possible here—that is answer enough. It is an illusion to suppose that there is any well-founded conception of the reasonable that is independent of human nature, and of the substance of human life as we know it, by which a judgement could be reached on some further question of the reasonableness or not of conventions that have the property mentioned in the penultimate paragraph of Section 3 above and of observances which agents can perceive as having moral beauty. (Hume sees no special reasonableness in the promptings of self-interest.) Let the critics who say they want more get for themselves a notion of the reasonable that presupposes nothing at all about human nature. If they want more, let them say what more they want in those terms. Their difficulty will be this, that

Where passion is neither founded on false suppositions, nor chooses means insufficient for the end, the [theoretical] understanding can neither justify nor condemn it. It is not contrary to [theoretical] reason to prefer the destruction of the whole world to the scratching of my finger. It is not contrary to [theoretical] reason for me to choose my total ruin, to prevent the least uneasiness of an *Indian* or person wholly unknown to me.[10]

[10] Hume, *Treatise*, II. III. iii. 416 (with interpolations of reinterpretative intent marked in square brackets).

The reasonableness of the convention (not the reasonableness of individual prudence!) helps to constitute its moral beauty and the moral beauty of its observances. Its moral beauty affords one part of what gives any individual agent a good reason to observe it. Is there nothing more to say? Not really.

If a man have a lively sense of honour and virtue, with moderate passions, his conduct will always be conformable to the rules of morality; or if he depart from them, his return will be easy and expeditious. On the other hand, where one is born of so perverse a frame of mind, of so callous and insensible a disposition, as to have no relish for virtue or humanity, no sympathy for his fellow creatures, no desire of esteem and applause; such a one must be allowed entirely incurable, nor is there any remedy in philosophy. For my part, I know not how I should address myself to such a one or by what arguments I should endeavour to reform him. Should I tell him of the inward satisfaction which results from laudable and humane actions, the delicate pleasure of disinterested love and friendship, the lasting enjoyments of a good name and an established character, he might still reply that these were perhaps pleasures to such as were susceptible of them; but that, for his part, he finds himself of quite a different turn and disposition. I must repeat it; my philosophy affords no remedy in such a case, nor could I do any thing but lament this person's unhappy condition. But then I ask if any other philosophy can afford a remedy.[11]

5. Before we conclude the exposition of Hume's system, there is at least one loose end to be attached.

In the final analysis, Hume's aetiology of morals successfully subsumes the artificial virtues, different though they are from 'humanity, benevolence, friendship, public spirit, and other social virtues of that stamp'.[12] But how clean an exit does his idea of convention furnish from the circle that he began by complaining of finding within the apparent rationale of acts of justice?

Any careful or complete reply to this question will have to acknowledge that Hume's answer to the difficulty that he professed to find depends crucially on his silently revoking the proposition which, in expounding his infamous circle, he treats as axiomatic—the proposition

---

[11] Hume, 'The Sceptic' (1742), in *Essays*, 159–180, pp. 169–70.

[12] Hume, *Enquiry*, Sect. iii, p. 204. What is more, the contrast between the natural and artificial is not simply an oddity arising from Hume's need to defend this aetiology of morals. The distinction can be marked by reference to the striking way in which the artificial virtues verify and the natural virtues falsify the general claims Aristotle enters about virtue and acting virtuously at *Nicomachean Ethics* 1103^{a}31–2. See my 'Eudaimonism and Realism in Aristotle's *Ethics*: a Reply to John McDowell', in R. Heinaman (ed.), *Aristotle and Moral Realism* (London, 1995), 119–31.

about what we look to 'when we praise any action'. Once room is made
for the artificial virtues within the theory, it is simply impossible to
persist in Hume's claim that an 'external performance has no merit'.
Indeed Hume himself will need to claim that there is 'moral beauty' in
an observance. He says this without any regard to the original axiom.
If there can be moral beauty in an observance as such, then any non-
accidental performance of some act that is sanctioned by convention does
pro tanto have some merit. It follows that it is all right to say that a just
act is an act that conforms to a convention or system which is useful in
a certain way. In truth, it is neither necessary nor possible to do the
opposite and define the justice of an act via the justice of a person. What
after all is a just person? A just person is a person with a strong attachment to certain *practices* and *outcomes*, namely those singled out in certain particular conventions which Hume thinks of him as wanting the
life he leads in community with others to be shaped and constrained by.

If this is correct, then there is no room for Hume to persist in the
claim that 'virtuous actions derive their merit only from virtuous motives,
and are considered merely as signs of those motives'. By the Humean
theory itself, just acts and just motives depend for their merit on their
conformity to practices that are in a certain way beneficial—and could
even be subjected to the additional test of the sacred principle of consent.

Finally, consider the nature of the question of how beneficial a given
convention is. Like the question of how beneficial an action is, this question depends for its answer on our extending moral evaluation from
states of character to states of affairs. Hume, like Aristotle, Nietzsche,
and countless other pre-modern moralists, would nowadays be classified as a 'virtue theorist'. But it is evident that at this juncture Hume's
system affords a vantage point to look forwards to theories of a different kind, namely those like J. S. Mill's that define acting rightly in terms
of the states of affairs that result from doing the act. What is more,
from the special vantage point of Hume, we may start to conceive of an
account of these matters that looks beyond J. S. Mill and all the confusion and turmoil that the theories of his inheritors have occasioned.
What a grown-up moral philosophy might attempt is an account of morality that embraces the full gamut of moral predications, seeing them as
mutually irreducible and mutually indispensable, allowing no primacy to
character traits *or* practices *or* states of affairs—or allowing primacy
to all at once. Such a theory, being neither consequentialist nor virtue-
centred, might take on some of the subtlety of the moral phenomena
themselves and of our moral deliverances upon them.

9

Does Moral Virtue Constitute a Benefit to the Agent?

BRAD HOOKER

1. INTRODUCTION

Something is instrumentally beneficial to someone if it is a means to some further thing that itself constitutes a benefit to that person. Being morally virtuous is often instrumentally beneficial to the agent. It can bring the agent pleasure and peace of mind and such social rewards as others' co-operation and respect.[1] But as my title indicates, this essay is about constitutive benefits rather than instrumental ones. Different theories of individual welfare—of what makes a person's life go well or badly for him or her—differ over what things *constitute* benefits to people. What do the main theories of individual welfare say about whether moral virtue constitutes a benefit to the agent?

Theories of individual welfare fall into three main categories: hedonism, the desire-fulfilment theory (sometimes called the preference-satisfaction theory), and the list theory.[2] Hedonism claims that how beneficial something is to us is entirely a matter of how much pleasure

---

[1] But a long-standing dispute exists over whether having moral dispositions always has enough instrumental benefit to the agent to outweigh the costs to him or her of developing or retaining those dispositions. For an excellent discussion of this issue, see G. Sayre-McCord, 'Deception and Reasons to be Moral', *American Philosophical Quarterly* 26 (1989), 113–122.

[2] Though this way of dividing the theories is common, the terminology comes from D. Parfit, *Reasons and Persons* (Oxford, 1984), Appendix I, except that what I call the list theory he calls 'the Objective List Theory'. I have deviated from his terminology in order to inhibit the assumption that the list theory, which is a view about what constitutes individuals' welfare, is committed to an objectivist or realist view about the nature of prudential values. As I explain in 'Theories of Welfare, Theories of Good Reasons for Action, and Ontological Naturalism', *Philosophical Papers* 20 (1991), 25–36, the list theory of welfare is compatible with anti-realist metaphysical views (such as projectivism) and with expressivist views about the nature of evaluative judgement.

(or reduction of pain) we get from it. The desire-fulfilment theory maintains that the best life for us in self-interested terms is whichever one involves the maximum fulfilment of desire. And the list theory maintains that how beneficial some things are to us is not just a matter of how much pleasure we get from them or of how much they fulfil our desires. In the next section I discuss what hedonism and the desire-fulfilment theory say about whether being virtuous constitutes a benefit to the agent. I shall then turn to the list theory. What hedonism and the desire-fulfilment theory say about whether being virtuous constitutes a benefit to the agent is fairly straightforward. Figuring out what the list theory says about the matter is more difficult. Therefore, most of the essay will be on the list theory.

Being a virtuous person is a matter of having and acting on a set of character traits, or settled dispositions.[3] Which dispositions? I would like to leave this somewhat open. But I will focus on other-regarding dispositions (such as dispositions to be just, trustworthy, generous, etc.). The traditional problem of reconciling virtue with self-interest focuses, of course, on other-regarding virtues.[4]

Someone might suggest that worrying about whether moral virtue benefits the agent is deeply confused, since being honest, fair, kind, etc. *for the sake of benefits to oneself* is not *moral* virtue.[5] That may be true. But we can nevertheless be interested in whether having moral virtues constitutes a benefit to the morally virtuous person.

2. HEDONISM AND DESIRE-FULFILMENT THEORY

Many philosophers who have discussed the relation between self-interest and morality have been hedonists about welfare. According to hedonism,

---

[3] See Aristotle, *Nicomachean Ethics* (= *NE*) 1105ª30–31.

[4] After all, the potential for conflict between self-regarding virtue and self-interest is fairly slight. In any event, my question is whether *moral* virtue constitutes a benefit to the agent. The focus on *moral* virtue leads to a focus on other-regarding virtue, since morality is (at least primarily) concerned with how one treats others—see T. Nagel, *The View From Nowhere* (New York, 1986), 197; B. Williams, *Ethics and the Limits of Philosophy* (Cambridge, Mass., 1985), 12–13; B. Gert, *Morality* (New York, 1988), 5; R. Brandt, 'Morality and its Critics', *American Philosophical Quarterly* 26 (1989), 89–100, p. 99; and Julia Driver's essay in the present volume.

[5] F. H. Bradley wrote, 'what is clear at first sight is, that to take virtue as a mere means to an ulterior end is in direct antagonism to the voice of the moral consciousness' ('Why Should I Be Moral?', in his *Ethical Studies*, 2nd edn. (Oxford, 1927), 58–84, p. 61). See also H. A. Prichard, 'Does Moral Philosophy Rest on a Mistake?' and 'Moral Obligation', in his *Moral Obligation* (Oxford, 1949), 1–17, 87–163; and N. Lemos, 'High-Minded Egoism and the Problem of Priggishness', *Mind* 93 (1984), 542–58.

although being morally virtuous may be *instrumentally* beneficial to you in that it brings you pleasure, being morally virtuous is not *in itself* a self-interested good. Hedonists would say that your acting morally, say, refraining from cheating someone, brings you some benefit only if it brings you some pleasure. Being moral is not what constitutes the benefit to you; instead, the benefit to you is constituted by whatever pleasure you get as a result of your moral behaviour. Note this consequence: if the chief pleasure you get out of being morally virtuous comes from your thinking you are, then you might be better off not *actually* being morally virtuous but merely *believing* falsely that you are—because actually being morally virtuous can carry considerable costs.

Most philosophers today who are not hedonists about welfare accept the desire-fulfilment theory of welfare. The desire-fulfilment theory maintains that the best life for you in self-interested terms is the one involving the greatest fulfilment of the desires you have in that life. Such a theory takes into account the *number* of desires that get fulfilled, the *relative importance to you* of your various desires, and *how long* they last.[6] But these and other complications can be ignored here. The main difference between the desire-fulfilment theory and hedonism comes out in cases in which you have a desire that is fulfilled without your getting any pleasure from this fact, because, for example, you do not know that it has been fulfilled. In such cases, the desire-fulfilment theory maintains that the fulfilment of that desire constitutes a benefit to you; hedonism maintains that it does not.

Proponents of the desire-fulfilment theory of welfare distinguish between *desiring something as a means to some further thing* and *desiring something as an end in itself*. A stock example of a desire for something as a means to some further thing is the desire to go to the dentist. In contrast, one's own pleasure is something typically desired for its own sake. And other things are desired in this way—for example, many people desire both personal autonomy and knowing the truth about important matters at least partly for their own sakes. Desire-fulfilment theorists couch their theory in terms of desires for ends—only fulfilment of these desires constitutes benefits to the agent. I thus have no need to refer to desires for things as means. So I shall use the term 'desires' to refer to desires for ends.

---

[6] For a discussion of the intricacies of this kind of theory, see Parfit, *Reasons and Persons*, Appendix I. See also P. Bricker, 'Prudence', *Journal of Philosophy* 77 (1980), 381–401; and J. Griffin, *Well-being: Its Meaning, Measurement, and Moral Importance* (Oxford, 1986), Part One.

One version of the desire-fulfilment theory says the fulfilment of any desire of yours, even if that desire is based on faulty reasoning or mistaken beliefs, constitutes some benefit to you. A more restrictive version of the theory claims instead that something constitutes a benefit to you if but only if it fulfils your 'informed' desires, that is, desires that are not based on illogical reasoning or false empirical beliefs. Mark Overvold persuasively argues for further restrictions on which desires are to count in the assessment of someone's welfare: the only desires that should count are the agent's desires for things that involve the agent in some way.[7] But many moral desires pass all these tests. Examples might be people's desires that they be kind, that they be fair, that they be honest, and, more generally, that they live a moral life. Holders of the desire-fulfilment theory would conclude that the fulfilment of any of these moral desires constitutes a benefit to these people. So, on this view, being morally virtuous constitutes a benefit to the agent if *but only if* the agent has the relevant desires. We might say that, on this view, moral virtue *contingently* constitutes a benefit to the agent.[8]

Desire-fulfilment theorists would add, however, that the fulfilment of any moral desire will also constitute a *loss* to the agent if the fulfilment of that desire causes some other present or future desire of the agent's to go unfulfilled. This kind of loss might be greater than the benefit constituted by the fulfilment of the moral desire. When that is the case, and there are no relevant side-effects, the fulfilment of that moral desire is, on balance, against the agent's self-interest.

3. THE LIST THEORY OF WELL-BEING

The rest of this essay is about the other main theory of individual welfare, the list theory.[9] The list theory holds that how beneficial some

---

[7] M. Overvold, 'Self-Interest and the Concept of Self-Sacrifice', *Canadian Journal of Philosophy* 10 (1980), 105–18. See also Parfit's discussion of what he calls 'the Success Theory' (*Reasons and Persons*, Appendix I). In my 'Overvold's Contribution to Philosophy', *Journal of Philosophical Research* 16 (1990/1), 333–44, I argue that Overvold's restriction should be glossed as proposing that the only desires that count are ones for events or states of affairs in which the agent is an essential constituent.

[8] Some desire theorists might be uncomfortable with any talk of being moral's *constituting* a benefit to the agent. They might say that, in so far as having moral dispositions has prudential value for someone, it has this prudential value not really because the dispositions are moral, but only because the person desires to have those dispositions.

[9] For some excellent defences of the list theory, see D. Brink, *Moral Realism and the Foundations of Ethics* (Cambridge, Mass., 1989), 221–36; T. M. Scanlon, 'Value, Desire, and Quality of Life', in M. Nussbaum and A. Sen (eds.), *The Quality of Life* (Oxford, 1993), 185–200. See also R. Nozick, *The Examined Life* (New York, 1989), especially ch. 10.

things are to us is not merely a matter of how much pleasure they give us or of how much they fulfil our desires. Some of the things that might be listed as having this status as prudential goods are autonomy,[10] friendship, knowledge of important matters, achievement, and perhaps the appreciation of beauty. List theorists can add that our pleasure also constitutes a benefit to us.[11]

We can distinguish between at least three general types of list theory. According to one type, certain things are good for me even if I do not desire them or get any pleasure from them (though pleasure itself is an additional good). According to the second type, a necessary condition of something's being beneficial to me is that I get pleasure from it, but how much pleasure I get from something is not the only factor in determining how beneficial to me the thing is. So, on this second view, playing push-pin and appreciating excellent poetry might be equally pleasant for me, but the latter is better because it involves appreciating beauty, while the former does not. The third type of list theory makes a connection with desire rather than pleasure. This type holds that a necessary condition of something's being beneficial to me is that I desire it, but how much or how long I desire it is not the only factor in determining how beneficial to me the thing is. On this third view, although I may desire push-pin as much as excellent poetry, poetry is nevertheless better. For the purposes of this paper, however, I can remain neutral on the question of which of these three general types of list theory is best.[12]

What is the relation of the list theory to perfectionism? Perfectionism is a sub-species of the list theory. Perfectionism differs from other kinds of list theory in claiming that we ascertain what gets on the list by

---

[10] For the best discussion of autonomy's place on a plausible list, see R. Crisp, 'Medical Negligence, Assault, Informed Consent, and Autonomy', *Journal of Law and Society* 17 (1990), 77–89, pp. 81–4.

[11] One commentator suggested that I manifest a male bias by not listing marriage and children. Of course, marriage and children can be sources of friendship, pleasure, achievement, and knowledge. But do they have a place on the list apart from their connection with those other goods? I will not take sides on this matter here.

[12] But for useful discussion, see W. Frankena, *Ethics*, 2nd edn. (Englewood Cliffs, NJ, 1973), 91; Parfit, *Reasons and Persons*, 502; and G. Trianosky, 'Rightly Ordered Appetites: How to Live Morally and Live Well', *American Philosophical Quarterly* 25 (1988), 1–12, pp. 3–4. See also C. Korsgaard's discussion of the idea that getting pleasure out of something can be the condition of that thing's having value without the thing's being valuable *merely* as a means to pleasures: 'Two Distinctions in Goodness', *Philosophical Review* 92 (1983), 169–95, pp. 186–7. Especially clear and persuasive on all this is R. Crisp, 'Sidgwick and Self-Interest', *Utilitas* 2 (1990), 267–80, sections ii and iii. I will not venture into the vexed question of how Aristotle's view of a person's good relates to those above, but see R. Kraut, 'Two Conceptions of Happiness', *Philosophical Review* 88 (1979), 167–97, esp. pp. 170–7, 181.

considering essential, distinctive, or characteristic human capacities or activities. That is, other kinds of list theory would reject the idea that your having or exercising X constitutes a benefit to you if and only if X is an essential, distinctive, or characteristic human capacity or activity. These list theories would rely on some other way of coming up with a list, such as direct appeal to intuition about self-interested value, for example. I later offer my proposal for how to determine what we think should be on the list.

Some people might reject the particular list of goods I have mentioned because they think some other list is superior. Other people might reject the whole idea of a list theory because they think it a dangerous pretence. Although this essay is not about which of hedonism, the desire-fulfilment theory, and the list theory is the most plausible theory of well-being, I will indicate why a list theory is not so odious as to be beyond discussion.

Many people reject the list theory because they think it has outrageously paternalistic implications: they see looming the spectre of people's imposing 'the good life' on others. However, the list theory identifies autonomy as one of the prudential values. It *might* even go so far as to give overriding importance to autonomy. Therefore, the list theory itself might prohibit what we intuitively think of as objectionable paternalism.[13] Furthermore, even if autonomy were *not* one of the things on the list, paternalism would be in the offing *only* if *morality* requires or permits forcing things on people that they do not want. But morality might not require or permit this. So even if the list theory did not itself have the resources to block objectionable paternalism, the list theory could be combined with a moral theory providing the necessary prohibitions.

So, do the most plausible versions of the list theory hold that moral virtue constitutes a benefit to the agent? In the next section, I shall consider the best arguments I can think of for concluding that moral virtue does constitute a benefit to the agent.

4. THREE ARGUMENTS FOR THINKING THAT VIRTUE CONSTITUTES A BENEFIT TO THE AGENT

Here is one such argument. Knowledge of important matters is on the list. What is right and what is wrong are important matters. Therefore,

---

[13] This point is made in a number of places (e.g., J. Finnis, *Fundamentals of Ethics* (New York, 1983), 50; Griffin, *Well-being*, 71; T. Hurka, 'Perfectionism', in L. and C. Becker (eds.), *The Encyclopedia of Ethics* (London, 1992), vol. 2, pp. 946–9, see p. 949; and Hurka, *Perfectionism* (New York, 1993), 148–56).

one of the things on the list is knowing what is right and what is wrong. Furthermore, knowing right and wrong brings with it moral motivation. Hence, moral virtue is a necessary concomitant of something on the list. Let us call this *the argument from knowledge.*

Obviously, many things about this argument are controversial. First, whether there really is moral knowledge is controversial. Second, it is controversial whether, even if there is moral knowledge, moral knowledge necessarily brings with it moral motivation.[14] Third, it is controversial whether, even if there is moral knowledge and there is a necessary ('internal') connection between it and moral motivation, this moral motivation must be sufficient to qualify one as morally virtuous.[15] For some hold that, although anyone who knows that certain acts would be morally wrong must have *some* motivation to avoid these acts, this motivation might not be particularly strong. Being morally virtuous, however, involves having certain very strong (if not overriding) motivations. Therefore, if moral knowledge does not necessarily bring with it strong moral motivation, one can have moral knowledge without being morally virtuous. In fact, the only people who *would* accept the argument from knowledge are those who think that there is moral knowledge and that it necessarily brings with it moral motivations that are sufficiently strong to qualify a person as virtuous.

I turn now to a more promising argument. One premiss of this argument is that the most plausible versions of the list theory will have achievement on the list. The other premiss is that living a truly moral life is an achievement. From these premisses it follows that moral virtue gets on the list because being morally virtuous is a kind of achievement. Call this *the argument from achievement.*[16]

Why think that living a moral life is a significant achievement? Given

---

[14] Some representative examples of philosophers who deny that there is a *necessary* connection between moral judgement and motivation are W. Frankena, 'Obligation and Motivation in Recent Moral Philosophy', in A. I. Melden (ed.), *Essays in Moral Philosophy* (Seattle, 1958), 40–81; D. A. J. Richards, *A Theory of Reasons for Action* (Oxford, 1971); and Brink, *Moral Realism and the Foundations of Ethics*, ch. 3.

[15] Endorsements of what we might call 'internalist cognitivism' about moral judgements appear in H. Sidgwick, *The Methods of Ethics*, 7th edn. (London, 1907), 34; J. McDowell, 'Non-Cognitivism and Rule-Following', in S. Holtzman and C. Leich (eds.), *Wittgenstein: To Follow a Rule* (Oxford, 1981), 141–62, pp. 154–5, 161, nn. 19 and 20; T. Nagel, *The Possibility of Altruism* (Oxford, 1970), 8–9, and *The View From Nowhere*, 138–52, esp. pp. 139, 144, 148, 149; D. McNaughton, *Moral Vision* (Oxford, 1988), 46–50. See also S. Scheffler, *Human Morality* (New York, 1992), chs. 4–5.

[16] For hints of the argument from achievement, see Griffin, *Well-Being*, 69–70, 132. Frankena presents the following similar but more general argument: other things being equal, one's life goes better to the extent that it involves excellences; being moral is a kind of excellence; therefore, moral virtue does, other things being equal, benefit the agent

that writing a great book is an achievement that makes someone's life
go better in self-interested terms, why wouldn't righting a great wrong
be one too? Or consider the case of someone who succeeds in rescuing many innocent people from a genocidal army. Indeed, living a moral
life even in a less heroic, more humdrum fashion is quite an achievement.[17] So, given that two people have led lives with the same amount
of *non*-moral achievement, but one has been moral and the other has
not, the moral one's life has contained more achievement overall than
the other's has. All else being equal, the life involving greater overall
achievement (in this example, the moral person's) does seem superior
from the point of view of the list theory.

A note of caution: the conclusion just reached was *not* that moral virtue is *always* more beneficial to the agent than his or her other alternatives. Being moral is only one kind of achievement. Achievement is only
one of the goods on the list. Thus, even if moral virtue does constitute
a benefit to the agent, there may be cases in which moral virtue brings
such large losses in terms of the other things on the list that the greatest
net benefit for the agent lies in not being moral. Such cases, I believe,
are common.

Moreover, what of success in immoral schemes? Are they also
achievements that constitute benefits to agents? Consider the career of
the manipulative rake who achieved the status of being the best seducer in
eighteenth century Paris. Imagine that, although he made a game of breaking hearts and disrupting lives, no one ever got back at him because of
the overriding need to keep the nature of his predatory activity (seduc-
tion) secret. I just do not know what to make of the idea that agents'
immoral achievements constitute benefits to them.[18]

Even if we reject that idea, we are left with the conclusion that moral
virtue is only one kind of achievement and achievement is only one
of the goods on the list. We might wonder whether we could not have

---

(*Ethics*, 91, 93–4). But the argument from achievement seems to me more persuasive
than the argument from excellence.

[17] See Susan Wolf's probing account of what being a moral saint would be like: 'Moral
Saints', *Journal of Philosophy* 79 (1982), 419–39. She pictures the moral saint as being
'dominated by a commitment to improving the welfare of others or of society as a whole'
(p. 420). One difference between her paper and this essay is that I am concerned mainly
with virtue as a matter of conforming to the *requirements* of everyday, common-sense
morality. I presume this falls well short of being *dominated* by a commitment to improving the welfare of others or of society as a whole.

[18] For an impressive defence of the idea that immoral achievements can constitute addi-
tions to aggregate good, see Hurka, *Perfectionism*, 19–20, and index s.v. 'Perfectionism,
Moralistic'.

reached a more cheering conclusion. More specifically, while not forgetting that being morally virtuous is a kind of achievement, we might wonder whether moral virtue has a less subordinate, less attenuated place on the list. We might ask whether it also has a place on the list at the same level as knowledge, friendship, pleasure, and achievement. Does moral virtue stand shoulder to shoulder with these other values? Let me mark the status on the list that knowledge, friendship, pleasure, achievement, and perhaps the appreciation of beauty have by referring to them as *fundamental categories of prudential value.* So another way of asking whether moral virtue has a place on the list at the same level as knowledge, friendship, pleasure, and achievement is to ask whether moral virtue is also a fundamental category of prudential value. I take up this question in the next section.

5. THE SYMPATHY TEST

How sorry we feel for someone is influenced by how badly from the point of view of his own good we think that person's life has gone, that is, by whether we think his life has lacked important prudential goods. Consider someone whose life has been predominantly painful and contained little knowledge or achievement or appreciation of beauty, though it has involved some deep, long-lasting friendships. We would feel sorry for the person who had this life, because of the prudential goods his life lacked. But our sorrow for the person would not be as great as it would be if his life had not contained friendship. That is, if his life had not contained friendship, we would feel even sorrier for him. Or if two people's lives have contained the same amounts of pleasure, knowledge, and autonomy, but one has contained significantly more achievement than the other, we feel sorrier for the person whose life has contained less achievement.

We could try applying this line of thought to the question of whether we think moral virtue is a fundamental category of prudential value. Consider two people who lead sad and wretched lives. Suppose that one of these two people is morally virtuous, and that the other is not. Let us use the name 'Upright' for the one who is morally virtuous, and the name 'Unscrupulous' for the one who is not. We would *not* feel *sorrier* for Unscrupulous. This suggests that we do not really believe that moral virtue has the same status on the list as pleasure, knowledge, achievement, and friendship. I will refer to this argument as the *argument from lack of sympathy*.[19]

The argument is inadequate as it stands. For one of its premisses is this: If (1) two people are as much alike as possible except that one's life contains something which the other's does not and (2) we do not feel sorrier for the one whose life lacks this thing, then the explanation is that we do not really think this thing is one of the fundamental categories of prudential value. This premiss, however, needs amendment. But I will argue that, with this premiss amended, the argument will have considerable force.

Admittedly, even after the amendments to that premiss are added, the argument holds out no hope of convincing either people who *do* feel sorrier for Unscrupulous or people who confidently believe that moral virtue *is* on the list as a fundamental category of prudential value. Thus the argument from lack of sympathy is addressed only to those of us who (a) do not know what we think about whether moral virtue is a fundamental category of prudential value and (b) do not feel sorry for the immoralist. Obviously, I would not be discussing this argument if I did not think this is a large group. The question, then, for those of us in this group is whether the reason we lack sympathy for Unscrupulous is that we do not believe moral virtue is a fundamental category of prudential value (though we might not initially realize this).

The argument from lack of sympathy presupposes that we can believe something without knowing that we believe it. And it presupposes that this holds true for evaluative beliefs as well as for non-evaluative ones. It further presupposes that these beliefs can sometimes be brought to light by reflection on our sentiments. These presuppositions seem justified. Suppose that I am initially unsure whether a given kind of act is morally wrong. Then I realize that I would not only resent someone's doing that kind of act to me but also feel the resentment justified. One possible explanation of my having these sentiments is that I really think that kind of act is wrong. So, my becoming aware that I would have these sentiments might show me a moral belief I did not know I had.

I shall now consider objections to the argument from lack of sympathy. These objections all have the same structure. The argument from lack of sympathy depends on the idea that the explanation of our not feeling

[19] See A. Sen, 'Plural Utility', *Proceedings of the Aristotelian Society* 81 (1980/1), 193–215, p. 203.

sorrier for Unscrupulous is that we really think moral virtue is not one of the fundamental categories of prudential value. The objections I consider suggest that there is some other explanation, and thus that we might not feel sorrier for the immoral Unscrupulous than for the moral Upright even though we think that Unscrupulous's life does indeed go worse.

For example, the following explanation may be offered of why we do not feel sorrier for Unscrupulous. Feeling sorry for someone essentially involves sharing in or taking on (in some sense) that other person's unpleasant feelings or mental states. Thus, what explains our not feeling sorrier for Unscrupulous than for Upright is that the amount of unpleasantness Upright and Unscrupulous experience is the same.

But the analysis of feeling sorry for someone that is presupposed by this objection is too narrow. It is not true that whenever I feel sorry for someone I am sharing in, or taking on in some sense, that other person's feelings or mental states. Nor is it true that I can feel sorry *only* for those people who are having (or have had or will have) unpleasant mental states. To take a familiar example, suppose that Laura's husband is having affairs in spite of his solemn promise to her that he would not do this and in spite of her extremely strong desire that he not do it. Suppose he is so adept at orchestrating matters that she will never in any way be aware of his affairs. I may feel sorry for her even though I am completely convinced his affairs will not cause her to have less pleasant mental states. Given this case as I have set it out, what would be eliciting my sympathy for her could not be thoughts about unpleasant mental states she will have experienced. It would instead be the thought that she is deceived about a central aspect of her life. Likewise, how sorry we feel for Upright or for Unscrupulous in our test case need not be determined solely by how much unpleasantness they suffer.

Someone might now object that we *do* feel sorry for Unscrupulous on account of Unscrupulous's missing out on the prudential good of being moral, and that the reason we do not feel sorrier for Unscrupulous than for Upright is that our sympathy for Unscrupulous is counterbalanced by our sympathy for Upright. And the reason we feel sorry for Upright is that Upright is not getting more prudential goods than Unscrupulous, which is an injustice to Upright, given that Upright has been moral and Unscrupulous has not.

This objection can also be answered. We just need to add further stipulations about Upright and Unscrupulous. Suppose Upright and

Unscrupulous have lives maximally full of (exactly equal amounts of) pleasure. Upright's life contains some moral pleasure[20] unavailable to any immoral person, such as Unscrupulous; and Unscrupulous's life has some pleasures unavailable to any morally good person, such as Upright. Suppose also that both Unscrupulous and Upright have lives maximally full of (exactly the same amounts of) knowledge of important matters, friendship,[21] autonomy, and the appreciation of beauty. And let us suppose their lives are full of (exactly the same amounts of) overall achievement (Upright's achievement of being morally virtuous is offset by the non-moral achievements of Unscrupulous). They thus have had lives full of exactly the same amount of each of the list's goods—with the disputed exception of having led a morally virtuous life. Now, since Upright has a life filled with all the goods one could hope for, it cannot be the case that she has been harmed or disadvantaged by the injustice to her of Unscrupulous's getting all the same goods without having to be virtuous. Since Upright lacks nothing, how can we feel sorry for her? And if we cannot feel sorry for Upright, then the objection we are considering is a non-starter.

Someone might now object that the reason we do not feel sorrier for Unscrupulous is merely that we do not feel at all sorry for someone whose life has been as rich as Unscrupulous's. After all, we have only so much sympathy to go around. And all of it is naturally directed at people much worse off than Unscrupulous.

This objection can be circumvented. Assume Unscrupulous lives in a wonderfully fortunate world in which every other individual's life is at least as good in self-interested terms as Unscrupulous's. No one in Unscrupulous's world is a better candidate for our sympathy. So, if we *still* don't feel sorry for Unscrupulous, this cannot be because our sympathy is used up on other people.

Another possible objection is that the real reason we do not feel sorry for Unscrupulous is that we do not feel sorry for people who miss out

---

[20] As Aristotle famously said, 'it is the mark of virtue both to be pleased and to be pained at the right objects and in the right way' (*NE* 1121^{a}3–4; see also 1099^{a}7–21). And Sidgwick acknowledged that 'the sacrifice of sensual inclination to duty is disagreeable to the non-moral man when he at first attempts it, but affords to the truly virtuous man a deep and strong delight' (*Methods of Ethics*, 150).

[21] It would be absurd to suggest that an immoral person such as Unscrupulous could not have friends: has no pirate or gangster ever had friends? To be sure, having a friendship with someone involves caring about his or her welfare. So in order to have friendship Unscrupulous must have some concern for the welfare of *some* other people (his friends). But this on its own is far too little to qualify his life as a moral one.

on some prudential good *through their own fault.* If I repeatedly pass up opportunities to obtain knowledge and to develop friendships, then the fact that I live an ignorant and friendless life is no reason to feel sorry for me. Likewise, the fact that Unscrupulous did not lead a moral life is no reason to feel sorry for Unscrupulous, since he missed out on the benefit through his own fault.

There are two good answers to this objection. One is that we can have sympathy for someone even while we recognize that his predicament is his own fault. Fault does not *always* shut off sympathy. Sometimes we recognize that people are to blame for, say, ruining their lives, and yet we simultaneously feel sorry for them because of what they have brought on themselves. For example, we might blame Jack for being so imprudent as to marry (or divorce) Jill, but nevertheless feel sorry for him. Or we might blame the people of a country for being so gullible and short-sighted as to elect their present ruler, but still feel sorry for them. Now, given that in some cases fault and blame do not preclude sympathy, we should demand some explanation of why sympathy is absent in the case of our reactions to Unscrupulous.

The other good answer to the objection that we do not feel sorry for Unscrupulous because he is at fault is as follows. Suppose Unscrupulous grew up with no exposure to the influences that typically form moral dispositions in people (e.g. morally good role-models). Suppose that anyone with Unscrupulous's upbringing would turn out to lack moral dispositions. It is then hard to think that Unscrupulous's turning out as he did is his fault. And if Unscrupulous's turning out to lack moral virtues is not his fault, our not feeling sorry for Unscrupulous cannot be explained by reference to the matter of fault.

It might now be said that we cannot help but feel contempt for Unscrupulous, and that this contempt precludes whatever feelings of sorrow we might have for him. I doubt, however, we always feel contempt for people who are not moral. Moreover, contempt does not always shut off sympathy. There are contemptible characters in literature for whom we manage to feel some sympathy—think of some of the characters in Shakespeare's tragedies (Edmund in *King Lear*, for example, or Richard III). Closer to home, many of us manage to have simultaneous feelings of contempt and sympathy *for ourselves.* So the fact that contempt does not *always* preclude sympathy presents us with this question: Why think that what keeps us from feeling sympathy for Unscrupulous is contempt, rather than the belief that Unscrupulous is not worse off in self-interested terms than Upright?

Someone might now say that the right explanation of our not feeling sorry for Unscrupulous is that we have some other negative feeling toward immoralists, such as indignation.[22] Well, does indignation toward someone *always* preclude sympathy for him? If it does not, then we are owed an explanation of why it *does* so in the case of Unscrupulous. Admittedly, feeling sympathy for people at the same time as one feels indignation towards them may be rare. But it happens sometimes. Some of us felt at least a little sorry for Richard Nixon when he had to leave office (because of the humiliation, etc.) even though we at the same time thought he richly deserved moral censure and felt indignant toward him for what he had done. Thus, since indignation does not *always* preclude sympathy, I see no reason to think that the best explanation of what keeps us from feeling sorrow for Unscrupulous is our indignation toward him.

Where does all this leave us? Unscrupulous and Upright have exactly the same amount of all the values on the list, with the disputed exception of moral virtue. They even have the same level of achievement, because Unscrupulous has some extra non-moral achievements compensating for Upright's moral achievements. If we do not feel sorrier for Unscrupulous than for Upright, one possible explanation of this is that we do not really believe Unscrupulous's life has gone worse in self-interested terms than Upright's. I have discussed a number of other possible explanations. Some of these explanations I have rejected. The rest I have undercut by designing the situation so that none of them will work. We are left, I think, with two possible alternative conclusions.

If we still do not feel sympathy for Unscrupulous even with the situation designed so as to preclude the other possible explanations, we might conclude that the best explanation of our lack of sympathy for Unscrupulous is that we do not think Unscrupulous's life has gone worse in self-interested terms. If we do not think Unscrupulous's life has gone worse in self-interested terms, then we must think that Unscrupulous's lacking the moral virtue that Upright has does not make Upright's life go better in self-interested terms. In other words, we apparently really believe moral virtue does not have a place on the list other than as a subcategory of achievement.

The other possible conclusion is that the argument from lack of sympathy breaks down. I have had to stipulate many conditions, some quite far-fetched, in order to prevent explanations other than the explanation

---

[22] This objection comes from Alan Goldman.

that we do not really believe Unscrupulous's life has been worse in self-interested terms. As these stipulations mount up, so wanes our ability to decide whether we feel sorry for Unscrupulous. It may wane so far that our thinking about whether we would feel sorry for him fails to deliver any result.

Which of these alternative conclusions is most plausible? I tentatively accept the conclusion that the argument from lack of sympathy shows that moral virtue has no place on the list other than as a subcategory of achievement. Admittedly, my favouring this conclusion might be partly motivated by the suspicion that thinking about what we would feel sorry for someone for lacking is our best hope as a method of figuring out what we think are the fundamental categories of prudential value. If this method cannot help, I do not know where to turn.[23]

[23] For helpful comments on earlier drafts of this paper, I am grateful to Charlotte Brown, Robert Ginsberg, Alan Goldman, James Griffin, John Heil, Thomas Hurka, Rosalind Hursthouse, Martha Klein, Penelope Mackie, Al Mele, Mark Nelson, Ingmar Persson, John Robertson, Eldon Soifer, and Gabriele Taylor. I am especially grateful to John Bogart, Roger Crisp, Andrew Moore, Mark Overvold, and Peter Vallentyne, each of whom commented on more than one draft. Work on an earlier version was completed with the help of a Grant-in-Aid from Virginia Commonwealth University. Ancestors of the paper were presented at meetings of the Pacific Division of the American Philosophical Association, the Southern Society for Philosophy and Psychology, and Oxford University's Wolfson Society.

10

Deadly Vices?

GABRIELE TAYLOR

The vices, I take it, are the opposites of the virtues. This does not imply that every vice can neatly be paired off with a virtue. But it does imply that where virtues are thought to be beneficial, vices are harmful; while virtues are thought to contribute to human good and to be needed in human life, vices on the contrary are corruptive of such good and are an obstacle to human flourishing. Given these general descriptions both may then be classified according to who precisely benefits or is harmed by the exercise of a particular virtue or vice, whether or not its exercise requires a certain type of motivation, or what sorts of unfortunate human inclination they respectively counterbalance or encourage. So we may for instance identify a class of 'social virtues' necessary for the smooth running of society; a class of 'other-regarding virtues' the exercise of which is intended to benefit particular persons other than the agent herself, and where each exercise has to be motivated by concern for that other in order to count as an instance of a relevant virtue; and a class of what are sometimes labelled 'self-regarding virtues', which do not require such motivation and which, while they may or may not benefit others, are thought to profit primarily the agent herself.[1] The vices may be grouped similarly: some may be undermining of a harmonious life in society, some may harm individuals other than the person acting viciously, and some may be destructive mainly of that person herself.

An account of the virtues should explain in precisely what way they are needed in human life, and the extent to which we have reason for

[1] Classifications along these lines, though not always so labelled, are suggested by, e.g., G. H. von Wright, *The Varieties of Goodness* (London, 1963), ch. 7; P. Foot, 'Virtues and Vices', in her *Virtues and Vices* (Oxford, 1978), 1–18; J. Wallace, *Virtues and Vices* (Ithaca, NY, 1978), preface.

cultivating this or that particular virtue. Presumably some are needed
more than are others. In certain cases, I think, this is best done negat-
ively, i.e. by investigating the vice(s) which a cultivation of some virtue
is designed to prevent. It seems to be true particularly of some members of the 'self-regarding' class that an account of the nature and
degree of damage engendered by the vice serves to demonstrate the need
for countervailing virtues, the importance of which might otherwise be
underestimated. I shall therefore concentrate on those vices which are
thought to harm primarily the person possessing them, and ask what
exactly that harm might amount to. By being harmful to her they are,
probably inevitably, also harmful to others. But the harm to others is
not necessarily prompted by malicious motives on the part of the agent.
The coward, for example, may harm others in that she will fail to help
them on those occasions when doing so would involve facing danger,
which she cannot bring herself to do however compassionate her thoughts
and intentions may be. A person possessing such vices, therefore, need
not be immoral or wicked in the sense of denying that the well-being of
others need ever be a reason for action, or of thinking that in the cause
of her own advancement any means is justified. Since the harm is prin-
cipally to the agent herself, and since it is unlikely that any sane person
would want to harm herself, it seems that these vices must be unwanted
by those prone to them. So what has here gone wrong?

There is a familiar pattern of faulty practical reasoning into which
some self-regarding vices may quite plausibly be fitted. A person acts in
a cowardly fashion, for instance, if believing herself to have an overriding reason for facing the danger confronting her she nevertheless
does not do so; she is a coward if in such circumstances she mostly or
always does not act as she herself believes she should; she acts against
her own better judgement. Alternatively, she may be less clear-sighted
about what she ought to do for either prudential or moral reasons: she
may misread the situation and inaccurately weight the reasons she has
for or against facing the danger precisely because her timidity prevents
her from being clear about what it is more or less worth while for her
to do. Her judgement is clouded, her reasoning based on faulty premisses. The disadvantages of either form of cowardice are obvious: she
will not achieve what she herself wants to achieve; her life will by her
own standards not be as good as it might have been. She will fail herself
and others on all those occasions where she should act in spite of what
she perceives as some risk. In extreme cases, seeing danger everywhere
and not facing it, her life will be in a mess. This will have repercussions:

she will be a nuisance to others, which will worsen her position, contribute to her misery, and so on. There are therefore good practical reasons for cultivating the virtue of courage.

If the coward nevertheless does not act on, or does not see, these reasons, then maybe the answer to the paradox of persisting in a course of conduct which is harmful to oneself is that in being weak or muddled she is a helpless victim of her feelings rather than an agent in control of her life. To accept, or dispute, this type of answer is to raise a problem I shall not deal with here, viz. that of responsibility. The vices, as well as being harmful, are thought to share with the virtues the characteristic of being subject to the will. This must be so, for we blame people for their vices and thereby imply that the exercise of control is possible, so that they can fairly be held responsible, at least to a degree, for their possessing them. Perhaps the notion of control has been given too much prominence. To make this aspect the focus of attention tends to result in undue emphasis being placed on matters of the will, on intention, choice, decision, and consequent action. But to isolate merely these features is to ignore the complexity of the phenomenon and leave quite unexplained the nature of the kinds of harm inflicted by characteristics we pick out as vices.[2]

The two cases of cowardice as I have described them may give the impression that, if not in practice then at any rate theoretically, they can be clearly separated from one another, the flaw of one type of coward being in the will, that of the other in their faculty of judgement. But notoriously, the phenomenon of weakness of will needs explaining: the person concerned is in the paradoxical position of both accepting that she has an overriding reason for acting in a certain way and yet, since she does not act accordingly, also rejecting it as overriding. Her acceptance seems intellectual merely, without emotional backing; there is a lack of whole-heartedness in her assessments of and attitudes towards her circumstances. If so, then there is here a connection with the second case envisaged, for the clouded judgement, too, was linked with emotional attitudes.

In some cases, at least, a more detailed scrutiny of these interrelated

---

[2] Relevant discussions of responsibility may be found in R. M. Adams, 'Involuntary Sins', *Philosophical Review* 94 (1985), 3–31; and H. Frankfurt, 'Identification and Whole-heartedness'; J. Fischer, 'Responsiveness and Moral Responsibility'; and J. Sabini and M. Silver, 'Emotions, Responsibility and Character', all in F. Schoeman (ed.), *Responsibility, Character, and the Emotions* (Cambridge, 1987), 27–45, 81–106, and 165–75, respectively.

features is of interest in itself, as well as yielding a clearer picture of the nature of the harm entailed by some specific vice. This, I think, is so in the case of the so-called 'deadly sins', given that label because they are said to bring death to the soul, and thus to constitute the most fundamental ways in which human beings may go wrong: pride, envy, covetousness, gluttony, sloth, lust, and anger are to be seen as different forms of corruption of the self and so totally destructive of a flourishing life. To think of these (or any other) vices as so fundamentally damaging must mean that the kind of harm elicited from the model used for cowardice is relatively superficial. That harm was, after all, contingent on the circumstances of the person's life. It is at least conceivable that she may encounter only a few and unimportant occasions where danger should be faced, that she has 'moral luck' either in this respect or in that the consequences of her timidity are not as harsh as has been envisaged; maybe her charm is such that there are always friends ready to help. For anything to count as a *deadly* vice such contingencies are presumably beside the point. In order at least to indicate the complexity of this type of vice I shall concentrate on only one of the traditional deadly sins. Though occupying perhaps a unique place among them,[3] it is nevertheless representative of the group in showing the undermining flaws to be in a person's inner emotional life and attitudes rather than in her intention and action.

II

Looking at the history of the concept of acedia or sloth, it is clear that it has been used to refer to many different though presumably related phenomena. In the course of the Middle Ages, the understanding of acedia as a sin shifted from viewing it as a kind of depression and boredom with a specifically monastic form of life to seeing it as a moral perversion of human nature in general, which might be manifested by anybody. Naturally enough, cutting across this development, the features of acedia emphasized by the scholastics differed from those expounded in the more popular literature, designed to be practical and concrete. The latter tended to look at the vice from an 'external' point of view, as it shows itself in behaviour. The slothful neglect their religious duties,

---

[3] Dante e.g. presents sloth as the only deadly sin which is a defect in love rather than excessive or misdirected love (*The Divine Comedy*, II. xviii).

they do not say their prayers, they sleep through the sermon. They are lazy and idle. The 'internal', scholarly viewpoint, by contrast, concerns itself with the state of the person's soul or mind: it is, after all, possible that she may be outwardly punctilious in performing her duties but do so in the wrong spirit, full of doubt or without joy, for example. 'Sloth' therefore spans a wide range of both behavioural and mental phenomena, of which among the most commonly mentioned are laziness, idleness, complacency, cowardice, lack of imagination, irresponsibility, boredom, uneasiness of mind, restlessness of body, verbosity, idle curiosity, melancholy, and despair.[4] Only some of these characteristics are likely to be associated with slothfulness today, where (if we think in these terms at all) we think of the slothful as being generally inactive, lazy, and indolent. If sloth is a vice, then it seems a wholly negative and relatively harmless one: the slothful may not do much good, but they do not do much harm, either. Our view of it tends to pick out the behavioural features of the sin rather than internal states like boredom or despair, which makes it hard to see why it should have been regarded as a deadly sin at all.[5]

Behaviour by itself is not a good indicator of the vice, for what is seen as laziness or idleness may not at all connect with a slothful state of mind, and conversely, the relevant state of mind may not express itself in that type of behaviour. To be slothful is to be in an inactive and indolent state, but again, not all such states need be destructive in the sense required for there to be a vice. It is a specific form of indolence which has to be identified.

A person may be in an indolent mood: she does not feel like doing anything at all. The mood itself may be felt as pleasant or unpleasant. At one extreme of the range of possible responses she may feel pleasantly lazy and relaxed, at the other feel unpleasantly inert, unable to move herself. Either way, short-lived and infrequent moods of this kind are unlikely to do much harm; feeling pleasantly lazy and free from demands may on the contrary be a healthy state which it is good every now and

---

[4] For the history of the concept, see S. Wenzel, *The Sin of Sloth: Acedia in Medieval Thought and Literature* (Chapel Hill, NC, 1967). The individual items on the list given are sometimes regarded as aspects of sloth, sometimes as 'daughters', i.e. as vices which are dependent on sloth, of which sloth is the origin.

[5] An essay on sloth by Evelyn Waugh starts with these remarks: 'The word "Sloth" is seldom on modern lips. When used, it is a mildly facetious variant of "indolence", and indolence, surely, so far from being a deadly sin, is one of the most amiable of weaknesses. Most of the world's troubles seem to come from people who are too busy.' ('Sloth', in R. Mortimer (ed.), *The Seven Deadly Sins* (London, 1962), 57–64.)

then to experience. The person who possesses the vice is not merely occasionally in the relevant mood of indolence; she has the character-trait slothfulness. To ascribe a character-trait is to label and so try to impose some order on a whole complex of behaviour and states of mind. We take ourselves to be isolating certain dominant tendencies to behave and dispositions to have certain thoughts and feelings which will help us to explain particular actions and reactions and to predict how she will behave and feel on other occasions. Such 'explanations' may be quite minimal and tell us no more than that such behaviour and thoughts are only to be expected. But explanations in terms of character-traits may also be more substantial, in that they may shed light on conduct or feelings which are not usually thought typical of the character-trait in question. Those who are slothful may tend to be in the relevant mood for prolonged periods and behave in a manner expressive of this mood. But while I shall treat this position as the paradigm case of the vice, it is not the only way in which sloth may manifest itself.

Being in the mood of not wanting to do anything that needs effort may or may not be accompanied by the thought that none the less the situation is such that some effort is required. In each case further distinctions may be drawn. In the first case, the person who believes that no effort is required of her may do so on the grounds that, as it happens, there are at present no demands on her, that at the moment at least there are no duties to fulfil or prudential steps to be taken. It is this view of the situation which is most likely that of the person feeling pleasantly lazy. Alternatively, she may view the situation not as providing a temporary respite from such demands, but as being typical of many in her life in simply not offering anything worth making an effort for.

In the second case, those who believe that they should make some effort and resist their present state of indolence may see the demand to exert themselves as either externally or internally imposed. The protagonist of Goncharov's novel *Oblomov* will serve as an example to illustrate the difference. When we first meet Oblomov, in a state of complete physical and mental indolence, he is inclined to take the first, external, view of the situation. He can see that there is some urgency for him to bestir himself if various catastrophes are to be averted: unfortunately, the world is so arranged that he cannot do what he wants to do without having to expend some effort. But any kind of effort, in his view, interferes with enjoyment and should be avoided at all cost. The best he can do, therefore, is to forget about the demands of everyday life and return to his bed and enjoyable day-dreams. But although in this way he manages for much of the time to escape from thoughts of the unpleasantness of everyday demands on him and to enjoy his idleness, his state is clearly a precarious one. It seems that effort is required to ensure a more or less effortless enjoyment of life, and this effort he will not make because it will interfere with his enjoyment of an effortless life. There is something irrational in this state of affairs, an indication, perhaps, that here we have one form of sloth the vice. On the other hand, the irrationality of his situation is a contingent one, depending on the particular circumstances of his life. If the manager of his estate were an honest man, if his landlord were more considerate and his servant not so lazy, he might be able simply to enjoy his idleness. It is at least not clear that in such circumstances his indolence would amount to sloth.

Sometimes, however, Oblomov's mood changes: occasionally he sees that there are worthwhile things to achieve in life, which he will not achieve because he will not make the effort, because he cannot get himself sufficiently engaged with what he thinks worth while to push him into activity. When in these moods, the demand for effort is of the second, 'internal', type and is not contingent on the specific unfortunate states of affairs which happen to obtain. The external demands were just a nuisance, but what he now sees as requiring effort is the achieving of something which is worth while in itself. When in this mood, he sees himself, rather than his specific circumstances, as being the obstacle to his ever leading an admirable sort of life.

A person who tends to remain in a state of indolence in spite of recognizing that there are urgent external demands will no doubt possess a number of failings: she will be typically self-indulgent and weak-willed and probably cowardly in failing to face up to the realities of life. All these are serious defects, but not, perhaps, deadly sins. Given such demands she will be unable to enjoy the kind of idle existence she plans for herself. At a later period in his life, however, Oblomov appears to have achieved just that. His circumstances have altered: an energetic friend keeps an eye on his estates for him and secures a steady income; a devoted woman is prepared to look after him without asking anything in return. There are no more demands on him; he remains totally inactive and, it seems, is content. There is, on the face of it, nothing destructive about this state, so it may be that, though hardly admirable, this form of indolence does not add up to the vice. I shall return to this point.

Where, however, the demands are internal ones, the person herself believes that there is a worthwhile life for her to lead if only she could make the requisite effort. Since she does not do so she is a failure in her own eyes and cannot be content. She does not or cannot move herself sufficiently to make her life worth living. But a self seen as failing to be engaged in worthwhile activities presents itself as a worthless self. Hence a person in that state will take a gloomy view of herself, which will tend to be self-perpetuating: a worthless self is not worth taking trouble over, so there is no point in making any kind of effort on its behalf by finding worthwhile things for it to do. So she may as well give up the thought of leading a worthwhile life; there is no reason for her to bestir herself.

In all essentials this state of mind is also that of the person who acknowledged no internal demands at all, who could see nothing in the situation worth making any effort for. This is so because forms of evaluative awareness of the world cannot be separated from conceptions of one's own position in the world so assessed, and vice versa. Seeing nothing in the world worth engaging with, she also sees no reason to engage herself with such a world. So she, too, is confronted by a self not meaningfully employed. The difference in the two states described is merely one of emphasis: in the first case the person concerned will be more likely to blame herself for this dismal state of affairs; in the second she may tend to see the fault in what she finds is on offer. Their common feature is that both are in a state of boredom.

We may be bored by this or that, on some specific occasion. Boredom, in this case, has an 'object': the lecture, her chatter, the interminable play. If I am bored by the lecture then I see nothing in it to engage my attention and interest, maybe because it offers nothing new, maybe because it is above my head. But here I am; I have to do something with the time I was supposed to fill by listening. I may be able to divert myself by thinking about something else and so keep myself occupied. If so, then, although bored by the lecture, I am not bored. But I may not succeed in diverting myself. In that case the 'object' of my boredom, the lecture, figures in my thoughts as an irritant, as an obstacle to not being bored; it is that which prevents me from doing something with this time which, as things are, hangs heavy on my hands. So I feel caught: that which is supposed to occupy my time does not in fact do so but merely prevents me from making a better use of it. I naturally want to escape from this situation.

The state of boredom is a negative one which we experience as unpleasant and so want to avoid if possible. In all cases time is the enemy. It is there to be done something with, but no content offers itself, and

without content it passes extremely slowly, making it even more difficult to find something to fill it with. Of course, on those occasions
where there is an 'object' perceived by me to be causally responsible
for my inability to deal with time, it is relatively straightforward to
remedy my state by removing myself physically from the obstacle or
by developing techniques for preventing the object of boredom from
inducing a state of boredom.[6] Boredom threatens to be a serious evil
only when neither type of escape is possible, and this is paradigmatically
the case when boredom is 'objectless', when it is a mood rather than
an emotion.

Moods are objectless in the sense that there is no specific thing,
situation, or event which can be picked out and described independently
of the mood itself and which the state is 'about'. This is not to say that
the mood in question may not have been caused by some specific event,
but even where it is so caused, and even where the person is aware of
her mood's causal antecedents, it is not *felt* as motivated by particular situations. While she may be aware of causal links, she does not
experience them as such, and consequently her state is not 'about' what
she may recognize as its cause. When in a mood-state, therefore, it is
not a specific situation she will see in a certain light, as, e.g. threatening
or insulting; her mood will colour everything in her perception. It is
a constitutive feature of moods that they involve a way of seeing the
world. They are distinguished from each other by the particular way in
which the world is seen: in moods of elation everything is perceived
as attractive and attainable, in moods of depression everything appears
gloomy or irritating, the worthwhile out of one's reach. The difference
between emotions and moods is reflected also, of course, in the person's
actions and reactions. When in a mood-state, her tendency to behave in
certain ways will not have a specific focus but will manifest itself more
generally in an increased or decreased interest in the world around her,
a greater readiness to be provoked, discouraged, or encouraged.[7]

A person who is bored by some specific situation finds nothing of
interest in that situation, sees nothing in it she can engage with. If she
is in the mood-state of boredom then she can see nothing at all in the
world to interest her, nothing that is worth engaging with. But if there

[6] Some people say that they do not mind being bored. I think they must mean that they
have a technique for dealing with what bores them; it is inconceivable that they should
not mind being in a state of boredom.

[7] Recent discussions of moods can be found in N. Frijda, *The Emotions* (Cambridge,
1986); and C. Armon-Jones, *Varieties of Affect* (London, 1991).

is nothing to engage and interest her then life will seem quite mean-
ingless. '[T]he only thing I see is emptiness, the only thing I move
about in is emptiness. I do not even suffer pain,' says Kierkegaard's
aestheticist.[8] Nothing is seen as either pleasurable or painful, so that
nothing is seen as differentiated from anything else. In a world so seen
no particular course of action will seem more attractive than another;
there is nothing to engage one's desires and move one to act. Hence the
bored will also tend to be indolent; not seeing any point in doing anything, they are inclined to do nothing and experience themselves as
inert, as being heavy on their own hands.[9]

It is this experience which is typical of that form of indolence which
is sloth. To be in a slothful mood is to be in a state of which the interrelated components are feelings of physical and mental inertness and
a cognitive appraisal of the world as not worth engaging with. And
so, maybe, a slothful person is one who is inclined to be in that state.
But this move is too simple; to pinpoint the vice, more needs to be said
about the nature and dimensions of this form of indolence. Aquinas, in
reply to the objection that sloth cannot be a mortal sin since even the
virtuous may suffer from it, makes the point that there may be an
inclination towards such a state even in holy men, but they are not
therefore sinful because they withhold rational consent.[10] I want to
incorporate this point by offering one possible interpretation of what it
is to consent to one's state.

In order to do so, further distinctions between mental states need
to be drawn: I have spoken of moods of boredom and indolence. But
moods may be thought of either as occurrent or as standing. For a
person to be in some occurrent mood is for her to see the world in the
relevant way and to have the experience of so seeing it, to have the
appropriate feeling. To have the experience of seeing nothing worth
making an effort for, for example, is to feel inert. I shall speak of a
person who is in an occurrent indolent mood as being in a state of
indolence.

It is occurrent moods which have the two elements spoken of earlier:
a form of awareness and an experienced consciousness on the agent's
part of this awareness. A 'standing mood' refers to the former only.

    [8] S. Kierkegaard, 'Diapsalmata', in *Either/Or*, vol. I (Princeton, NJ, 1971), 17–42, p. 36.
    [9] John Casey gives a description of the feelings pertaining to sloth in ch.3 of *Pagan
Virtue* (Oxford, 1990).
    [10] *Summa Theologiae* 2a2ae, question 35, article 3 ('Sin's consummation is in reason's
consent'), Blackfriars edn., 60 vols. (Oxford, 1972), vol. xxxv, p. 29.

Occurrent moods are changeable and may be quite short-lived. The standing mood, the relevant form of awareness, may live and die with the person's experience of it. But it may also outlast it; it is compatible with a whole range of other occurrent moods. I shall refer to a person's standing mood as her frame of mind. A frame of mind which is long-lasting may be called an attitude, and if that attitude is dominant in a person's life in that it governs a high proportion of her moods and behaviour, then it will be a character-trait.

Reference to a standing mood will be explanatory. It will be explanatory in the minimal sense if what is 'explained' is the corresponding occurrent mood; but it will offer a more substantial explanation when the occurrent mood is a different one. Not thinking anything worth making an effort for minimally explains her present inertness, but more substantially explains, for example, her present hopelessness or despair. The claim here is that her frame of mind is causally responsible for her present state of mind; a causal connection not hard to explain since the given view of the world and herself is naturally undermining of all hope and joy. In this sense despair and hopelessness are indeed 'daughters' of acedia.

The distinction between occurrent and standing moods was introduced to explain how 'consenting to one's state' might be understood: it is to let the state of mind turn into a frame of mind which comes to dominate one's life. It is to be uncritical of that form of awareness and hence not to try to modify it in any way but to let it become established. The slothful, then, are not those who are merely inclined to be in the occurrent mood of indolence, but are those who do not oppose such inclination even in thought, who by not attempting to alter their vision of the world encourage those occurrent states which are causally dependent on that frame of mind.

The most important aspect of this form of consent is to allow oneself to take the relevant particular view of oneself: that the self is a worthless one. There is no point in engaging such a self. The form of awareness is that of boredom. As earlier it was the lecture or play that was seen by the person as the obstacle to her doing something with the time there was, it is now herself in the state of inertness that is the obstacle. Evidently, she cannot remove herself from herself as she could remove herself from the lecture, nor can she comfort herself with the thought that the spell of boredom will end when the lecture is over. It is the self so perceived which is the 'object' of sloth and is the source of its destructiveness. The slothful person will not be able to respect or like herself and thereby precludes even the possibility of her leading a flourishing life.

III

Constitutive of the vice, on this account, is a certain view of the world and of the self, and hence a shift in vision the only remedy. In the paradigm case the slothful person's frame of mind will be operative in states of indolence and tend to manifest itself also in states of hopelessness and despair. But there are other, less obviously destructive cases of sloth. At one period in his life Oblomov appears to be no longer in the grip of indolence. He is attracted to Olga, and under her influence seems to be leading a more or less normally active life. Nevertheless, although no longer idle, there has, I think, been no fundamental change; basically he is as indolent as he has ever been. Yet activity, on the face of it, is incompatible with indolence, and is often prescribed as its cure. Kant, as is only to be expected, speaks of activity as part of life's sustenance. 'It is by his activities and not by enjoyment that man feels that he is alive,' he says.[11] Kierkegaard's aestheticist, however, expresses the opposite view: he thinks of activity as being a kind of restlessness which is incompatible with the spiritual life. Seen in this way, idleness is a good rather than an evil. Hence merely being active or non-idle is not a desirable state. It is, according to him, enjoyment rather than activity with which we should fill our lives.[12]

Both sides have a point, and their respective points are acceptable once their different understandings of 'activity' are disentangled. Kant thinks of being active as implying a whole-hearted and rationally justified commitment on the part of the agent. The aestheticist, by contrast, has in mind a 'being busy', a form of being active which lacks the implication of fully engaging the agent and being worth the effort expended on it. It is activity and not busyness which is incompatible with indolence. This is not to deny that busyness may well be a way of not consenting to one's state, if embarked on in the hope that it will turn into activity. But I shall ignore this possibility and assume no such motivation.

The person who is merely busy may or may not believe at the time that what she is doing is worth while. In the latter case she knows

---

[11] 'Occupation', in Kant's *Lectures on Ethics*, tr. L. Infield (London, 1930), 160–2, p. 160.   [12] 'The Rotation Method', *Either/Or*, vol. 1, 279–96, p. 285.

herself to be unengaged and is only superficially different from the slothful person so far described. But even temporary engagement is no indication of activity rather than busyness. Kant remarks that 'The present may, indeed, seem full to us, but if we have filled it with play, etc., the appearance of fullness will be confined to the present. Memory will find it empty.'[13] The valid point here is not whether we have filled the time with play or work but whether looking back we think of it as a superficial filling only, and so a waste of time. Looking back we find that what we took to be a worthwhile engagement was nothing of the sort.

The person's own view, either at the time or in retrospect, is then one indication of her being busy rather than active. But the superficiality of the engagement may also show itself in a lock of being goal-directed: since her commitment to whatever she is doing is a merely shallow one it will not generate reasons for embarking on a coherent, life-guiding plan of action. Oblomov is stimulated or bullied by Olga into periods of non-idleness, but his engagements remain isolated occurrences with no aim or cohesion. A person who is busy, therefore, while not outwardly idle, is nevertheless indolent. Her frame of mind has not changed, though she may be more successful in avoiding the corresponding state of mind. In such a case her life is quite likely to exhibit that form of restlessness which in medieval literature was cited as a consequence of sloth.

The possibility of busyness has introduced a variation and complication into the paradigmatic case of slothfulness initially discussed. The indolent person is not now totally unengaged, but her engagement is a shallow one. If aware of its superficiality she will still tend to find time heavy on her hands, and experience herself as inert and bored; consequently she, too, is prey to depression and despair. On the other hand, being engaged at all, if only temporarily and superficially, may offer a distraction, a way of avoiding such low states of mind, and in particular may enable her to avoid taking such a grim view of herself. The obvious disadvantages of living with a wholly negative view of oneself make it tempting and natural to try to persuade oneself that one is active and not merely busy. But if, as claimed earlier, the requisite view of the self is an essential ingredient of the vice, then busyness would after all seem to offer an escape, provided she manages to hide her lack of proper engagement from herself. For such self-deception to succeed she would have to make it appear to herself and others that her engagements are not merely shallow, that they do generate life-guiding commitments. If

[13] Kant, 'Occupation', p. 160.

it is possible so to deceive oneself then it would be impossible to tell that she is merely busy. But given that her frame of mind is that of the slothful, the coherence in her life will be sham; she will not really care.

But why should this matter? If no one, including the person herself, can tell whether her life is sham and her engagement shallow, then it seems that it will make no difference at all to her, and the remedy to suggest to those who are disposed towards sloth is to try to practice self-deception until they are perfect at it. It would certainly prevent them from suffering hopelessness and despair, which are consequent only on facing the situation. But it seems paradoxical to suggest that possession of a vice can be avoided by such means. On the contrary, deceiving oneself should surely make matters even worse?

It is, however, not possible for a person in the given frame of mind to deceive herself to the extent envisaged. In her view there is nothing worth taking trouble over, and this includes herself. It is true that this frame of mind need not manifest itself in certain specific states of mind, such as hopelessness and despair. But it will have some causal efficacy: some states or attitudes are incompatible with it. It is a frame of mind which precludes doing anything with joy, and in particular, it makes it impossible to respect or love oneself. Consequently, the self-deceived person will not be able to avoid taking a negative view of herself. It is indeed part of her self-deception that she will not articulate this view, that she will not spell it out to herself, but it will nevertheless be operative in everything she does. It is in this sense that self-deception cannot be complete. While self-deception may save the person concerned some actual suffering, it does not enable her to lead a flourishing life; and rather than being a means of escape from the vice it constitutes a form of consenting to it.

IV

Traditionally the seven deadly sins are thought of as exhibiting misguided or deficient love. It is a consequence of the characteristics of the vice outlined above that the slothful, not being engaged with anything, do not love anything, and this includes themselves. Self-love does not normally appear on any list specifying virtues, for it is thought that we can be trusted to love ourselves anyway, the danger being that we love ourselves too much rather than too little. But the nature of the harm suffered by the slothful seems to imply that such a virtue is required, though of course not any kind of love will do. Self-concern is presumably that kind of love which we are so prone to that it is more likely to be an obstacle to virtuous behaviour than itself a virtue. Equally, the self-indulgence of an Oblomov is the wrong type of love, if love at all. Self-indulgence is not only compatible with self-contempt, it may even be its ground; it is constitutive of one manifestation of sloth. This suggests that it is perhaps self-respect rather than self-love that is required. The slothful's lack of self-respect is indeed fundamentally damaging, and the possession of it, therefore, secures freedom from the vice. A Kantian notion of respect, however, with its requirement that it be based on admirable characteristics and hence universalizable, implies a degree of detachment and rationality which seems inappropriate in the virtue set in opposition to a vice anchored in the person's affective state. The characteristics of the opposing virtue should be such that they counter the emotional as well as the cognitive aspects of the vice, the feelings of inertia as well as the specific mode of awareness. The person possessing the virtue will, therefore, not only differentiate between the more or less worthwhile and hence think of some things as being more worth achieving than others, she will in particular experience herself as being engaged with the worthwhile, with what she thinks worth caring for. Sloth and its countervailing virtue may then be seen as manifesting themselves in opposing forms of self-consciousness.

One implication of the form of consciousness constitutive of the virtue is that it will generate self-respect, not in the sense of a favourable self-assessment, but in that a self discriminating between the more or less worthwhile will at the same time be self-discriminating, i.e. be aware of what is more and what is less worth her making an effort for. If engaged accordingly she will necessarily respect herself: to respect oneself is to be conscious of being valuably employed. It does not require a self-consciousness in the sense of being aware of oneself as being so employed; her consciousness is directed rather at what she cares for, not at herself as caring for these things. But in being self-discriminating she cannot be indifferent as to whether or not she is engaged with what strikes her as worth while, and so she cares about her caring.[14] Since in this sense she may be said to care for herself,

[14] This is a point made by Harry Frankfurt in 'The Importance of What We Care About', in the collection of that title (Cambridge, 1988), 80–94, and further discussed by Annette Baier in 'Caring about Caring: a Reply to Frankfurt', in her *Postures of the Mind* (London, 1985), 93–108.

there is here one reason why 'self-love' is not an inappropriate label for this virtue.

Possession of the virtue, corresponding to possession of the vice, has two interrelated aspects: a certain perspective on the world and a feeling response. The fact that she believes what she is doing worth while provides her with reason for further pursuing it and for embarking on related projects. Particularly relevant in the present context is her being (obliquely) aware of herself being so engaged. She will, as a consequence, be feeling alive. At the very least she will not be in the grip of feelings of apathy and inertia, for she will be doing something with herself rather than be an obstacle in her way. Awareness of doing something with oneself is itself a source of pleasure and a stimulation for further activity, thus providing further reason for remaining involved, and a sense of being in control. In contrast to the slothful she not only is able to live with herself, she is in a position to enjoy living with herself. For this reason, too, the virtue opposing the vice of sloth may be spoken of as self-love.

Considerations of this kind indicate that self-deception cannot be a way of escaping from the vice. For the inertness and lack of all pleasure in anything one does and hence in oneself, which is consequent on the given frame of mind, will remain and affect one's being, however much one may try to shut one's mind to it. The self-deceived suffer from that malady of spirit of which one indication is the lack of harmony between motivation and evaluation: they do not care for what moves them to act,[15] and consent to their state by disguising this split from themselves. Nor is contentment with one's state an indication that all is well with one's life. If it is true that a degree of self-love, in the sense given, is a necessary antidote to sloth, then an Oblomov undisturbed by external demands has not escaped from the vice, even if he is content with his state. He, too, has consented to his indolence by his having reconciled himself to the withering away of whatever internal demands he once experienced.

[15] See M. Stocker, 'The Schizophrenia of Modern Ethical Theories', *Journal of Philosophy* 73 (1976), 453–66. As he points out, harmony between one's motives, reasons, values, and justifications, while a mark of the good life, does not by itself imply moral worth.

How Emotions Reveal Value and Help Cure the Schizophrenia of Modern Ethical Theories

MICHAEL STOCKER

Many modern ethical theories are schizophrenic—allowing, even requiring, a split between value and motivation. They see no need for values to serve as motivations, and they hold that motivations are irrelevant to the value of what is done or even intended.[1] To explain and justify these splits, it is held that value and motivation are distinct and that it can be 'for the best' if values are not sought directly, perhaps are not even recognized as values. It is concluded that ethical theories can well be esoteric, self-effacing, or schizophrenic (to use, respectively, Sidgwick's, Parfit's, and my terms).

I suppose this could be for the best, much as it could be for the best if people never existed or ceased existing soon: i.e. the universe might contain most value that way. But neither is best for us. Neither tells us how best to live, nor even how to live well. Whether or not those theories are right about total value in the universe, they are not right about us, nor are they right for us. They are not good ethical theories.

Those theories misunderstand, and often do not allow for, large and important parts of human life, including such important goods as love and friendship. For here, motivation and value must come together if the goods are to be actualized: if I do not act for your sake, then no matter whether what I do is for the best, I am not acting out of friendship. And whether or not friendship is for the best, human life without

---

[1] I have discussed these issues in 'The Schizophrenia of Modern Ethical Theories', *Journal of Philosophy* 73 (1976), 453–66; 'Values and Purposes: The Limits of Teleology and the Ends of Friendship', *Journal of Philosophy* 78 (1981), 747–65; and 'Act and Agent Evaluations', *Review of Metaphysics* 27 (1973), 42–61.

friendship is hardly human life. So too, those theories fail to see the extent to which we guide and understand ourselves in terms of our values, and how what we value makes us the sorts of persons we are and societies the sorts of societies they are. Those theories thus fail to see how our values enter directly into so much of our life, and so much of moral importance for us.

These criticisms and more positive views are central to Aristotelian and virtue ethics. I will expand on them by exploring some relations between emotions and value. As will become clear, emotions do not allow for that ethical schizophrenia. To the extent, then, that emotions are central to ethics, ethics, too, should not be schizophrenic.

How important, then, are emotions for ethics? During the last hundred years or so, they have generally been deemed not all that important. But earlier in our tradition, the dominant view was that emotions have central evaluative importance. For example, Aristotle thought that to be a good person, one must have the right emotions. This goes well beyond holding that emotions help make a life good, perhaps in the way that utilitarianism and Kantianism can allow emotions to be important because of the pleasure or pain they involve. Aristotle also held that having the right emotions is necessary for being a good person, indeed for knowing what to do and how to live.

Many nowadays find this claim, especially its last part—that evaluative knowledge requires emotions—difficult to accept, or even to see how it could be right. They think emotions either destructive of, or at least irrelevant for, ethics and especially evaluative knowledge. I will argue for the earlier view. Although I will be supporting an Aristotelian position, I am not all that concerned whether my position is his. And I do hope that what I say will be acceptable to, and useful for, ethicists of many different persuasions.

I will argue for two interrelated claims, one about constitutive relations between emotions and values, the other about epistemological relations between them. Constitutively, I start by showing how emotions might seem external to values, only pointing to them. I conclude by showing how emotions are internal to value, in fact so internal that they are inseparable from it or are even forms of it. Epistemologically, I start by showing how emotions provide evidence for value. I conclude by showing how emotions are expressions of, and may even be, evaluative knowledge. Emotions, thus, show why we cannot accept schizophrenic, esoteric, self-effacing ethical theories.

1. SOME EPISTEMOLOGICAL CONNECTIONS
BETWEEN EMOTIONS AND VALUE

It is once again coming to be widely seen that emotions—or at least many of them—contain, have as components, values or evaluative judgements. These contained values or judgements can be revealed by investigating the emotions. Aristotle's account of anger in his *Rhetoric* shows these interrelated points clearly. He writes, 'Anger [*orgē*] may be defined as a desire accompanied by pain, for a conspicuous revenge for a conspicuous slight at the hands of men who have no call to slight oneself or one's friends.'[2] Further, according to Aristotle, to be slighted is to be denied due importance and proper respect. So, angry people must take it that, without proper justification, they have been dealt the moral or moral-like harm of being denied proper respect.

Thus—assuming that my anger is sufficiently like that described by Aristotle—my anger at your being slighted can show that I still care about you as a friend. Similarly, my boredom at a concert may show that I do not value the music or the performance.

Emotions thus provide us with information about value. They also have other systematic epistemological connections with value. I will briefly sketch how having emotions is important for making good evaluations.

This last sort of connection is, of course, central to many psychoanalytic theories.[3] As Guntrip says, 'As a result of ... [their] lack of feeling, schizoid people can be cynical, callous, and cruel, having no sensitive appreciation of the way they hurt other people.'[4]

We can also see such connections in our normal, everyday world. Suppose I think that a visitor might be coming and that her visit would be good for my family. Typically, this can be enough to get me to hope that she comes. But it might not be enough. Here are some reasons why: I might be physically or emotionally tired, perhaps worn out; I think it would be good for the family if she came, but would be 'too much' for me; I am suffering from depression; I am bitter at the world; I have little heart for company now; I do not like her.

I think we can accept that these emotion-defeating conditions are also all likely to interfere with my making sound evaluative judgments,

---

[2] Aristotle, *Rhetoric*, tr. W. R. Roberts (Princeton, NJ, 1984), 1378^{a}30–2.
[3] See, e.g. D. Shapiro, *Neurotic Styles* (New York, 1965), and H. Guntrip, *Schizoid Phenomena, Object Relations and the Self* (London, 1968).   [4] Guntrip, ibid. 44.

e.g. about her coming. For example, my weariness can easily interfere with my seeing how good it would be if she came. So too, my self-absorption can prevent me from hoping that she will come if this will be good for my son but not me; and it can also prevent me from appreciating how good it will be even for him. Similarly, my emotional distance from my son can explain at once why I do not hope, for his sake, that the visitor will come and also why I do not see how good it would be for him if she did.

Now, my claim is not that if one has defective or distorted emotions, or if one is emotionally distant, or, at an extreme, if one is affectless, one must make errors about value. Often at least, we can correct for those conditions. For example, knowing that I am played out, I pay special attention to sources of value that, in my state, I would otherwise be inclined to overlook. Or knowing that I do not much care about you, cannot warm to you, I take special pains to make sure I give your interests due weight.

But it is easy to overestimate how well, how easily, and how long we can correct for those conditions which at once impair our emotions and also our epistemological, judging relations with value. Our will, our attention, our vigilance are sooner or later all too likely to fail.

It might seem that what I have really argued for is that the epistemological relations emotions have with value and evaluation are only external or indirect. For it might seem that what helps or hinders the epistemological work is not emotions, but rather the various conditions which figure in having or not having emotions. Along these lines it could be held that if a self-absorbed person fails to see others' interests, or if having seen them fails to be moved by them, the real explanation would lie not in the emotions of self-absorption, but in the patterns of thought, attention, and desire that underlie self-absorption. Similarly—to turn now to a favourite example of a bad and disruptive emotion—it will be held that it is not anger that misleads, disrupts, and is destructive of proper thought and action, but its patterns of thought, attention, and desire, e.g. the short-sightedness that anger can involve, the restriction of attention to wrongs one has suffered, and the desire for revenge.

So, the conclusion would not be that correct evaluative understanding comes from correct emotions, and incorrect evaluative understanding from incorrect emotions. Rather, it would be that typically and for systematic reasons, correct evaluative understanding and correct emotions come together, as do incorrect evaluative understanding and incorrect emotions.

There may well be something to this. But I am unsure. First, consider what occasioned it: the fact that someone who has self-absorbed emotions can take corrective epistemological action. But this line of thought seems to show too much. After all, someone who has self-absorbed patterns of thought, attention, and desire can also take corrective epistemological action. Should we—and those suggesting that those patterns, rather than the emotions, are epistemologically relevant—conclude from this that those patterns, too, are epistemologically irrelevant?

Second, it seems to me that in making the distinction between emotions and patterned thought, attention, and desire, we may have carried philosophical analysis too far, leading to misleading artificiality, or at least a mistaken psychology. For that distinction points to, if it does not rest on, a potentially worrisome, and often undesirable and unhealthy, split. It is, after all, part of the core of the common ego defence, and neurotic style, of intellectualization.[5] When it becomes general and typical of significant portions of a person's psychic life, that distinction typifies and is constitutively central to the affect-denying world of alienated work, repression, dissociation, and more severe schizoid phenomena.

We have yet to be sure about the relations between evaluative understanding and emotions. But I think we have seen enough to take seriously, and perhaps accept, the claim that people who have correct emotions, because they are such people, can be well-placed to make correct evaluations, and people who have incorrect emotions, because they are such people, can be poorly placed to make correct evaluations.

Here we should remember that it is a long- and soundly established part of our ethical tradition, and most others, that being good at noticing and appreciating value—being a good judge—is of utmost value. It is, of course, instrumentally valuable. But in addition, being a good judge is, itself, an important internal part of what it is to live well and to be good.

2. EMOTIONS HAVE EVALUATIVE IMPORTANCE BY BEING VALUABLE

I want now to turn to some further constitutive relations between emotions and value. I will sketch how emotions are essential constitutents of many of our important, and also unimportant, activities and relations,

---

[5] See A. Freud, *The Ego and the Mechanisms of Defence*, tr. C. Baines (London, 1937), and Shapiro, *Neurotic Styles*.

and thus of much of our lives. What I want to urge about emotions is found in, or at least suggested by, Aristotle's accounts of pleasure and pain in the *Nicomachean Ethics*. So let us turn very briefly to those accounts. In VII. 13, Aristotle identifies pleasure with *energeia*, i.e. value-made-actual or unimpeded activity. In X. 4, he says that pleasure is the natural concomitant of *energeia* in that it perfects or completes *energeia*: 'pleasure completes the activity . . . as an end which supervenes [on the activity] as the bloom of youth does on those in the flower of their age.'[6] As we will see, emotions stand to value in these two related ways.

For present purposes, what is important about Aristotle's accounts of pleasure is the view of pleasure that it is, or is the natural concomitant of, the actualization of value. Put far too simply, it is pleasant to have what one thinks good come to be—especially if one makes it come to be, i.e. achieves it. Again far too simply, this is what pleasure is or what has pleasure as its natural concomitant.

If this is right, this helps show why emotions reveal value—according to Aristotle, anyway. For as he sees matters, emotions constitutively involve pleasure and pain—'By the emotions I mean . . . in general the feelings that are accompanied by pleasure and pain;'[7] and given his accounts of pleasure and pain, emotions thus constitutively involve value.

An example might help here. For me to take pride in an achievement of mine is for me to take pleasure in and from the achievement. This is a pleasure that, as we could say, binds up the achievement, me as the achiever, the way I did it, and the like. And for me to take such bound-up pleasure is for me to take pride in my achievement. We thus see how emotions can, in themselves, be valuable. So too, we can see why values and our pleasure—e.g. the pleasure we take in ourselves for and in realizing them—are just too bound up together to single out either one as the one that has real importance. As Aristotle says,

whether we choose life for the sake of pleasure or pleasure for the sake of life is a question we may dismiss for the present. For they seem to be bound up together and not to admit of separation, since without activity pleasure does not arise, and every activity is completed by pleasure.[8]

I want to say something along similar lines for at least some emotions. They are themselves of value, or they and the values they embody 'seem bound up together and not to admit of separation'.

I am not claiming this of all emotions. So, excitement at the thought

[6] Aristotle, *Nicomachean Ethics* [= *NE*], tr. W. D. Ross (Princeton, 1984), 1174[b]31–3.
[7] *NE*, tr. H. Rackham (Oxford, 1943), 1105[b]21–3.   [8] *NE*, tr. Ross, 1175[a]18–21.

of, or produced by, a roller-coaster ride may well not show any value or any valuing.[9] But such inseparability does hold for some—and, I think, many—emotions.

Let us turn again to my example of pride. I find it hard to take seriously the claim that pride is not, in itself, good or bad. Bad pride is easy: it can involve an overestimation of what one did, oneself for doing it, one's right in doing it, and so on. It is as easy to see why bad pride is, in itself, bad, as it is to see why lying to oneself or perhaps others is bad. Indeed, part of what makes bad pride bad seems often to be the deceptions and lies it involves.

Good pride is also easy—especially if we take care that such pride does not move over into bad pride, such as being too full of oneself. I mean, who can doubt the goodness of young children's pride in mastering their body and mind: in walking, in running, in climbing, in learning to read and write, and so on? Or the goodness of an author's quiet satisfaction, even rather loud exultation, perhaps up to and including a wild glorying, in finally completing after all these many years a very fine piece of writing; or such pride had by a sculptor upon completing a wonderful statue; or by a woodworker on completing a wonderful bedroom suite?

Again, we must take some care. This pride might well be objectionable if these proud people give no recognition, perhaps no thanks, to others—neither their parents, nor their teachers, nor their fellows. And it would be objectionable if they seriously overrate the work, or themselves for accomplishing it. But unless one thinks that whatever a human achieves is really due to someone else, or is really very poor, these are simply matters over which to take care. They limit good pride, rather than showing it impossible.

This, of course, is just what we should expect—or expect me to say. For I have already stated my view that some pleasures are good and good in themselves. The question may remain, Why is such pride good? Or, if the answer to that is clear enough, the question may be, How is such pride good? In many cases at least, the answer can be given in the form suggested by the X. 4 account of pleasure: 'pleasure completes the activity . . . as an end which supervenes [on the activity] as the bloom of youth does on those in the flower of their age.' Pride completes the activity this way, too.

Especially when we consider activities in terms of what is done, they

---

[9] For a discussion of near-constitutional and non-value-based character differences which centre around liking and disliking such activities, see M. Balint, *Thrills and Regressions* (London, 1959).

can seem perfect—and from that standpoint may well be perfect—even if the agents take no pride or other pleasure in the activities or in their doing them. A philosophy paper does not seem to be a better philosophy paper because the philosopher takes pride or other pleasure in it or in doing it.

But when we focus more on the agents and their activity, it does seem that proper pride makes the activity even better—at least in the sense of an added bloom. There is now the agents' recognition of what they did and how they acted, and this recognition is accurate and appreciative and pleasurable. Even if these do not make the product any better, they do make the production, the producing, better.

Let us now turn to some emotions whose value seems to fit more with the model of pleasure given in VII. 13, where pleasure is identified with the perfect activity, i.e. with value made actual. I will start with the more interpersonal emotions, or group of emotions, that inform play: e.g. the emotions that inform loving play between a child and parent, or those that inform the engaged play of children, or the playful and amusing conversations of good friends. As it seems to me, one can see easily that such emotions are, in themselves, good by seeing why those engaged in these forms of play might care whether they or their partners in play have the emotions.

We can see this, I think, from the other side, by imagining cases where the affect and emotional engagement are missing. To this end, we should imagine an emotionally engaged child playing with an affectless parent, or children playing affectlessly with other children or with their own toys, or your friend talking with you about playful and amusing matters, but affectlessly, not engaging emotionally with you.

If one were to ask exactly why one might want, for oneself and for others, the emotional engagement, the answer can be given simply in terms of the engagement. One wants, and quite properly so, engagement—emotional engagement—with those one plays with. Indeed, one of the important reasons for playing is to be emotionally engaged with the play, with oneself, and with others.

The point can easily be generalized. One quite often wants engagement with others. One wants them to share our joy and grief; one wants to share their joy and grief; and one wants all the people involved to want such a shared life. One wants to live with others, one wants a social, interpersonal life; and, to a greater or lesser extent, depending on the details of the engagement, one wants the engagement to be emotional—constituted in part by emotional interpersonal relations.

It must be emphasized that what one wants, as well as constituting value, can also be informed by value. This is most easily seen by looking at the engaged care we want to give and receive, e.g. in friendship and love. Here we want not just emotional engagement; we also want the good of the person cared for to be a focus of the engagement. Put another way, to act out of friendship is to act for the sake of the friend.

To be sure, not all relations between people need have emotions as constituents. So, cancer patients may judge their cancer surgeon in just the ways they would judge a cancer-fighting drug or a cancer-fighting computer-driven automated laser: not in terms of emotional involvement, but simply in terms of costs and benefits, e.g. as determined by survival rates, pain, gain or loss of functions, and the like. The thought here might be that where some end E can be achieved either by a mechanism or a person, there is no difference between E-as-done-by-a-mechanism and E-as-done-by-a-person.

But while some cancer patients have that view, in fact many do not.[10] Many of them complain that their surgeons are too technocratic, too concerned with mere effectiveness and survival rates. These patients thus do not view their surgeons as mere means, mere mechanisms for ridding them of cancer. This seems a correlative of how they want their surgeons to view them. They want their surgeons to be concerned and involved with them as people, not just as 'sites' for operations. In these cases, then, medical patients do not see what their doctors do to them just in terms of what this may achieve. What is done is also seen as human acts, with emphasis on both 'human' and 'acts'. (What is done is thus seen as, or something very close to, Aristotelian activities, *praxeis*, rather than means, *poiēseis*.)

Much the same holds for acts considered from the perspective of agents. We often care about the emotions with which we act. So, we are often not indifferent between doing or producing something and its simply existing. We want to do the act or produce the effect. This goes well beyond saying that we can be concerned that we, as opposed to someone else, do the act or produce the effect. It also says that we can be concerned that we be agents: that we, as agents, do or produce it.

These last comments give us reason to examine the evaluative implications of two distinctions. The first is the one between those

---

[10] I am indebted here to Robert W. Daly, MD. My thanks are also owed him for discussion of other issues in this paper and for showing me his articles, 'Schizoid Rule-Following', *Psychoanalytic Review* 55 (1968), 400–14, and 'The Specters of Technicism', *Psychiatry* 33 (1970), 417–32.

activities that are constitutively emotional and those that are only perfected by emotions. For as just said, what we often want is not simply to do something, e.g. write a good philosophy paper—where what we do is not made better by our pleasure in doing it. We can want to be engaged in the activity. What we here want is emotionally engaged activity, rather than alienated, machine-like, dead activity. At the extreme, we want not to be like Guntrip's schizoid who feels no interest in objects either in consciousness or in the outer world.[11]

The second distinction is between emotions and activity. For, as also just said, what we often want is emotionally engaged activity. It is, of course, possible to have activity without emotion. And it is possible to have emotions without activity. Sometimes, as in the case of pity for the dead, no action may be possible. But at other times, lack of activity bespeaks a moral or personal problem. Sentimentalism is just one of these problems—as is the view that experiences are what are important, and, at an extreme, that being a spectator is the proper way to live. Here I would simply suggest that any evaluatively adequate account of emotions, or of people as emotional, will yoke emotion and action together. My argument for the evaluative importance of emotions is in no way an argument against the evaluative importance of action.

This concludes the argument of this section. We have seen that we want many of our important activities and relations to be infused with emotions. We might thus extend Socrates' dictum that the unexamined life is not worth living by adding that neither is the unfelt life. Less grandly, I want my beloved to care for me not simply because that shows that she values me. I also want to be held warmly, in her heart, her mind, and, perhaps, her arms.

3. HOW EMOTIONS HELP WITH EVALUATIVE KNOWLEDGE

I want now to turn to some other ways emotions reveal value. As before, here too there will be two interrelated themes, the constitutive and the epistemological. I will focus on how emotions are constitutive of what is known in some evaluative knowledge, and how emotions allow for such knowledge.

The constitutive theme takes off from what has just been shown: that

[11] Guntrip, *Schizoid Phenomena*, 30.

emotions are central to the nature, meaning, and value of a great deal of human life. It offers an epistemological extension of this. It is that if we are unable to see, understand, and appreciate the emotions of others, we will be unable to see, understand, and appreciate a great deal of what their relations, activities, and lives are, and are like, for them. So too for us and our emotions and for understanding ourselves.

This failure, if I am right, will be thoroughgoing and deep. It will not be a failure in some separable, perhaps important, but ultimately non-essential, part of a person. It might well have been such a failure, if emotions were only an important but separable feature of a person, in much the way that, as it might be thought, whether a person lives in New York City or Boston is an important but separable, and non-essential, part of a person. But, if I am right, emotions are centrally important and both evaluatively and conceptually essential to our activities, relations, and lives. What our activities, relations, and lives are, and what they are for us, and the value they have all depend essentially on our emotions.

So, Aristotle's account of anger shows us not only the values and the evaluatively charged life of people with those emotions. It also shows us how those emotions are essential constituents of those values and lives. For only with those emotional structures can Aristotle's people live in the particular ways they do. More generally, as Charles Taylor has argued so persuasively, much of our ethically important life—extending well beyond the intimate and personal—involves emotions, and is caught up in and constituted by emotions.[12]

Indeed, as argued by P. F. Strawson in 'Freedom and Resentment', emotions are constitutive of human life.[13] Having and being the subject of reactive attitudes is central to being and being recognized as a person; and also, having shared reactive attitudes is central to being a community. With Strawson, I would hold that we have no idea what a human community that lacked reactive attitudes would be like, or even whether it would be possible.

Let us now turn to my second theme, which is directly epistemological—having to do with how emotions help us see and understand these values. My central claim here is that one of the central ways to

[12] See, for example, his article 'Self-Interpreting Animals', in his *Human Agency and Language, Philosophical Papers*, vol. 1 (Cambridge, 1985), 45–76. See also M. Walker, 'Morality and the Emotions: Getting Things Right', unpub.
[13] *Proceedings of the British Academy* 48 (1962), 187–211. I am grateful to Laurence Thomas for discussion on Strawson and other issues in this work.

gain an understanding of, especially, such emotions and relations is by means of emotions. So, we learn the nature and meaning—the value—of love, say, by experiencing loving and being loved.

Quite generally, we learn emotions—how and when to have them, how to recognize our own and those of others, their significance, and so on—by engaging emotionally with others. In much the way that we learn and understand language—what we and others mean by what we and they say—we learn and understand emotions—what we and others mean by our and their emotional expressions. This of course allows for and, I think, requires being able to do this on one's own, by imagination—both linguistic imagination, often called thought, and emotional imagination, rarely called thought. (I will return to this parallel below.)

This, if right, allows us to justify and see the importance of the claims by Murdoch, Blum, and Nussbaum that loving attention and other forms of emotional knowledge are essential for ethical knowledge.[14] For, as I see matters, their claims develop naturally from, and are grounded in, the situations they discuss: e.g. for Murdoch, the mother-in-law coming to understand and appreciate her daughter-in-law; for Blum, person-to-person relations, including friendship and intimacy; for Nussbaum, family relations as depicted in Henry James's novels. What is evaluatively important about these situations is importantly, and often largely, the emotions and the emotion-based and emotion-expressing relations that make them up—that make them the very interesting and evaluatively important situations they are.

Put briefly, then, my suggestion is that many situations which are importantly constituted by emotions, can be best understood by emotional engagement. This can be taken as making what I hope by now is the uncontentious claim that it is by means of, or through, emotional engagement that we understand those situations. It can also be taken as making the far more difficult claim that the emotions and emotional engagement provide—because they embody, express, and really are—the evaluative knowledge. Emotions are necessary for evaluative knowledge of such situations precisely because emotionally engaged people, in their emotional engagement, embody, express, and thus really have evaluative knowledge.

[14] I. Murdoch, *The Sovereignty of Good* (London, 1970); L. Blum, *Friendship, Altruism, and Morality* (London, 1980) and 'Iris Murdoch and the Domain of the Moral', *Philosophical Studies* 50 (1986), 343–67; M. Nussbaum, *Love's Knowledge* (Oxford, 1990). My thanks are owed Margaret Walker for discussion of these and other issues.

This is to say that the evaluative knowledge we are here concerned with is deeply practical. Not only is this practice in the sense of doing, but also, this practice is knowing practice. It embodies and expresses the knowledge.

This can be taken in a relatively mild and unfreighted way. The practice might be important or necessary only in the way that leading someone to your house embodies and expresses your knowledge of how to get there—knowledge you might be unable to express by using a map or verbally. Here we think it obvious that there is a way to articulate the knowledge—a way that is or can be possessed by others—that you can only show.

But much the same point can be made where it is unclear whether there is, or even could be, an articulation of the knowledge. Here we might think of knowledge of a dance performance. I mean a particular dancing, by a particular dancer, on a particular occasion. We might well think that there is no notational system which could accurately get all the important details—not just where the feet should be in a given temporally ordered sequence, but also how the arms should be, the suppleness or rigidity of the arms, the forwardness or the modesty of the torso, and so on. In this case, a movie, or a series of movies so that no part of the dancer is hidden, might be necessary.

Similarly, we might well think that there is no way to give a general and fully detailed account of how a parent can play well with a child, and that there is no way to give a general and fully detailed account of how to keep up an amusing conversation with a friend. One could, of course, make general points—e.g. continue at the same level of intensity. But, the present claim would have it, the detail of evaluatively informed ways to continue can only be shown. And now there is the problem that we might need more than movies to do the showing. We might also need 'recordings' of the participants' minds.

But even so, I can see the force of the thought that the movies show something external to them, and that this could be articulated if only we had a good enough notational system—perhaps the movies themselves could be taken to be such a system. The idea here is not that there is a general articulation of what makes play or conversation good or bad, and that this is shown in or by the movies. Rather, the thought is that there could be an articulation of what makes a given episode of play or a given conversation good or bad.

Let us use this to put a claim—whether or not it is Aristotle's—that emotions are necessary for evaluative knowledge. The claim would be that the general knowledge, or what it is knowledge of, is too complex and difficult to articulate and can only be shown in and by means of emotions. It could, none the less, hold that there might well be a knowledge-giving, discursive, articulate commentary about some, or even all, particular cases. And it could also hold that what is known in ethics, in contrast with how we know it, has no essential connection with emotions.

Now, I do think emotions would be shown to be important for evaluative knowledge if they were shown to be important in this way. However, there is a far stronger position, which correspondingly accords far more epistemological importance to emotions. Here we might hold that the knowing emotional engagement is a primary way or a typical way, whether or not it is the only way, to have and express the knowledge. A related way to put this is that we have knowledge in and of practice: the knowing practice embodies, expresses, and really is the knowledge. Somewhat more strongly, it could be held that the emotional practical knowledge has epistemological priority over other knowledge, e.g. articulated and reflective theory and knowledge. As we might say, the heart has its reasons which reason does not, perhaps cannot, have.

This conception of practical knowledge might seem difficult and unusual. Whether or not it is difficult, I do not think it is so unusual—as is shown by the following parallels of philosophy, conversation, and art. For philosophy, we should compare the different epistemological roles of philosophy, that is, work produced by and taken up by philosophers, on the one hand, with, on the other hand, the canons of and for philosophy, which we use to criticize philosophy and to guide our students and ourselves in the doing of philosophy. In important ways the doing of philosophy has epistemological priority over the reflective, articulable knowledge about this.

Good conversation is explained and characterized in terms of the activity of good conversationalists, not in terms of rules, e.g. rules of grammar, of niceties about seriousness, topicality, politeness, and the like. That good conversationalists converse in a certain way, and accept the conversation as good, shows that it is good—not just as a matter of evidence, but more as a matter of recognition and constitution.

Finally, so far as beauty and knowledge of beauty is concerned, it seems that mature artists, or their works, embody, express, and thus really have knowledge of beauty. They or their works have epistemological priority over aesthetics considered as reflection and articulation.

It is absolutely clear that these are examples of knowing, intelligent activity. It is also absolutely clear that they, or their agents, embody, express, and are guided by value. Otherwise, it would simply be a mystery how those activities so regularly achieve value.

As this shows, we cannot accept views holding that evaluative knowledge requires the use and knowledge of principles. And we now see how to reject the claim that since or in so far as, e.g. maternal care is bound up with emotions and does not proceed via evaluative principles about what is good for the child, it cannot be knowing, intelligent, and evaluatively guided activity.

Does theory—understood largely in terms of principles, reflection, and articulation—play any role? We might start our answer with the claim of Barnett Newman, an abstract expressionist of the New York School, who said that 'aesthetics is to me as ornithology is to birds'. Taken strictly, this allows that aesthetics might be a source of knowledge, if not for him and perhaps other artists then for other people. And, quite generally, knowledge does seem accessible in different ways —e.g. by and through practice and also by and through theory, and by emotional or non-emotional means.

This last is entirely consistent with holding that if theory provides such access, practice has epistemological priority over theory. Here we might remember Aristotle's 'second-best' advice: if you yourself lack proper ethical understanding, e.g. because you lack proper emotions, you can none the less, to some extent anyway, act well by following the lead of a good person, who has correct emotions.

Perhaps, however, theoretical knowledge can harm practice, e.g. by interfering with the sort of engagement good practice requires. We could consider artists who take art to be the implementation of a theory, taking art to be good to the extent it fulfils the criteria of the theory. Here we may have artists who look to rules and critics, rather than themselves, for guidance and direction—and who, not surprisingly, produce modish, stylized, routinized, or merely academic art.

Much the same holds for play, conversation, and other emotional interchanges. Here we might think of those who look to rules and 'experts' to find out how play, conversations, and other emotional engagements 'should be', rather than attending to and engaging with the activity, themselves, and others involved in the activity—and who, not surprisingly, are not attuned to the activity, themselves, and those others.

None the less, it does seem that even in these cases of strong practical knowledge, we can have articulable knowledge—especially if it is gained through reflection on knowing emotional engagement. Further, reflection and articulation may in all sorts of intelligent ways change, or call for a change in, the practice. This can still allow that the practice—modified to take account of the articulated knowledge—retains epistemological priority over both the reflective knowledge that led to the change and reflective knowledge about the now-changed practice.

Let us now apply this discussion of strong practical knowledge to Aristotle. Since he held that each good person requires correct emotions to know how to act and how to be, it might seem that he would agree with Newman's claim transposed to ethics. This may be right about the usefulness, the practicability, of a reflective, articulable ethics. But even a Newman-like claim is not strong enough to capture Aristotle's claim that ethics does not admit of a complete, detailed account. For Aristotle's claim is also that there is no account of ethics that is as complete, even if as useless, as ornithology is for birds.

Taking these points into account, we now get a strong reading of Aristotle's claim that emotional engagement is necessary for evaluative knowledge. It is that good and wise people, those who are *phronimos*, are emotionally engaged. And because they are good, wise, and emotionally engaged, they embody, express, and determine what is morally correct.

It remains to be seen where emotional practice is necessary. This work has suggested at least two areas: where emotions help constitute values, and where lack of emotions is due to features of the person which also make the person a bad evaluative judge.

4. HOW EMOTIONS HELP
JUSTIFY EVALUATIVE KNOWLEDGE

In the previous section, I showed how we may use, and may have to use, emotions and emotional knowledge to gain knowledge of values and other forms of evaluative knowledge. But there is still something to be shown: whether and how what we thus gain is knowledge. How, if at all, do emotions enter into not just what is known, but also into the knowledge? How do emotions enter into justification of claims of evaluative knowledge?

This is to ask what probative force, if any, is to be attached to emotions and the values they help constitute and in this and other ways reveal. For it does seem that we must investigate the moral correctness of emotions before allowing them to show us what is morally correct.

So, for example, if the anger described by Aristotle is itself deplorable, it is difficult to see how the values it reveals and helps constitute should be accorded much, if any, positive weight.

We can take this as asking about the standpoint from which we are to assess such anger and other emotions. Some think that for quite general reasons, we must here have recourse to theory and articulate principles. And some think that since emotions are in question, we must find a standpoint that does not involve emotions. But, as I see matters, at least many of the most important ways to make such assessments make use of emotions.

I do, of course, see how emotions can be criticized for success or failure in serving certain values, for perpetuating certain values and disvalues—e.g. the anger described by Aristotle may well give expression to and also perpetuate improper hierarchies. However, these criticisms importantly and typically involve emotions, or what can be understood only in terms of emotions.

I have two interrelated sorts of reasons for holding this. The first is found in Taylor's and Strawson's arguments that many of our most important evaluations of emotions themselves, and of social and other structures that depend essentially on them, are made, and perhaps can be made only, in terms of other emotions and emotionally-constituted structures. As Taylor put it, in order to understand what it is for me to experience shame, we are referred to what 'shows me up to be base, or to have some unavowable and degrading property, or to be dishonourable. In this account, however long we carry it on, . . . we cannot escape from these terms into an objective [and non-emotional] account'.[15]

The second is that many criticisms of emotions and structures which depend on them are made against some conception or other of human, primarily social, life. And human, especially social, life is through-and-through affectively infused and in large part constituted by emotions. One central set of standards for a life has to do with the way it meets and fulfils various emotional requirements: whether a life satisfies affective needs is one important consideration in judging its success or failure. And this success or failure is itself understood and evaluated in terms of affectivity: what is important about the satisfaction or lack of satisfaction of such affective needs is not, or not simply, some other thing. It is also the satisfaction of those needs. My reply, then, to the worry about the need to evaluate emotions is that we can and do evaluate

---

[15] Taylor, 'Self-Interpreting Animals', 55.

emotions in terms of the human and social lives they foster or hinder; but these lives are in part constituted by and evaluated in terms of emotions and met or unmet emotional needs.

In conclusion, then, emotions are essential to value and are themselves valued and valuable. They are forms of lived, engaged, human value. In addition, emotional knowledge—knowledge and understanding of emotions and the knowledge shown in emotions—is important, often vital, for knowledge and understanding of value, because much of this knowledge is emotional knowledge.

This is important on its own. It is also important for its implications about esoteric or self-effacing ethical theories. The values of the emotions, including of course the emotional practices, discussed here are in the emotions and emotional practices themselves. Their value does not lie in some other and esoteric or self-effacing value or goal. Indeed, esotericism and self-effacement are destructive of these values. To see just how important emotional values are, and how many values are emotional, is to see how little room is left for esoteric and self-effacing ethics. In this way then, a study of emotions helps reveal value at the same time as it helps cure the schizophrenia of modern ethical theories.[16]

[16] My thanks are owed to the many philosophers who read or listened to and commented on earlier drafts of this work. Along with those already mentioned, I am pleased to thank Lawrence Blum for showing me his 'Emotion and Moral Reality', unpublished; Henry Richardson for discussion and for showing me his 'The Emotions in Reflective Equilibrium', unpublished; and Jonathan Adler, Jonathan Bennett, Jeff Blustein, Chris Gowans, Elizabeth Hegeman, Frances Howard-Snyder, Lynne McFall, and Graeme Marshall.

MacIntyre on Modernity and How It Has Marginalized the Virtues

ANDREW MASON

The revival of interest in the virtues in moral theory has had its counterpart in political theory: political philosophers have been concerned with the role of the virtues in justifying social, political, and economic arrangements, and have explored the issue of what institutions can provide space for the virtues to flourish. Alasdair MacIntyre's *After Virtue* was a seminal contribution to this debate. MacIntyre not only gave an account of the virtues, but also employed that account to launch an attack on liberalism, by arguing that the institutions it defends undermine rather than foster the virtues. I propose to examine MacIntyre's account, and then to turn to some of the responses it has provoked. I shall argue that MacIntyre makes an important criticism of liberalism which liberals have not yet fully answered, but which also creates problems for his own account.

1. MACINTYRE'S ACCOUNT OF THE VIRTUES

MacIntyre's account of the virtues is Aristotelian in inspiration, although unlike Aristotle's own account it gives an important role to the concept of a practice. He employs the term 'practice' in a semi-technical way, meaning by it

any coherent and complex form of socially established cooperative human activity through which goods internal to that form of activity are realised in the course of trying to achieve those standards of excellence which are appropriate to, and partially definitive of, that form of activity, with the result that human powers to achieve excellence, and human conceptions of the ends and goods involved, are systematically extended.[1]

As examples of practices, MacIntyre gives football, chess, farming, the enquiries of physics, chemistry, and biology, the work of historians, and painting and music. He claims that the concept of a practice is central to an adequate understanding of the virtues: virtues can be characterized, at least in part, as acquired human qualities the possession and exercise of which tend to enable us to achieve goods which are internal to practices.[2] Goods are internal to a practice if they cannot be achieved except by participating in it (or a related practice), and if they can only be identified and recognized through that participation.[3] MacIntyre contrasts internal goods with external goods. The latter are only contingently related to practices, and could in principle be obtained independently of them; he has in mind mainly prestige, status, and money.[4]

MacIntyre provides us with an implicit account of what makes a set of social and political arrangements justifiable: they are justifiable if and only if they facilitate the leading of a good life. In order to do so they must sustain the practices which supply goods that would otherwise be unavailable, the traditions which transmit and shape these practices, and the communities within which people can pursue the good life effectively. It follows that social and political arrangements are justifiable only if they foster the virtues, for it is the virtues which in various ways enable people to achieve goods internal to practices and lead a good life (though of course, MacIntyre's account does not regard the virtues as merely means to these ends, for they are conceived as partially constitutive of the ends themselves). MacIntyre is in effect claiming that only social and political arrangements which sustain practices, and make possible the effective pursuit of the good, *respect* the virtues.

MacIntyre's central claim in *After Virtue* is that the social and political conditions typical of modernity are hostile to the virtues. Modern

[1] A. MacIntyre, *After Virtue: A Study in Moral Theory* (London, 1981; hereafter referred to as *AV*), 175.

[2] *AV* 178. This provides only part of MacIntyre's account of the virtues: see *AV* 187–207 for the other elements that he adds to it.   [3] *AV* 176.

[4] It is rather surprising that the concept of a practice does not loom large in MacIntyre's more recent book, *Whose Justice? Which Rationality?* (London, 1988), given its centrality to the account of the virtues in *After Virtue*. As David Miller points out, however, MacIntyre does speak in the more recent book of 'types of systematic activity', and distinguishes between the goods of excellence and the goods of effectiveness, a distinction which is closely related to his distinction between internal and external goods. See D. Miller, 'Virtues, Practices and Justice', in J. Horton and S. Mendus (eds.), *After MacIntyre* (Cambridge, 1994), 245–64, p. 248.

societies are marked by intractable disagreements over moral and political issues, including disputes over what it is to lead a good life. These
disagreements are rationally irresolvable because conflicting positions
employ a variety of incommensurable premises, involving concepts that
originally derived their meaning from different historical contexts. Modern concepts (such as 'rights' and 'utility') are in MacIntyre's view
entirely bogus, whereas older ones (e.g. 'desert') have been deprived of
the surroundings which were essential to their meaning.[5] He argues that
the virtues cannot flourish when dislocated in this way because many of
them can be adequately understood only by reference to a shared conception of the good for man:

> In a society where there is no longer a shared conception of the community's
> good as specified by the good for man, there can no longer either be any very
> substantial concept of what it is to contribute more or less to the achievement
> of that good. Hence notions of desert and honour become detached from the
> context in which they were originally at home. Honour becomes nothing more
> than a badge of aristocratic status, and status itself . . . has very little to do with
> desert. Distributive justice cannot any longer be defined in terms of desert
> either . . .[6]

As a result, virtue terms such as 'justice', 'desert', and 'honour' become
redefined as dispositions necessary to produce obedience to the rules
of morality.[7] MacIntyre argues that this understanding of the virtues
is inadequate because some particular virtues (e.g. chastity) cannot be
coherently understood in this way; furthermore, there will be no agreement on the nature and content of the virtues which can be reconceptual-
ized along these lines, since there is no agreement on moral rules. Under
these circumstances the application of virtue terms becomes unclear, and
the virtues themselves become marginalized.

MacIntyre also thinks that modernity is unfriendly to the virtues
because it transfers work from the household to the market: the market cultivates the vice of acquisitiveness,[8] and work becomes simply
a means to external goods, rather than a practice which involves the
exercise of the virtues in realizing its internal goods. Let me quote
MacIntyre at some length, since I think his argument here is an important one:

---

[5] See my 'MacIntyre on Liberalism and its Critics: Tradition, Incommensurability and
Disagreement', in Horton and Mendus (eds.), *After MacIntyre*, 225–44, for a more detailed
discussion of MacIntyre's diagnosis of why modern moral and political disagreement
is so intractable.   [6] *AV* 215.

[7] *AV* 216, and ch. 16, *passim*.   [8] *AV* 237.

As, and to the extent that, work moves outside the household and is put to the service of impersonal capital, the realm of work tends to become separated from everything but the service of biological survival and the reproduction of the labour force, on the one hand, and that of institutionalized acquisitiveness, on the other. *Pleonexia*, a vice in the Aristotelian scheme, is now the driving force of modern productive work. The means-end relationships embodied for the most part in such work—on a production line, for example—are necessarily external to the goods which those who work seek; such work too has consequently been expelled from the realm of practices with goods internal to themselves. And correspondingly practices have in turn been removed to the margins of social and cultural life. Arts, sciences and games are taken to be *work* only for a minority of specialists: the rest of us may receive incidental benefits in our leisure time only as spectators or consumers.[9]

According to MacIntyre, the modern economic order marginalizes practices, and the pursuit of external goods predominates in it. The practices which remain are under constant threat of corruption by acquisitiveness: the pursuit of external goods often comes into conflict with the realization of the goods internal to practices,[10] and corruption of a practice occurs when its participants pursue external goods at the expense of its internal goods, i.e. when in these circumstances the pursuit of external goods becomes the primary or overwhelming motivation for engaging in it.

MacIntyre's critique of modernity—in particular, his account of why it provides a hostile environment for the virtues—extends to liberal theory, which he sees as its main representative.[11] He argues that liberal theory embodies the deficiencies of modernity and possesses its own shortcomings. First, he claims, liberal theory has a flawed understanding of the virtues because it draws on the modern conception of them as dispositions or sentiments which will produce in us obedience to certain rules; as a result, liberalism cannot provide the basis for a shared view of the virtues. Second, liberalism is hostile to the virtues because it is in the service of the market, which cultivates vices such as acquisitiveness and individualism, and banishes work from the realm of practices. Third, liberal theory also contains an essential commitment to the idea that the state should be neutral between competing conceptions of the

---

[9] *AV* 211.   [10] *AV* 183.

[11] MacIntyre thinks that all modern political ideologies—what he refers to as 'modern systematic politics'—are hostile to the virtues, but he focuses his attention on liberalism. He seems to think that at root socialism, Marxism, and conservatism (for example) are just variants of liberalism in disguise. See W. Galston, *Liberal Purposes: Goods, Virtues, and Diversity in the Liberal State* (Cambridge, 1991), 67.

good, and hence cannot cultivate the kind of moral outlook, involving core moral qualities such as justice, honesty, and courage, which are central to practices.[12]

2. SOME PROBLEMS WITH MACINTYRE'S ACCOUNT

MacIntyre's account of why modernity is hostile to the virtues, and why liberalism cannot accommodate them, is problematic in several respects. He maintains that the pervasive and intractable disagreement which is characteristic of modernity undermines many of the virtues: they cannot flourish where there is radical disagreement because they rely on the existence of a shared conception of the good. But why does it follow that the virtues must suffer when there is no agreement on a substantive conception of the good?

Consider again MacIntyre's discussion of distributive justice, which provides a good illustration of the sort of argument he employs. He maintains that the virtue of justice was originally understood in terms of desert, judged on the basis of the contribution an individual made to the shared conception of the community's good. When consensus on the community's good was eroded, however, the virtue of justice came to be understood as a disposition to obey the rules or principles of justice. This generated radical disagreement on the nature and content of justice as a virtue, since there were, and continue to be, different conceptions of the rules of justice.

What exactly is MacIntyre's point here? He might be saying that the virtue of justice will be marginalized because it will be conceived as secondary to the *rules* of justice. But why can't justice, albeit variously understood, flourish as a virtue even if it is conceived as a disposition to obey the rules of justice? Even if the virtues lack justificatory primacy—because our ultimate justifications for what we do would have to be couched in terms of the following of rules rather than some conception of a virtuous person—it does not follow that their cultural status must be diminished. Virtue terms could in principle continue to be widely used in ordinary discourse, and the virtues themselves could continue to be highly valued.

MacIntyre might mean instead that the virtue of justice, when it is understood in the way he thinks it should be—i.e. as a quality which

[12] See *AV* 182.

is necessary to sustain practices, which involves an ability to judge impartially people's contribution to a practice or, more generally, to the community's good, and also includes a disposition to reward them according to that contribution—will be marginalized. But if the virtue of justice is conceived as a disposition to obey the *rules* of justice, it could then be understood as a disposition to follow the rule that people should be rewarded in accordance with their contribution to the community's good. There is no obvious reason why that conception should not gain adherents in modern societies; indeed, it seems to be one of our ordinary understandings of what justice requires.[13] MacIntyre might reply that this is not enough: that the virtue of justice, properly conceived, will flourish only if it is widely believed that justice requires contributions to the community's good to be rewarded, *and* only if there is a widely shared conception of that good.[14] But how would MacIntyre justify that claim? It begins to look as if it is a tautology in disguise: justice, conceived (at least in part) as a disposition to reward people according to what they deserve on the basis of their contribution to the good of the community, will not flourish where there is radical disagreement, since part of what it is for it to flourish is for people to share a conception of the community's good and to believe that contributions to it should be rewarded.

There is perhaps another way of construing MacIntyre's argument, however, which avoids the charge that it rests on a mere tautology. MacIntyre might be maintaining that justice, conceived in the way he recommends, cannot flourish as a virtue unless that conception of it is widely accepted because otherwise there cannot be the shared practices on which the exercise of many of the virtues, including justice, depends. This would resonate with his insistence in another context that 'I am never able to seek the good life or exercise the virtues only *qua* individual.'[15] The survival of a practice depends on a measure of consensus about its point, and about the goods which it supplies, for only where such a consensus exists is co-operation possible, and co-operation is required if anyone is to realize the goods internal to it. But this argument would not warrant the conclusion that there needs to be a shared

---

[13] David Miller argues for the stronger claim that 'the modern age has not witnessed the decline of the notion of desert, but if anything its apotheosis' because in modern societies 'it is easier to draw a line between someone's personal qualities and accomplishments and their ascribed social position' ('Virtues, Practices and Justice', 257–8).

[14] See *AV* 143: 'the social presuppositions of the flourishing of the virtue of justice in a community are therefore twofold: that there are rational criteria of desert and that there is socially established agreement as to what those criteria are.'   [15] *AV* 204.

conception of the virtues and of the good life across a whole society for the virtues to flourish: the virtues might also flourish in a society made up of a number of different practices, each practice involving a group of individuals who shared a conception of the good, and hence who could co-operate with each other in pursuit of it.

If the virtues really could not flourish under conditions of radical disagreement, then the appropriate conclusion would seem to be that they are doomed to wither away. Liberals, such as John Rawls, are surely right when they maintain that disagreement over comprehensive conceptions of the good is an inescapable feature of the modern predicament, barring the oppressive use of state power.[16] MacIntyre would reject that idea because he thinks that the kind of radical disagreement which currently exists can be overcome and that we can reach agreement, at least on a partially comprehensive conception of the good.[17] He believes that rationally compelling reasons can be given in favour of *one* tradition of moral and political thought and practice and that adherents of others could therefore be given irresistible reasons for abandoning them. Since the relevant tradition—some heir of Aristotelianism—is informed by a determinate conception of the good for man, it is not dogged by radical disagreement.[18]

In *Whose Justice? Which Rationality?*, MacIntyre provides the account of rationality which he thinks entitles him to argue that a suitably revised Aristotelian account—one which incorporates the insights of Augustinian Christianity, and in effect constitutes a form of Thomism—rationally requires our allegiance.[19] Rationality, in MacIntyre's view, is always relative to a tradition of thought and practice. Different traditions have their own norms of rational enquiry and practical rationality, but this does not mean there is no rational way of choosing between them. Traditions may be subject to epistemological crises: a tradition T1 may

[16] This is what Rawls refers to as the fact of pluralism: see his 'The Idea of an Overlapping Consensus', *Oxford Journal of Legal Studies* 7 (1987), 1–25, p. 4. In my *Explaining Political Disagreement* (Cambridge, 1993), I defend a qualified version of the claim that central moral and political disagreements are likely to persist.

[17] In Rawls's view, a doctrine is fully comprehensive 'when it covers all recognized values and virtues within one rather precisely articulated scheme of thought, whereas a doctrine is only partially comprehensive when it comprises certain (but not all) non-political values and virtues and is rather loosely articulated' (J. Rawls, 'The Priority of Right and Ideas of the Good', *Philosophy and Public Affairs* 17 (1988), 251–76, p. 253).

[18] MacIntyre does, however, allow that there will continue to be some moral and political disagreement—for example, in cases where goods conflict and choices are tragic (see, e.g., *AV*, 208–9).

[19] See *Whose Justice? Which Rationality?*, esp. chs. 1 and 18.

face a crisis in which it confronts and fails to deal adequately with what
is for it an important incoherence, whereas another tradition T2 can
provide a cogent and illuminating explanation, by the standards of T1,
of why this incoherence has arisen. Epistemological crises can therefore
give rationally compelling reasons for giving up a tradition of thought.[20]
MacIntyre thinks that this is what has happened to liberalism: it has
faced an epistemological crisis and has been defeated by it, and Thomism
has emerged as clearly rationally superior by its own standards and by
the standards of liberalism.[21] But this is an unlikely description of what
has happened, even if there is much to be said in favour of Thomism.
If we accept the idea that norms of rational enquiry are relative to traditions, it is implausible to suppose that a rationally compelling case
could be offered in favour of any particular tradition: the more likely
situation is that several different traditions will have a claim to superiority and none will be able to *demonstrate* its claim, in the strong sense
of providing what are for others rationally compelling reasons to give
up their traditions.[22] If that is so, then there are grounds for supposing
that disputes between different traditions will persist.

MacIntyre rejects all forms of 'modern systematic politics' (i.e. liberalism, socialism, conservatism, etc.) on the grounds that none of them
can accommodate the tradition of the virtues, but it becomes unclear
whether in doing so MacIntyre can provide scope for an account of the
state's legitimate functions. He accepts that some tasks performed by
the modern state will continue to be necessary: 'the rule of law, so far
as it is possible in a modern state, has to be vindicated, injustice and
unwarranted suffering have to be dealt with, . . . and liberty has to be
defended in ways that are sometimes only possible through the use of
governmental institutions.'[23] But how, for example, is MacIntyre going
to answer the following question: What happens if people are unable to
take care of themselves, perhaps because they are sick or disabled, or
perhaps simply because they are out of work? MacIntyre seems to suggest that it is impossible to give an abstract, non-contextual answer to
this question. There may be some value in refusing to give a universal
answer to it, but we might legitimately demand an answer in relation
to the forms of community MacIntyre is seeking to put in place of modern

---

[20] See MacIntyre, *Whose Justice? Which Rationality?*, 364–5.
[21] See *AV* 241, 244. Strictly speaking, it is only in *Whose Justice? Which Rationality?*
that MacIntyre identifies Thomism as the victor, and accords liberalism the status of a
tradition.
[22] See my 'MacIntyre on Liberalism and its Critics' for further discussion of this point.
[23] *AV* 237.

institutions. Ideologies such as liberalism and socialism at least give answers to the problems thrown up by modern industrial societies, which MacIntyre does not.[24]

3. LIBERAL ACCOUNTS OF THE VIRTUES

There are a number of possible moves that liberals can make in response to MacIntyre's claim that they are unable to respect the tradition of the virtues. Some liberals, such as William Galston, have argued that MacIntyre is wrong to suppose that liberalism is committed to neutrality, and have sketched a picture of the human good which they think liberalism presupposes or should presuppose; they have then sought to relate the virtues (albeit indirectly) to the good, conceived in this way.[25] Others, such as John Rawls, have accepted that liberalism should in some sense be neutral between controversial conceptions of the good, but have argued that it is nevertheless committed to a thin theory of the good, which enables it (again indirectly) to accommodate the virtues. Contrary to appearances, however, the issue of whether liberalism is, or should be, committed to some kind of neutrality is of no great importance in understanding liberal responses to MacIntyre.[26] Liberals who take conflicting sides in the neutrality debate tend to employ essentially the same strategy in answering him: they argue that liberal theory can accommodate the virtues by understanding them in relation to a conception of justice, grounded in a minimal understanding of the good which is widely shared in modern societies. Broadly speaking, this is the strategy adopted by Rawls and Galston, despite their differences.

Rawls believes that it is possible to construct a theory of justice on the basis of common understandings, including ideas of the good, which are part of the public culture of modern democratic regimes. Liberalism need not, and should not, employ any particular comprehensive conception of the good in developing a theory of justice, since part of the purpose of doing so is to provide a means of justifying the basic institutions of society to those with widely different 'comprehensive'

---

[24] See Galston, *Liberal Purposes*, 70. MacIntyre's failure to address these problems is indicative of the general way in which he undervalues external goods relative to internal ones. Some external goods, such as health and security for example, do not appear in his standard list, but are surely of the first importance.

[25] See Galston, *Liberal Purposes*.

[26] Nevertheless MacIntyre is surely mistaken to suppose that some sort of commitment to neutrality is essential to liberalism.

conceptions.[27] He maintains that the conception of justice which can be worked up from our shared understandings provides us with an account of what it is to be a good citizen of a modern democratic state: a good citizen is someone who possess the various qualities which are required to enable them to act from the principles of justice which should govern the basic structure of society, and to sustain the institutions which make it up. According to Rawls, these include the virtues of social co-operation, such as civility and tolerance, reasonableness, and a sense of fairness.[28]

William Galston proposes that liberalism should be founded on a somewhat thicker (and hence more controversial and less widely shared) conception of the human good than Rawls permits. Galston argues that the relevant conception is nevertheless a minimal one, and therefore provides scope for the core liberal idea that the basic structure of society should allow people to hold, and act on, a variety of different conceptions of the good. This conception includes the following as goods: life, the normal development of basic capacities, the fulfilment of interests and purposes, freedom, rationality, social relations, and subjective satisfaction.[29] Galston views the liberal polity as a co-operative endeavour to create and sustain communities in which individuals may pursue and, as far as possible, achieve their good. He argues that it should fulfil this purpose by designing institutions and formulating policies which promote the good, conceived in the minimal way he recommends. Since the polity is understood as a co-operative venture, members of it may make special claims on one another: they may make claims of need, based simply on their membership of the community; they may make claims of desert, based upon their contribution to the community—in particular to 'the cooperative endeavour to create opportunities for the good life';[30] and they have entitlements which arise from their voluntary choices, after the claims of need and desert have been met. Galston makes space for a conception of liberal virtues by construing them mainly in an instrumental fashion, as dispositions which sustain liberal institutions, i.e. those institutions which embody liberal purposes, and which distribute goods in accordance with liberal claims.[31]

[27] See e.g. J. Rawls, 'Justice as Fairness: Political not Metaphysical', *Philosophy and Public Affairs* 14 (1985), 223–51.

[28] See Rawls, 'The Priority of Right and Ideas of the Good', 263.

[29] Galston, *Liberal Purposes*, 174–7.   [30] Ibid. 185.

[31] Galston allows that many of these virtues will also sustain other social orders, and indeed that some will be necessary to sustain any polity. He also argues that some liberal virtues should be understood non-instrumentally—for example, the disposition to take responsibility for one's life (ibid. 230).

Steven Macedo has also argued at some length that liberalism can make space for the tradition of the virtues. Compared to Rawls's and Galston's accounts, the structure of the theory he develops is much less clear,[32] yet he ends up with a conception of the virtues which is strikingly similar to theirs in crucial respects. He argues that ordinary citizens and public officials must possess particular virtues if liberal principles (such as the principle of equality of respect for persons) and liberal values (such as the public justification of policy and institutions, and self-directedness) are to be realized.[33] These include tolerance, openness to change, self-control, and broad sympathies.[34] He also argues that citizens require particular virtues to flourish in a liberal order,[35] and that a liberal society promotes certain types of character;[36] these ideas, suitably qualified, would also be acceptable to both Rawls and Galston.

Despite their differences, the way in which Rawls, Galston, and Macedo make room for a range of virtues within their versions of liberalism is fundamentally the same. They each provide a list of virtues which are construed primarily as dispositions which sustain liberal institutions, i.e. the institutions which embody liberal principles and values. Galston and Rawls in effect argue against MacIntyre that there is sufficient agreement in modern societies on a minimal conception of the good for this to generate considerable agreement on the principles of justice which should govern these societies, and hence to underpin broad agreement on a particular set of virtues. (Galston differs from Rawls, however, in thinking that the relevant conception of the good will be more controversial.) They can both allow that there may be a greater range of virtues than those they mention, and indeed can grant that some of these may be of intrinsic rather than merely instrumental value. It is open to them to argue that liberal theory need not and should not presuppose that these qualities are virtues because they form part of comprehensive, and hence more contestable, conceptions of the good.

4. WORK, PRACTICES, AND THE MARKET

Rawls and Galston show that liberalism can accommodate a range of virtues by construing them in an instrumental fashion, as dispositions

---

[32] I think that this is because Macedo wants 'to avoid the theoretical debate about whether "the right" is prior to "the good" or vice versa' and the issue of how thick a theory of the good is implicit in liberal practice. See S. Macedo, *Liberal Virtues: Citizenship, Virtue, and Community in Liberal Constitutionalism* (Oxford, 1990), 5.

[33] Ibid. 99, 240, 256, 260, 265, 275.   [34] Ibid. 128–9, 271–2.

[35] Ibid. 128–9, 240, 267.   [36] Ibid. 213, 266–7.

required to sustain liberal institutions. Their accounts of the relevant virtues, and the way in which they are related to institutions, also have at least two advantages over MacIntyre's: first, they do not assume the possibility of agreement on a comprehensive conception of the good; second, they give systematic answers to the question of how certain external goods (such as money) should be distributed amongst citizens. But neither Rawls's nor Galston's account shows any real appreciation of MacIntyre's idea that practices, and the virtues the exercise of which they make possible, are marginalized within the modern economic order.

In the passage I quoted in Section 1, MacIntyre makes several claims only one of which I am going to defend, namely that the capitalist market makes it extremely difficult for work to be a practice for many people: work often does not supply internal goods and is mainly a means to external ones. This claim is based on some plausible assumptions about the dynamics of the capitalist market, and the pressures it places on the organization of the workplace, though the reality is more complex than MacIntyre acknowledges.

For MacIntyre, the work of the professional academic and of the professional artist are paradigm cases in which work constitutes a practice (though he would no doubt raise worries about the extent to which these forms of work have been corrupted by the pursuit of external goods). His paradigm case in which work falls short of being a practice is the production line. Those who work on production lines do so *only* in order to acquire the external goods which are necessary for them to survive. Presumably this is because work on a production line is insufficiently complex to provide opportunities to realize internal goods and to develop human powers to achieve excellence. Such work will almost always involve the repetition of simple tasks and hence lack the variety and depth that is required for it to constitute a practice.

Between the relatively clear cases in which work is a practice and those where it fails to be one, there is a large grey area. For example, can the work of a nurse constitute a practice? What about the services provided by a plumber or an electrician or a salesman? Nursing would seem to be sufficiently complex to provide the opportunity to realize internal goods and to develop human powers to achieve excellence. So too would electrical work and plumbing. Salesmanship might count as a practice in some cases, such as when it involves the possession and exercise of specialist knowledge in matching a product to a customer's needs, e.g. in selling computing systems. MacIntyre could of course argue that these forms of work can constitute practices but are prone to corruption by external goods. But it would be inadvisable for him to rest very much of his case for the marginalization of the practices by the market on this contention. Though the pursuit of external goods can come into conflict with the realization of internal ones, the two sorts of goods often seem to be in harmony. An electrician is likely to receive many of his contracts as a result of personal recommendation, and these will be based on his achievement of the standards of excellence which govern electrical installation. In many circumstances, an electrician will be rewarded with a continuous supply of external goods only if he is a good electrician. Similarly, a salesman who selectively represents, or misrepresents, the truth about the product he is selling runs the risk of losing future custom, so will generally have an interest in selling products which really do meet the customer's needs. Of course, this interest may not be overriding on any particular occasion, so the prospect of immediate external goods may triumph, but there are limits to how often that can happen and business remain good. So if MacIntyre's case for the marginalization of the practices is to be plausible, it must rest in large part on the idea that the market puts constraints on the way in which services are provided and production is organized which mean that work is incapable of being a practice for many people. Though this claim can be exaggerated, I think that there is kernel of truth in it which can be best perceived by considering the kind of pressures which the market exerts upon work.

The capitalist market is driven primarily by the desire of employers to maximize profits (or at least to make healthy profits) and hence by the desire for efficiency. Though companies are generally run by managers rather than owners or shareholders, managers will retain their positions, and be judged as successful, only if they provide owners or investors with a good return on their capital. Even those who work in the public sphere, i.e. directly or indirectly for the state, cannot be entirely insulated from market pressures. Sometimes it will be efficient to organize work so that it is a practice. When it is a practice, job satisfaction will be higher, since engaging in practices involves the exercise and development of a range of human capacities; as a result, workers are more likely to be self-motivated, and good workers may be easier to recruit, so the process will in certain respects be made more efficient. But it would be naïve to suppose that this is likely to be the case in general: in manufacturing, production lines are often going to be the most efficient way of organizing and controlling production. Since production lines can be used to set the pace of work, allowing workers greater autonomy is unlikely to lead to increased productivity. It also seems to be true generally that production and the provision of services become more efficient the more specialized they are.[37] If this is correct, then market pressures will mean that the tasks people perform will tend to become less and less varied, providing less and less scope for individuals to exercise a range of capacities, with the result that people's skills will often be developed at work in a very one-sided fashion. When this happens, work lacks sufficient complexity for it to be a practice, and it is difficult for it to involve the exercise of varied virtues, or indeed some specific ones. For example, the virtue of taking pride in what one does suffers: it makes sense to take pride in one's work only if one can see it as worth while, not merely in the narrow sense of providing something that people want, but in the wider sense of developing one's capacities and being a valuable activity in itself.

My general claim in defence of MacIntyre is that the capitalist market will favour work arrangements which are more efficient, since they will be more profitable, and these arrangements will often prevent work from being a practice. This point no doubt needs qualification to take into account the diversity of work for the market, but contains sufficient truth to provide some justification for MacIntyre's claim that the modern economic order is hostile to practices, and hence to the virtues. (I do not want to defend all of MacIntyre's claims about work and its relationship to practices: for example, he seems to think that pre-modern institutions allowed work to flourish as a practice, but that surely provides a misleadingly romantic view of how work was for most people under feudalism.)

Much of what I have said in support of MacIntyre resonates with Marx's writings on how the market affects the organization of production, but does not rest on Marx's contention that the interests of capitalists and workers are fundamentally opposed; indeed, it is compatible with allowing that everyone is better off, in terms of their share of certain important external goods, under some form of capitalism than they would be under any alternative form of economic arrangements.

As I remarked earlier, Rawls and Galston tend to ignore MacIntyre's claim that the practices are marginalized by the modern economic order. Rawls can perhaps be forgiven for this, since in his more recent writings

---

[37] Marx seems to believe that the tendency in capitalist societies is towards greater and greater specialization in the division of labour. See, e.g., K. Marx, *The German Ideology: Part I*, in R. C. Tucker (ed.), *The Marx-Engels Reader*, 2nd. edn. (New York, 1978), 146–200, pp. 150–1.

he is less interested in justifying particular institutions, such as the market, than establishing the principles of justice which should govern the choice of those institutions. In *A Theory of Justice*, however, Rawls has no doubt that these principles will favour the market in *some* form,[38] and once he comes to apply the principles he defends to the selection of institutions, he cannot avoid the issue of whether work should be organized so that it can be a practice. One of the principles he argues for—the difference principle—favours institutions which maximize the worst-off group's quantity of primary goods. Primary goods are defined as 'social conditions and all-purpose means to enable human beings to realize and exercise their moral powers and to pursue their final ends'.[39] Since Rawls rightly counts self-respect and self-esteem as primary goods (though he tends to conflate the two), the difference principle would favour institutions which allow work to be a practice over those that do not *if* that would increase the worst-off group's quantity of primary goods by providing them with higher levels of self-respect and self-esteem. Rawls gives no compelling reason for denying that the organization of work may have a profound effect on people's self-respect and self-esteem; he simply disregards that possibility.[40]

In *A Theory of Justice*, Rawls also presents what he calls the Aristotelian Principle as a plausible hypothesis about human motivation: 'other things equal, human beings enjoy the exercise of their realized capacities (their innate or trained abilities), and this enjoyment increases the more the capacity is realized, or the greater its complexity.'[41] He adds that if the Aristotelian Principle captures a relatively strong tendency, then 'in the design of social institutions a large place has to be made for it, otherwise human beings will find their culture and form of life dull and empty'.[42] It is difficult for him to avoid the conclusion that (other things being equal) institutions which allow work to become a practice should be favoured over those that do not.

Galston makes no effort to answer MacIntyre's criticism that the modern economic order marginalizes practices and hence the virtues. He argues that there are various 'liberal virtues' in the economic sphere, but these are conceived simply as character traits which are required for

---

[38] See J. Rawls, *A Theory of Justice* (Oxford, 1971), 270–4.

[39] J. Rawls, 'Kantian Constructivism in Moral Theory', *Journal of Philosophy* 77 (1980), 515–72, p. 526.

[40] For a related discussion, see G. Doppelt, 'Rawls' System of Justice: a Critique from the Left', *Nous* 15 (1981), 259–307.   [41] Rawls, *A Theory of Justice*, 426.

[42] Ibid. 429.

a basically capitalist market economy to run smoothly and efficiently.[43] If Galston had taken MacIntyre's analysis of work in a capitalist market economy more seriously, he might have been less complacent about whether it really does serve liberal purposes, or allow the virtues to flourish.

5. WHAT INSTITUTIONS WOULD RESPECT THE VIRTUES?

MacIntyre's solution to the marginalization of practices in modernity is difficult to discern. He writes: 'What matters . . . is the construction of local forms of community within which civility and the intellectual and moral life can be sustained through the new dark ages which are already upon us.'[44] But if a major part of the problem is that work is now largely at the service of impersonal capital, and hence cannot constitute a practice for most people, it is not clear how this is solved by constructing local forms of community, unless these somehow opt out of the capitalist system. If this is MacIntyre's thought, it begins to look as if he has a romantic yearning for pre-modern institutions which organized work around the household. But I take it that even if this were a genuine possibility (I doubt whether it is), it would not be an attractive one. Modern forms of technology are not compatible with this way of organizing work, and have brought enough benefits with them (even taking into account environmental disasters) for the idea of wholly abandoning them to be too desperate a solution; and in any case it would be a mistake to hold up pre-modern institutions as some sort of ideal to which we should aspire.

What then are the possibilities? We might simply conclude that work can never be a practice for many people, since much of it is by nature boring and repetitive; that if practices and the virtues are to flourish it will have to be outside of work—for example, in people's leisure activities. Capitalism has progressively increased the leisure time of working people (in the developed world at least) and is likely to continue to do so. But a large proportion of people's waking lives is still spent working, and there is no real prospect of this changing in the near future, so that would be an unhappy conclusion to arrive at.

---

[43] See Galston, *Liberal Purposes*, 223–4.   [44] *AV* 245.

Some socially necessary work is perhaps by its very nature incapable of becoming a practice, but it does not follow in a straightforward way that the people who do this work cannot be engaged in a practice for a significant proportion of their working lives. We can make a distinction between a job and the tasks which make it up. Some or all of the tasks which currently constitute some job may be intrinsically boring and repetitive, but an arrangement in which these tasks were rotated around a group of people, rather than given to just one person, could in principle allow a good proportion of each person's work to be a practice, even though it involved some mindless tasks.

Any moderately complex economy which is tolerably efficient will surely have to give a central role to the market in some form. F. A. Hayek argued convincingly that the system of pricing in market economies provides by far the best means of co-ordinating the plans of different economic agents, and that alternative ways of organizing production and consumption will lead to gross inefficiency when this is judged in terms of how successful they are in co-ordinating these plans.[45] But a market economy need not be capitalist. If, say, the cause of the marginalization of practices were not the market *per se*, but the capitalist market, then the solution might be to preserve the market but abandon capitalism, or, at least, to constrain it. (That solution would, of course, have to command widespread support; if it were to be successful, it would need to be a democratic choice.) There are different ways in which this might be done. One way would be to design a market in which a substantial proportion of the basic economic agents were co-operatives and leased capital from state banks. Co-operatives would be self-managing units, each of which made collective decisions about how the workplace should be organized, and competed against each other in a relatively free market.[46] Could that provide more space for

---

[45] See e.g. F. A. Hayek, 'The Use of Knowledge in Society', *American Economic Review* 35 (1945), 519–30, reprinted in his *Individualism and Economic Order* (London, 1949). For recent defences of Hayek, see D. Shapiro, 'Reviving the Socialist Calculation Debate: a Defence of Hayek against Lange', *Social Philosophy and Policy* 6 (1989), 139–59; N. Arnold, 'Marx, Central Planning, and Utopian Socialism', *Social Philosophy and Policy* 6 (1989), 160–99, esp. sect. iii. For a different view, see J. O'Neill, 'Markets, Socialism, and Information: a Reformulation of a Marxian Objection to the Market', *Social Philosophy and Policy* 6 (1989), 200–10.

[46] This proposal is of course radically underdescribed: on what basis would state banks decide to whom they are going to lease capital? Would wage labour be outlawed? What would happen if a co-operative were unable to compete successfully? See, e.g., J. Elster and K. Moene, *Alternatives to Capitalism* (Cambridge, 1989); J. Le Grand and S. Estrin (eds.), *Market Socialism* (Oxford, 1989); D. Miller, *Market, State, and Community:*

work to flourish as a practice in MacIntyre's sense? Perhaps, though it is difficult to be sure.[47]

Market forces would still operate and create a pressure towards efficient production, but the hope would be that (under normal circumstances) groups of workers would be in a position to choose to sacrifice some measure of efficiency in order to organize their work so that it enabled them to exercise and develop various human capacities, and exercise and develop various virtues in the process. They might, for example, opt for a system of task rotation. There is *some* reason to suppose that in relatively hospitable economic circumstances, workers would be able to place the internal goods associated with job satisfaction above the single-minded pursuit of external goods. In so far as workers would rather do jobs that have greater variety, and which allow the development of human capacities, they have an incentive to organize work so that it becomes a practice. In a capitalist market economy, in contrast, employers and managers have no incentive to organize work in this way, or to give workers a choice about whether to do so, unless this would increase profits. This suggests that it is likely that work would become a practice for more people under a market socialist system than under capitalism. This is all rather speculative, however. It is difficult to predict what decisions co-operatives would make in such a system. Workers in a co-operative might simply choose arrangements that they expected to maximize their profits, even if this prevented them from organizing their work as a practice. If a market socialist system were to function in the context of a global capitalist economy, then market pressures might be sufficiently strong for it to prove impossible for co-operatives to sacrifice any efficiency at all and still survive.

No firm conclusions have emerged from my discussion of whether and how work might become a practice for more people. I have argued that there is some truth in MacIntyre's claim that the modern economic order marginalizes practices, and hence the virtues, because it does not allow much of the work performed in it to be a practice. This is an

---

Theoretical Foundations of Market Socialism (Oxford, 1989), for discussion of these issues. John Gray transforms questions such as these into objections to market socialism: see J. Gray, *Beyond the New Right: Markets, Government and the Common Environment* (London, 1993), 92–9.

[47] Of course the case for market socialism does not rest solely on the idea that it would allow greater scope for work to be a practice. The main case for it, which I do not discuss in this paper, rests on grounds of social justice.

important claim that is neglected by his liberal critics. MacIntyre does not, however, offer us much by way of an alternative to the methods of organizing work with which we are familiar. I have suggested that there is perhaps an alternative: to restructure the market radically, so that workers come to have greater control over their working conditions. But even that might not produce the desired result. We may be forced to conclude that work can never be a practice except for a few, even though that would be an unfortunate conclusion for the many.[48]

[48] I would like to thank John Cottingham, Roger Crisp, Brad Hooker, David Miller, and John Preston for their helpful comments on the previous draft.

13

Feminism, Moral Development, and the Virtues

SUSAN MOLLER OKIN

How does virtue ethics look from a feminist point of view—that is to say, a perspective that expects women and men to be treated as equally human and due equal concern and respect? In this essay, focusing primarily on two accounts of virtue ethics—one of the earliest, Aristotle's, and one of the most recent, Alasdair MacIntyre's—I discuss three respects in which virtue ethics is problematic for anyone, however sympathetic, who approaches this mode of thinking about or practising morality as a feminist. My task in the first section is to enquire whether Aristotle's and MacIntyre's accounts of the virtues, in themselves, meet or fail to meet the feminist expectation of equal concern and respect for all human beings. My next task, following a negative finding on the first question, is to explore the problem that is inherent in these virtue theorists' accounts of early moral education, given their endorsement (or at least acceptance) of the belief that women are incapable of achieving truly 'human' virtue. Third, having shown that the two important examples of virtue ethics I examine involve considerable problems from a feminist point of view, I engage in discussion with those who, in recent years, claim to have found in virtue ethics something especially feminine, or even feminist. I end the essay by making some suggestions about what I consider to be a more tenable and appropriate feminist approach to the virtues.

1. THE ANDROCENTRISM AND ÉLITISM OF THE VIRTUES

'The virtues', in predominant conceptions from Homer to Alasdair MacIntyre and beyond, have often been presented as *human* virtues. But what have actually been emphasized and regarded as *unqualifiedly* virtuous are often qualities of character and abilities regarded as admirable only in free men of some social standing. That 'the virtues' are qualities attainable only by some—distinguished by sex, wealth, and social status—is abundantly clear in Homer. In the *Iliad* and the *Odyssey*, the highest words of praise, *aretē* ('virtue' or 'excellence') and *agathos* ('good'), *meant* that the individual to whom they were applied possessed both the internal skills and the external resources necessary for acting as a successful leader and warrior—a hero.[1]

The word *aretē*, itself is derived from *anēr*, meaning 'man' as differentiated from 'woman'. Only qualified and inferior forms of *aretē*, having to do with performing their respective supportive and subservient functions well, attach to women, slaves, and those free males who are unsuited, for whatever reason, to be heroes.

This is still the case, though slightly less obviously so, in the works of Aristotle. There is little doubt throughout Aristotle's ethics that, though the *eudaimonia* toward which it aims is ostensibly the human good (the good for the *anthrōpos*), his account of the virtues takes the perspective of the free, educated, and leisured male members of society. A number of feminist theorists, including me, have demonstrated the extent to which Aristotle's political and ethical arguments and conclusions *depend upon* the exclusion of free women, slaves of both sexes, and men engaged in manual labour both from 'the good life for a human being' and from citizenship in the best form of *polis*.[2]

By this account, it is inconceivable to regard Aristotle as a feminist, and it seems doubtful that one would find much in his politics and moral philosophy that might be useful to those thinking through issues from a feminist point of view. Recently, however, there has been some attempt to rehabilitate an Aristotelianism that can help to overcome (for feminists as well as others) some of the ostensible limitations of liberalism.[3] But we need to consider just how much revision of Aristotle must be done in order to achieve a theory that can be helpful in promoting

[1] This is well summed up by A. W. H. Adkins. See *Merit and Reponsibility: A Study in Greek Values* (Oxford, 1960), 32–3.

[2] See, for example, S. M. Okin, *Women in Western Political Thought* (Princeton, 1979), ch. 4; L. Lange, 'Woman is Not a Rational Animal: On Aristotle's Biology of Reproduction'; and E. Spelman, 'Aristotle and the Politicization of the Soul', in S. Harding and M. Hintikka (eds.), *Discovering Reality: Feminist Perspectives on Epistemology, Metaphysics, Methodology, and Philosophy of Science* (Dordrecht, Netherlands, 1983), 1–15 and 17–30 respectively.

[3] See, for example, L. Hirshman, 'The Book of "A"', *Texas Law Review* 70 (1992), 971–1012; M. Nussbaum, 'Aristotle, Feminism, and Needs for Functioning', *Texas Law Review* 70 (1992), 1019–28, and 'Human Capabilities, Female Human Beings', in M. Nussbaum and J. Glover (eds.) *Women, Culture, and Development* (Oxford, 1995), 61–104.

women's equality with men, and whether, once such revision is achieved, it is still possible to call the resulting theory Aristotelian.

Those, including me, who have concluded that Aristotle's philosophy is distinctly and thoroughly anti-feminist, have focused mainly on his instrumental treatment of free women as reproducers and household managers, who (together, of course, with slaves of both sexes and free manual labourers) liberate some men by providing for their day-to-day needs and enabling them to have the leisure needed to be a citizen or a philosopher—all in all, to achieve human flourishing or *eudaimonia*. We have interpreted the brief but key passages about women, their virtues, their roles, and their capacity for rationality that occur in the *Politics*, the two versions of the *Ethics*, and the *Rhetoric*, in the light of Aristotle's biological writings, particularly the *Generation of Animals*. Here, Aristotle clearly *assumes* women's inferiority. By a series of completely unsubstantiated assertions and invalid inferences (hardly characteristic of his other work) Aristotle concludes that women, 'a deformity of nature', came into existence only to perform their (lesser) role in the sexual reproduction of men.

As I shall explain, in my view this distortion of the respective roles of women and men in human life affects significantly a great deal of the rest of what Aristotle says. But some other scholars, while concerned with the equality and flourishing of women, disagree. Taking a far more positive view of what Aristotle's philosophy (without major revision) can contribute to feminism, they regard his reproductive biology—virulent sexism and all—as an aberration, best ignored.[4] How can we decide whether Aristotle's reproductive biology is just a piece of silliness we can disregard in order to appreciate and make use of other aspects of his moral and political philosophy, especially his account of the virtues? In order to consider the potential of Aristotelianism to be a non-sexist ethics, it is important to look closely at his account of the virtues, in order to see the nature and the extent of its androcentrism, and to point out some of the internal problems of such an ethic that are caused or exacerbated by such exclusivity. This will help us to see whether an Aristotelian type of ethic might be made at the same time more consistent and more universalizable.

[4] See Nussbaum, 'Aristotle', 1020–1. Nussbaum regards Aristotle's account of human reproduction as 'both misogynist and silly', and concludes that, were he to have applied his own methods properly, he 'would have ascertained that the capabilities of women were (as Plato already had argued) comparable to those of men'. She concludes that Aristotle can prove a valuable ally for feminists in search of a moral theory more adequate and complete than liberalism.

When Aristotle first embarks on his long discussion of the virtues in the *Nicomachean Ethics*, he mentions some aspects of human life that have nothing to do with human excellence (moral or intellectual virtue). He mentions, as a clear example, the 'vegetative' element of the soul: 'that which causes nutrition and growth'. Since it exists even in nurslings, embryos, and non-human species, and seems to function most in sleep, he concludes that 'it has by its nature no share in human excellence'.[5] We are left with a picture of humans, from the embryonic stage through to adulthood, as beings whose nutrition and growth is effected through the power of the most passive and least human part of their own souls. It is remarkable that Aristotle writes of nutrition and growth as something each person achieves alone, when in fact (apart from the workings of the digestive system) it is achieved only with the help of those—in his time, women and slaves—who provide the food and services required for even basic, let alone maximal, growth. This makes me question whether Aristotle was at all close to cognizance of either the extent to which human beings depend on others, or the material conditions necessary for human flourishing. He seems to have preferred to recognize the political, intellectual, and emotional interdependence of free and equal men rather than to acknowledge their day-to-day material dependence on the services and products of women and slaves.

Aristotle then proceeds to discuss the human virtues, dividing them into the moral and the intellectual. He argues that moral virtues are neither passions nor faculties but 'states of character', that virtuous behaviour of various kinds results from following the mean between two extremes, and that moral virtue as such is the disposition to choose the mean. The virtues Aristotle discusses explicitly and at some length are courage, temperance, liberality, magnificence, pride, good temper, friendliness, truthfulness (about oneself and one's abilities or accomplishments), ready wit, and, finally, justice—which is something of a 'catchall'. It includes both fairness in distribution and retribution, and behaviour that is in accordance with the law.

In the *Politics*, however, Aristotle makes it abundantly clear that all of these virtues are relative to persons and their social positions. Speaking of women and slaves relative to free men, he says:

[T]hey must all share in . . . [moral goodness], but not in the same way—each sharing only to the extent required for the discharge of his or her function . . . It is thus clear that . . . temperance—and similarly fortitude and justice—

---

[5] *Nicomachean Ethics* (= *NE*), tr. W. D. Ross (Oxford, 1925), 1102^a32–$^b12$.

are not, as Socrates held, the same in a woman as they are in a man. Fortitude in the one, for example, is shown in connexion with ruling; in the other, it is shown in connexion with serving; and the same is true of the other forms of goodness . . .[6]

We know from his biology that Aristotle considered women to be thoroughly inferior to men—'deviations' or 'deformities' in nature, existing solely so that men might be reproduced in such a way that their superior form or soul might be separate from their inferior matter or body.[7] We also learn from the *Politics* Aristotle's conclusion that women's power to reason must—as with others destined to perform certain functions—be proportionate and suitable to their function: though women have to a certain extent the faculty of deliberation, it is 'lacking in authority' in comparison with the fully authoritative reason of free men.[8]

If we were reading the *Nicomachean Ethics* alone, though, without knowledge of his other works, would we conclude that Aristotle's examples of the most important moral virtues apply to women as much as to men? I think even under these conditions it would be impossible to do this. Why? First, his discussion of the virtues is worded in terms of men, and many of his examples are explicitly from the male point of view. In his account of courage, he says that it is right, not cowardly, to fear insult to one's wife and children; in his account of how one cannot be unjust to oneself, his examples include not being able to commit adultery with one's own wife; his discussions of liberality and magnificence are all about money, to which most women of his time had little or no access.[9] One needs little interpretative skill to note the sexism implicit in his assertion that the proud man will have 'a slow step . . . , a deep voice, and a level utterance', as contrasted with him who has 'a shrill voice and a rapid gait'.[10] He differentiates clearly between 'political justice', which pertains to relations amongst free and equal men, and 'household justice', which applies between husbands and wives. He draws an analogy between the type of 'metaphorical' justice that operates between the rational and the irrational parts of a man's soul and the justice that exists between master and servant or husband and wife. Both of these,

---

[6] *Politics*, tr. E. Barker (Oxford, 1946), 1260^{a}14–24.

[7] *Generation of Animals*, tr. A. L. Peck (London, 1943), 727–30, 732, 738, 766–7, 775. For more extensive discussions of this, see Okin, *Women in Western Political Thought*, 81–3.   [8] *Politics*, 1252^b, 1260^a, 1277^b.

[9] *NE* 1115^{a}22–3; 1138^{a}25; IV. 1–2. It should be recalled here that the ancient Greek term for committing adultery (*moicheuein*) was reserved for sexual acts between a man and a married woman.   [10] *NE* 1125^{a}12–16.

he says, are like the 'mutual justice' between ruler and ruled.[11] There can be no doubt at all that, throughout Aristotle's account of the virtues, his subject—his potentially virtuous human being—is the free male head of a household.

In spite of all this, however, are 'the virtues' themselves necessarily male? In the lengthy passage from the *Politics* quoted above, Aristotle suggests that justice, temperance, and courage, for example, can be exhibited in different versions—those suited to persons who rule and those suited to persons who serve the former. Since he provides no examples, we are left wondering what virtues such as 'justice in a slave' or 'courage in a wife' might be like. In the light of Aristotle's teleology as a whole, and this passage in particular, it seems that they must be qualities that somehow resemble justice or courage in a free man, but that still enable slaves or women respectively to perform at least as well the functions required of them by free men. Courage in a woman or a slave, then, could hardly be exemplified by defying the command—however unjust—of a husband or master. Whatever such virtues are, and however pervasive such functionally defined virtues may have been throughout history, no such account of the virtues can free itself of sexism, racism, and assumptions about the naturalness of social hierarchies. Whether there can be a coherent and comprehensive set of 'non-gendered' virtues is an issue I shall take up later.

Aristotle, of course, was living in a society in which slavery and the subordination of women were by and large both taken for granted. Though some people, most notably Plato, at times questioned both of these systems of domination, most did not. Thus it is not remarkable— though it is course regrettable, given the extent of his influence—that Aristotle's theory of the virtues should reflect these conventionally held beliefs. With Alasdair MacIntyre, however, the situation is entirely different. His most influential works have been written during the last quarter of the twentieth century. But as we shall see, his attempts to breathe new life into an Aristotelian/Christian ethic of the virtues have failed to address adequately the social hierarchy and domination inherent in the Aristotelian tradition and, of particular interest to us here, to accommodate the changing status of women.

MacIntyre appeals to an Aristotelian theory of the virtues in reaction to what he sees as the philosophical weakness of, and the social damage caused by, liberalism. In *After Virtue*, he argues that we must return to the classical tradition of ethics, revolving around the concept of the

---

[11] *NE* 1134^{b}15–18; V, 11, 1138^{b}5–8.

virtues, if we are to be rescued from the incoherence of modern moral language and practice. Centred on Aristotle, with earlier roots in Homer, this tradition continues through the medieval variants of Aristotelianism combined with religion, experiences a brief revival in the Scottish Enlightenment, and unfortunately, according to MacIntyre, fades out after this and the contributions of a few other expositors, such as Jane Austen and the Jacobins.

In *Whose Justice? Which Rationality?*, MacIntyre follows up on his previous conclusions by attempting to evaluate the rationality of the traditions those in the Western world find available to them. He finds *his* most rational tradition in the Thomistic synthesis.[12] In contrast with modern liberal theories that value 'the capacity to detach oneself from any particular standpoint or point of view',[13] what characterizes the virtue ethics of the traditions he values is their thorough rootedness in the context of a particular social order. Specific social roles are the most fundamental assumptions on which the traditions build, and the virtues around which their ethics centre are the qualities necessary for the performance of these roles.

In spite of its still unfinished nature, MacIntyre's work has become a very influential example of virtue-centred moral philosophy, and is treated in some circles as a worthy critique of and substitute for contemporary liberalism. Some philosophers have criticized MacIntyre's Aristotelian project from various points of view, including its lack of political engagement and of consideration of 'hard cases'.[14] But few commentators have confronted the pervasive élitism of MacIntyre's defence of the traditions, and its equally pervasive sexism has only recently been challenged.[15] Indeed, just as there are feminists now looking back—not sufficiently critically, in my view—to Aristotle for

[12] MacIntyre does not think that the same tradition will be most rational, or practically suitable, for everyone. See *Whose Justice? Which Rationality?* (London, 1988), 393–4. With respect to how one is to begin to find out which tradition may provide one's moral framework, he says: 'The initial answer is: that will depend upon *who you are and how you understand yourself*' (my italics).

[13] A. MacIntyre, *After Virtue* (London, 1981), 119.

[14] See, for example, A. Gutmann, 'Communitarian Critics of Liberalism', *Philosophy and Public Affairs* 14 (1985), 308–22; H. Hirsch, 'The Threnody of Liberalism: Constitutional Liberty and the Renewal of Community', *Political Theory* 14 (1986), 423–49; W. Kymlicka, 'Liberalism and Communitarianism', *Canadian Journal of Philosophy* 18 (1988), 181–203; J. Wallach, 'Liberals, Communitarians, and the Tasks of Political Theory', *Political Theory* 15 (1987), 581–611, and 'Contemporary Aristotelianism', *Political Theory* 20 (1992), 613–41, pp. 625–7.

[15] See, however, John Exdell's excellent paper, 'Ethics, Ideology, and Feminine Virtue', in M. Hanen and K. Nielsen (eds.), *Science, Morality and Feminist Theory, Canadian Journal*

help in escaping what they perceive as the alienating individualism of liberalism, so also have some feminists looked to MacIntyre as an antidote to what they see as the prevailing Kantianism. But feminists need to be wary of such alliances.[16]

In MacIntyre's work, despite his rejection of Aristotle's biology and his adoption of gender-neutral language, the virtues are still centred around the lives of upper-status males.[17] His interpretation of Homer leaves one with the false impression that the epics are about communitarian cultures with traditions of mutually agreed upon and widely shared values. But we must confront the fact that its ethic was not one of genuinely 'shared values', but reflected the dominance of a male warrior élite. Given this, it is especially urgent that we evaluate that society and its ethic from the points of view of *all* of its members. MacIntyre's account of Aristotle's virtue ethics is just as inadequate in its attempts to deal with the problem of exclusivity and social domination. Much of the time, aided by falsely gender-neutral language, he writes as if the Aristotelian ethic were supposed to apply to all of us. He writes, for example: 'The soundness of a particular practical argument, framed in terms of the goods of excellence, is independent of its force for any particular person.'[18] The implication of much of his account is that all were eligible to share in the whole life of the *polis*. But of course this impression is false, and some of the time MacIntyre argues directly against it. He acknowledges that some goods were 'valued only for their own sake' and others 'only . . . valued as means to some further good'.[19] He points out that Aristotle's theory of political justice 'unfortunately' depends on his belief that farmers, artisans, merchants, and women cannot exercise the virtues 'necessary for participation in the active life of the best kind of *polis*'. But while acknowledging that Aristotle's social theory is 'deformed by his beliefs about women and about the nature of slaves', he does not explain how a modern Aristotelian like himself can overcome this rather large problem.[20]

---

of Philosophy, Supp. vol. 13 (1987), 169–99, esp. pp. 173–4, 179–82, 189–99; and S. M. Okin, *Justice, Gender, and the Family* (New York, 1989), 43–62, 69–72. Gutmann's and Kymlicka's critiques (see Note 14 above) briefly raise the problem of gender.

[16] See, for example, Annette Baier, 'What do Women Want in a Moral Theory?', *Nous* 19 (1985), 53–63, and 'The Need for More than Justice', in Hanen and Nielsen, *Science, Morality and Feminist Theory*, 41–56. Compare M. Friedman, 'Feminism and Modern Friendship: Dislocating the Community', *Ethics* 99 (1989), 275–90, and Okin, *Justice, Gender, and the Family*, 42–3.   [17] See Okin, ibid. ch. 3.

[18] MacIntyre, *Whose Justice? Which Rationality?*, 45.   [19] Ibid. 34.

[20] Ibid. 104, 121.

MacIntyre tries to replace Aristotle's metaphysical biology with his own emphasis on traditions and their 'practices'.[21] Practices are activities whose ends are internal to them. And the human virtues, in MacIntyre's account, are those qualities that enable people to carry out these practices well, and thereby to flourish. Perhaps this approach might help him to resolve some of the problems of domination discussed above. Despite his rather surprising readiness in *Whose Justice? Which Rationality?* to discard the family in order to respond to critics of Aristotle's subordination of women, in *After Virtue* MacIntyre does not ignore family life.[22] Rather, he includes 'the making and sustaining of family life' as a practice, along with others, such as playing games and following intellectual pursuits.[23] But unfortunately, this characterization of family life as a practice brings with it at least three problems, especially for a feminist trying to engage with and perhaps to make use of the theory.

First, in contrast to the practices MacIntyre most emphasizes, domestic life is not an elective but an *essential* practice for human flourishing. Without the child-bearing and nurturance that currently occur in families of one form or other, there would *be* no people to live 'the good life'. Second, as is surely obvious, past and present family arrangements make it considerably more difficult for women than for men to participate fully in intellectual, artistic, political, and other aspects of a flourishing human life. For both these reasons, practices within the household surely require closer ethical scrutiny than other practices that are less necessary for humans to flourish. However, instead of addressing this problem, MacIntyre goes in the opposite direction: he *denies* that, since the eighteenth century, family life has been a practice. Why? Because he considers that, from that 'key moment' when production moved outside of the household, what took place there was no longer within 'the realm of practices with goods internal to themselves'.[24]

John Exdell has addressed this problem very well. He argues that, though MacIntyre does not explicitly discuss the role of women in *After Virtue*, he perceives as pivotal the period when, with industrialization,

---

[21] See Andrew Mason's paper in the present volume.

[22] In *Whose Justice? Which Rationality?*, MacIntyre takes notice of the problem of Aristotle's sexism, only to suggest a solution for it that is utterly inconsistent with his own preference for the Thomistic tradition. He looks back to Plato for a means to eliminate or at least reduce women's inequality: abolish the family. For further discussion of the inadequacy of this solution, even within the framework of MacIntyre's own theory, see Okin, *Justice, Gender, and the Family*, 54–5.   [23] MacIntyre, *After Virtue*, 175.

[24] Ibid. 211.

women were transformed from skilled contributors to the household economy into either leisured ladies or (in the case of the vast majority) drudges as domestic servants or factory workers. As Exdell says:

In substance, MacIntyre's analysis suggests that when modern commercial society transferred production into the market, it also destroyed women's domestic labor as a practice. The reduction of women's sphere to 'homemaking' and the rearing of young children meant greatly reduced opportunities for realizing the various goods of self-development available to women practicing traditional productive skills.[25]

In so far as women (in addition to men who had become the employees of capitalists) were no longer engaged in human practices, they were *ipso facto* cut off from the exercise of the virtues. However, as Exdell goes on to argue, MacIntyre misses the important fact that, as most production moved out of the household, women were, increasingly, solely responsible for taking care of children—physically, emotionally, and intellectually. It is striking that MacIntyre appears to think that the work women did in pre-industrial society, such as making cheese and soap, and raising cattle and poultry, gave them more opportunity to exercise skill, creativity, and virtue than is available to women who take care of children. The child-centered virtues, so much needed in our homes as well as in our schools and communities, seem to have no home within MacIntyre's philosophy.

2. THE EDUCATION OF A VIRTUOUS CHARACTER

How are the virtues taught? Ethics of the virtues—most clearly in Aristotle's account, but also in others—depend heavily on moral education, by which the virtues are inculcated by example, practice, and the development of practical reason. Success in this results in the development of a person of good *character*. When we consider that, as I have shown, 'the virtues' are conceived of androcentrically and women's virtues are regarded as both distinct and inferior, and put this together with the almost universal fact of female early child-rearing, the question arises: how *can* very young children be educated so that their early habits instil in them virtuous character?

---

[25] Exdell, 'Ethics, Ideology, and Feminine Virtue', 180.

Aristotle considered the early environment of children extremely important for their moral and intellectual development. Thus, he wrote, 'the legislator should make the education of the young his chief and foremost concern'. It is seldom noted that, in his discussion of the ideal state, Aristotle takes up more space discussing this subject than everything else put together, or that what he means by 'education' actually begins before conception, and extends to the minutest details of family life.[26] He argued that early environmental factors, especially the influence of adults, were formative factors in the character of children. He says that we (meaning men) ought to be brought up with virtuous habits 'from our very youth', since the love of pleasure that so influences us is 'ingrained' in us; it has 'grown up with us all from our infancy'.[27]

How early *does* the moral development of children begin? Modern researchers—confirming Aristotle's observations or hunches—tend to think that it begins very early indeed. It is now widely agreed, as William Damon has recently noted, that signs of empathy and recognition of the emotional states of others can be observed even in infants: 'Most scholars believe . . . that the potential for moral-emotional reactions is present at birth.' He also writes: 'there is by now ample evidence of consistency and regularity in children's moral behaviour, and there are many indications that enduring aspects of character are indeed formed early.' 'By the age of four or five,' according to Damon, 'children can be interviewed about their views on moral standards like sharing and fairness.'[28] So, it seems, Aristotle was quite right to stress very early childhood influences on moral development.

But this led to a problem that he gives no indication of having recognized. Because of his convictions that the development of character was greatly affected by early influences and that the family was the best place to raise children, Aristotle thought that a crucial part of moral development, until the age of seven, should take place in the family, after which boys should be publicly educated. Therefore—given that he both clearly endorsed the division of labour between the sexes, and said care must be taken that 'very little of . . . [children's] time is passed

---

[26] *Politics* 1331ᵇ–1342ᵇ. The quotation is from 1337ᵃ11–12. For further discussion of this and of its implications for the supposed separation of private from political life in Aristotle, see Okin, 'Women, Equality, and Citizenship', *Queen's Quarterly* 99 (1992), 56–71.　　[27] *NE* 1103ᵇ24, 1105ᵃ1–2. See also 1119ᵇ and *Politics* 1334ᵇ.
[28] W. Damon, *The Moral Child: Nurturing Children's Natural Moral Growth* (New York, 1988), 7, 13–16, 35.

in the company of slaves'—there is little doubt that he envisioned, as the principal agent of this early development, the children's mother.[29] The resulting problem, beautifully explored by Nancy Sherman in *The Fabric of Character*, is that Aristotle, while perceptive in recognizing the importance of early character development, left it under the day-to-day influence of persons whom, as we have seen, he deemed not fully rational, and incapable of fully human, or indeed any but instrumental, virtue.[30] Aristotle clearly regards the close *attachment* between parents and their children as essential for the care and development of the latter. As Sherman says, moral education in the family, in Aristotle's account, is not only—although it is in part—a matter of learning practical reasoning; parents need to be 'ready-to-hand models for emulation, as well as attentive judges of the child's specific needs and requirements'.[31] Moral character is to be acquired through the formation of good habits, for which the example of one to whom the child is deeply attached is crucial. It is not a matter of learning rules and then how to apply them. But given the relative absence of the father in the private sphere, we must ask how a person who lacks practical reason and cannot be relied upon to control her own passions can be a good moral role model for a young child. Aristotle neither acknowledges nor addresses this 'glaring problem'.[32]

MacIntyre is less clear than some other philosophers in the virtues tradition about *who* should educate children morally. However, he clearly thinks that moral education results at least in part from children's imbibing the stories that emanate from 'their tradition'. 'Mythology, in its original sense,' he says, 'is at the heart of things . . . And so too of course is that moral tradition from heroic society to its medieval heirs according to which the telling of stories has a key part in educating us into the virtues.' The only way to answer the question 'What am I to do?' is to answer first the question 'Of what story or stories do I find myself a part?'[33] However, when MacIntyre gives some typical examples of these

---

[29] *Politics* 1336ᵃ39–41. For Aristotle's arguments (against Plato) in favour of families, see *Politics* 1261ᵃ–1262ᵃ. On keeping young children out of the company of slaves and on the age that domestic education should give way to public, see *Politics* 1136ᵃ⁻ᵇ. On the division of labour, see *Politics* 1252ᵃ–1253ᵃ and *NE* 1152ᵇ–1153ᵃ.

[30] N. Sherman, *The Fabric of Character: Aristotle's Theory of Virtue* (Oxford, 1989), 144–56, esp. 150–6.

[31] Ibid. 152. The passage from Aristotle that Sherman quotes to back this up in fact mentions the father, not the mother, but this is impossible to reconcile with what he says elsewhere about the household duties of women, the importance of very early childhood, and the greater attachment of mothers than fathers to their children.   [32] Ibid. 153.

[33] MacIntyre, *After Virtue*, 201.

stories and the parts 'we' play in them, while the male characters he mentions range widely, the only explicitly female characters are a wicked stepmother and a suckling wolf.[34] He gives no indication of having noticed this. But surely, faced with such a limited choice of roles—and they are not exceptional, given the misogynistic quality of much of 'our' tradition—girls are unlikely to learn much that is positive about how to develop good character from its stories.[35] This brings us to some questions of great practical as well as theoretical significance: Does education in the virtues require departure from usual divisions of labour between the sexes? And why has this not been commonly recognized? I think it does require such departure. I have shown here and elsewhere how moral philosophers throughout the ages have, on the one hand, recognized the crucial importance of the early years for the development of a child's moral character, but have neglected the fact that it has been *women*—whether mothers or servants, and almost always disadvantaged and subordinated both within the family and in society at large—who have played a vastly greater role in the early care of children than have men. Prominent philosophers, with the notable exception of John Stuart Mill, have failed to see that the environment of an unjust family—whether mildly but persistently unfair in its allocation between men and women, girls and boys of resources, work, power, and leisure, or grossly unjust to the point of persistent psychological, sexual, or other physical abuse—is hardly the best 'school of justice'.

In *Justice, Gender, and the Family*, following in the footsteps of Mill in this respect, I make a more positive argument—that by making families themselves more just, we can expect to foster the development of a sense of justice in children. Rather than being one among many co-equal institutions of a just society, a just family is its essential foundation.[36] Within virtue ethics it seems to be generally agreed that moral character as a whole derives largely from habitual virtuous behaviour, and that the example of others—especially others to whom one is closely attached—can be an important element in encouraging such behaviour. Thus if any of the vices—not only injustice, but also dishonesty, stinginess, cruelty, hypocrisy, cowardice, or failure to be nurturant—is frequently exhibited in the practices of parents, it seems unlikely that

[34] Ibid.

[35] The paradox that requires moral education to begin in very early childhood, yet excludes women from moral equality, is found not only in virtue ethics. See Okin, 'Reason and Feeling in Thinking about Justice', *Ethics* 99 (1989), 229–49, for a discussion of this problem in the moral theories of Kant and Rawls.

[36] Okin, *Justice, Gender, and the Family*, 17–23, 97–100, 185–6.

their children will learn the opposite virtues. The feminist implications of this more general argument are not difficult to see.

3. ETHICS OF JUSTICE, ETHICS OF CARE: IS VIRTUE ETHICS 'WOMEN'S MORAL THEORY'?

Another recent attempt to marry feminism with virtue ethics consists of pointing out the similarities between anti-Kantian accounts of ethical thinking, such as Aristotle's, Hume's, and those of various contemporary theorists, and the 'different voice' ethic of what is often referred to as cultural feminism.[37] Just as these alternative accounts of moral virtue stress practical reason and attention to context, rather than the deductive application of general laws or principles, so, cultural feminists claim, do women tend to think and act morally—eschewing general rules, principles, or rights in favour of attention to particular others and the details of the situation at hand. But there are at least three problems with this parallel. First, there are real dangers in the type of sex-stereotyping that can emerge from such claims; second, there are significant differences between virtue ethics and what has been put forward as women's different voice; and finally, there is considerable ambiguity and doubt surrounding the empirical claims about sex differences in moral development.

Centred around the work of Carol Gilligan, debate has now gone on for more than a decade about whether, and if so how, women's moral development and moral thinking differ from those of men.[38] Gilligan first performed the important function of challenging, as gender-biased, Lawrence Kohlberg's scale of moral development, which was based on the study only of male respondents, and which, when used to measure women's moral development, showed it to be typically inferior to that of men. On the basis of interviews with fairly small samples of highly educated women and men and a few girls and boys, Gilligan discovered not female inferiority, but difference. Specifically, she found

a mode of thinking that is contextual and narrative rather than formal and abstract. This conception of morality as concerned with the activity of care

[37] Some of the strongest claims for the similarity of virtue ethics to Gilligan's findings are made by Annette Baier in 'The Need for More than Justice' (Note 16 above), and 'Hume, the Women's Moral Theorist?', in E. Kittay and D. Meyers (eds.), *Women and Moral Theory* (Totowa, NJ, 1987), 37–55.

[38] C. Gilligan, 'In a Different Voice: Women's Conception of the Self and of Morality', *Harvard Educational Review* 47 (1977), 481–517; *In a Different Voice* (Cambridge, Mass., 1982).

centers moral development around the understanding of responsibilities and relationships, just as the conception of morality as fairness ties moral development to the understanding of rights and rules.[39]

For those familiar with the history of ethics and political philosophy, Gilligan's claims have a familiar ring, since the type of particularistic, contextual, caring morality that Gilligan and her colleagues find in highly educated, contemporary US women is in some respects the same type of thinking that past philosophers have attributed to women. But not only have the philosophers pronounced women morally *different* from men, as Gilligan does—at least part of the time; unlike Gilligan, they have pronounced women morally *inferior*, and therefore justifiably excluded from the rights of full citizenship. I have discussed this problem of moral sex-stereotyping at some length elsewhere, and shall not dwell on it here.[40] Rather, I shall discuss some similarities and differences between Gilligan's 'different voice' and virtue ethics, and then address some questions that have been raised about her empirical claims.

There is little doubt that the type of morality Gilligan finds more characteristic of women has a closer resemblance to virtue ethics than to Kantian ethics. As moral philosophers have pointed out, the more 'robust and realistic' conception she presents in contrast to the focus on rights and principles can be traced back to Aristotle.[41] Nevertheless, in spite of their similarities, such as the focus on context and personal responsibilities rather than on principles and rights, there are also important differences. Most importantly, Gilligan's different voice eschews not only rights, but justice, which is a crucial virtue for many virtue theorists, including Aristotle and Hume. While it is not difficult to argue that the development of a sense of justice and of principles of justice may depend upon the prior development of feelings of care, empathy, and responsibility for others, most moral and political philosophers who regard justice as a central virtue would be unwilling to see it *replaced* by such virtues as care and empathy.[42] In addition, as Michele Moody-Adams has pointed out, there are other important virtues—those having to do with respect

[39] Gilligan, *In a Different Voice*, 19.

[40] See Okin, 'Thinking like a Woman', in D. Rhode (ed.), *Theoretical Perspectives on Sexual Difference* (New Haven, Conn., 1990), 145–59.

[41] O. Flanagan and K. Jackson, 'Justice, Care, and Gender: The Kohlberg–Gilligan Debate Revisited', *Ethics* 97 (1987), 622–37.

[42] See Baier, 'Hume, the Women's Moral Theorist?', 42; Okin, 'Reason and Feeling in Thinking about Justice', 243–6; S. Benhabib, 'The Generalized and the Concrete Other: The Kohlberg-Gilligan Controversy and Moral Theory', in her *Situating the Self: Gender, Community and Postmodernism in Contemporary Ethics* (New York, 1992), 148–77.

for the integrity of persons, especially—that are ignored or diminished in importance by the different voice ethic.[43]

The third major problem of the claim that Gilligan's findings about women's moral thinking parallel virtue ethics is that the evidence that there is any clear difference between women's and men's moral thinking about hypothetical issues is itself highly questionable. As numerous critics of *In a Different Voice* have pointed out, Gilligan herself is quite ambiguous on the subject, disclaiming in her preface the degree to which she typically generalizes about women and men throughout the book.[44] Some critics have also argued that the disclaimer seems to be closer to the truth than the claims made in the book. John Broughton, for example, analysing a number of Gilligan's subjects' transcripts, discovered that many of the women and men—even some of those Gilligan presents as archetypes of their sex—speak in both the supposedly masculine and the supposedly feminine voice.[45] It is even less clear that any such difference that might exist between the sexes in thinking about hypothetical situations translates itself into differences in either moral thinking or decisions about real dilemmas.

Even if these difficulties did not exist, it is unclear what the real nature of the differences is: sometimes, the 'different voice' is represented as being less universalist in its judgements, as being more attuned to particular contexts and persons. But what does this really mean, and when *is* it morally appropriate to think in these different ways? There is a vast difference between a juror's finding a criminal defendant guilty or not guilty depending on whether the defendant was the juror's best friend or aunt, and taking particular facts about a person into account when determining a whole range of issues ranging from criminal sentencing to child custody. Indeed, because of the strong tendency in most people to be partial to those they like or love, it is for good reason that, in many but by no means all cases when they are acting as citizens or members of humanity in general, people are considered virtuous in so far as they treat others impartially—*without* regard to particulars about them.

[43] M. M. Moody-Adams, 'Gender and the Complexity of Moral Voices', in C. Card (ed.), *Feminist Ethics* (Lawrence, Kan., 1991), 195–212.

[44] For example, compare p. 2 of *In a Different Voice* with the concluding paragraph of chapter 3, p. 105. See Moody-Adams, 'Gender and the Complexity of Moral Voices', 197; Okin, 'Thinking Like a Woman', 156; and, for a more extended and somewhat more sympathetic treatment of the issue, J. Tronto, 'Beyond Gender Difference to a Theory of Care', *Signs* 12 (1987), 644–63, esp. pp. 644–8.

[45] J. Broughton, 'Women's Rationality and Men's Virtues: A Critique of Gender Dualism in Gilligan's Theory of Moral Development', *Social Research* 50 (1983), 597–642.

Another question arises from the claim of scholars, such as Annette Baier, who find value in the ethics of care that has been particularly associated with women, and who then find examples of this 'different voice' in the philosophy of Aristotle, MacIntyre, Hume, Adam Smith, or one of the other male proponents of virtue ethics. What could explain Hume's being any more 'uncannily womanly in his moral wisdom' than Kant? What *is* it about MacIntyre but not Rawls that admits the former, but not the latter, to the ranks of those to whom 'the status of honorary women' should be given?[46] The answer is certainly not obvious. A more plausible stance, in my view at least, is to acknowledge that, in almost all moral theories and systems of moral practice, the 'different voice' has been present to a greater or lesser degree. In recent years, such critics of the 'different voice as female voice' as Owen Flanagan and Kathryn Jackson, Joan Tronto, and John Exdell have all pointed out that ethics focusing on particulars, context, and responsibility, rather than on universality, rules, and rights, goes back at least as far as Aristotle and has been voiced by many men as well as many women.

4. TOWARDS A FEMINIST THEORY OF THE VIRTUES?

Ethics of the virtues, as we have seen, centre on human flourishing. Nussbaum's recent work emphasizes far more than most virtue ethics the material prerequisites for human flourishing.[47] But, so far as I am aware, almost no adherent of virtue ethics has yet addressed directly or faced the implications of the facts that, in virtually all human societies, women do far more than men to promote the day-to-day material and psychological flourishing of others, and that this promotion of the flourishing of others is not infrequently done at the expense of some aspects of their own flourishing. Rarely do we find, in lists of 'the virtues', the kinds of virtues that one needs in order to help others— whether children, the old, the ill or disabled, or merely those who are too preoccupied with their own concerns to take care of their daily needs or those of their children.[48]

[46] Quotations are from Baier, 'Hume, the Women's Moral Theorist?', 46, and 'What do Women Want in a Moral Theory?', 54.

[47] See, for example, M. Nussbaum, 'Human Functioning and Social Justice: In Defense of Aristotelian Essentialism', *Political Theory* 20 (1992), 202–46.

[48] Hume's account of the virtues, and Baier, in her account of it, provide rare exceptions. See the summary in Baier, 'Hume, the Women's Moral Theorist?', esp. 42–3.

What would such virtues be? At the forefront of them come the capacity to nurture, patience, the ability to listen carefully and to teach (sometimes mundane things) well, and the readiness to give up or postpone one's own projects in order to pay attention to the needs or projects of others. When we try to subsume these qualities under those that are usually named as virtues—justice, courage, honesty, generosity—they become distorted and strained. For example, few would be willing to praise as 'generous' or even 'kind' a parent who paid careful attention to her children's needs. Mostly, these qualities are simply *expected*—of *mothers*, at least; if praise or recognition is given at all for such nurturant attention, it is more likely to be given to those fathers who are truly participating parents. The presence of such qualities in mothers, unlike its absence, is usually taken for granted. This is probably why neither philosophers nor most other people tend to consider such qualities virtues. And it may also help to explain why so little attention is given to the irony that, under current social conditions, some of those who best exemplify these virtues—for virtues they undoubtedly are, however neglected—are thereby rendered economically and socially vulnerable.[49]

Some feminist authors, including Carol Gilligan, Nel Noddings, and Sara Ruddick, have written about the qualities of caring and particular attention, without explicitly connecting them with virtue ethics. And some female moral philosophers who may not necessarily think or have thought of themselves as feminists, such as Iris Murdoch and Simone Weil, *have* emphasized the type of virtue I speak of here: consider Weil's concept of 'attention' and Murdoch's concepts of 'the love . . . [that] is an exercise of justice and realism and really *looking*' and of its absence—the 'refusal to attend'.[50] Some recent Aristotelians, unlike MacIntyre, have recognized the need to add some 'gentler virtues' to those emphasized in the classical canon of the virtues, or have even tried to apply Aristotle's theory to feminist issues. But most of the 'new Aristotelians' have taken little or no notice of the urgent need to revise virtue theory thoroughly in order to correct for the fact that Aristotle and most other theorists of the virtues have taken much for granted. They have taken for granted that the goods and services that all in the community need both to develop and to live, in order even to *begin* to

[49] For further explanation of this point, see 'Vulnerability by Marriage', ch. 7 of Okin, *Justice, Gender, and the Family*.

[50] On Weil's concept of attention, see M. Dietz, *Between the Human and the Divine: The Political Thought of Simone Weil* (Totowa, NJ, 1988), 96–103, 125–31. For Murdoch on love and attention, see I. Murdoch, *The Sovereignty of Good* (London, 1970), esp. 91.

'live well', have been provided by categories of people to whom virtue ethics has either not been applied at all, or has been applied in only a very limited way.

Thus there has been, so far, little progress towards a specifically feminist account of virtue ethics. As I have argued here, many of those who find in virtue ethics the most comprehensive, consistent, and workable moral theory for the modern world still need to go beyond ignoring, while assuming that it will continue, what has traditionally been women's work. They need to include as human virtues (not just as adjunct 'feminine' virtues) the qualities needed to nurture, to take care of those who cannot take care of themselves, and to raise children to an adulthood in which they can both flourish as virtuous citizens and enable others so to flourish. They need also to examine whether acknowledging these virtues will involve simply *adding to*, or rather, more radically and extensively *revising*, traditional accounts of the virtues.[51]

[51] Many thanks to Brooke Ackerly for research assistance, and to Roger Crisp for helpful suggestions.

14

Community and Virtue

LAWRENCE BLUM

I

The revival of a virtue approach to ethics has been accompanied by a renewed concern with the notion of community, and many assume a close link between virtue and community. Yet most discussions of virtue proceed without ever mentioning community. The widespread assumption of a link between community and virtue may be due in part to the Aristotelian roots of virtue ethics, and to Alasdair MacIntyre's semi-Aristotelian *After Virtue*, probably the most influential single contemporary work in virtue ethics.[1] Both Aristotle and MacIntyre emphasize the fundamentally social nature of virtue—the way that particular forms of social life are linked with particular virtues.

Another source of the assumption of a close link between community and virtue may be the moral theory or family of theories that proponents of both community and virtue *reject*. These theories emphasize the primacy of the rational, autonomous individual in moral agency and in the normative foundations of political structures. Communitarians differ both in placing value on communal entities—a value not reducible to the value of rational agency—and (sometimes) in according communal entities a more fundamental place in the formation or constitution of the moral self. Virtue theorists see the foundations of virtue as lying not only in rational agency but also in habit, emotion, sentiment, perception, and other psychic capacities.

I wish to explore some of the possible links between virtue and community, with two ends in mind. First, I wish to indicate the multifariousness of such links, and thus to suggest that the ties between community and virtue are more significant than moral theory has taken

[1] A. MacIntyre, *After Virtue* (London, 1981).

account of. Second, I believe that some forms of community are crucial
to the maintenance of a moral psychology of excellence, and that community has often been a missing desideratum in the discussion of the
nature and development of admirable moral character.

The notion of 'community' is by no means a univocal one, and I will
not attempt a formal definition. We will see that different notions of
'community' are sometimes employed in different alleged links to virtue.
In general, however, by 'community' I mean more than the mere possession of a shared characteristic (such as being left-handed, or hailing
from Indiana). I require that status as a member of the community be
recognized by others within the community (and generally outside as
well), and that this status be significant (to a degree I cannot pin down
more precisely) to the individual member's sense of identity. I will generally have in mind communities bound together by either lineage or
location or both, though this feature is not absolutely essential.

Let me suggest six possible or claimed links between virtue and community that one can find in the virtue literature, especially in MacIntyre's
writings.

1. *Learning*. Virtues can be learned and nurtured only within particular forms of social life, including families. They are necessarily social
products and could not be generated *de novo* from individual reason or
reflection.

2. *Sustaining*. A second, stronger claim is that virtues can be *sustained* only in communities. MacIntyre says, 'I need those around me
to reinforce my moral strengths and assist in remedying my moral
weaknesses. It is in general only within a community that individuals
become capable of morality and are sustained in their morality.'[2] This
claim is stronger than (1); for it is consistent with (1) that even if their
original source and formation lies in communities, virtues, once originally
acquired, are able to be sustained solely through individual effort, and
in the absence of the social support MacIntyre refers to.

3. *Agency-constituting*. A somewhat more radical link is sometimes
suggested by MacIntyre—that our very moral identity, hence our moral
agency itself, is at least in part constituted by the communities of which
we are members. (A similar idea is suggested in Michael Sandel's *Liberalism and the Limits of Justice*.[3])

4. *Content-providing*. A different sort of link is that forms of com-

---

[2] A. MacIntyre, 'Is Patriotism a Virtue?', The Lindley Lecture, 1984 (Lawrence, Kan.,
1984), 10.   [3] M. Sandel, *Liberalism and the Limits of Justice* (Cambridge, 1982).

munal life fill in the detailed prescriptions that turn abstract principles into a lived morality. That is, our communities tell us how to apply our general moral principles to the world; without them we would not know what our principles bid us to do in the particular contexts of social life in which we operate. As MacIntyre says, 'The moralities of different societies may agree in having a precept enjoining that a child should honor his or her parents, but what it is to honor . . . will vary greatly between different social orders.'[4] It is only by living within a complex form of communal life that we can learn these particularities, not only cognitively, as one can learn the rules of another culture or community from reading a book, but in the lived way that requires forms of perception and consciousness, morally relevant situation-descriptions, habits of action, salience of certain considerations, and the like. Note, however, that the content provided need not be monolithic; the community's morality can involve internal variation and conflict, and can leave some room as well for individual interpretation.

This connection is distinct from the 'sustaining' connection. For the latter is consistent with our *knowing* what a virtue bids us to do independently of the community, yet requiring the community to sustain our acting on it. The 'content-conferring' connection denies the possibility of having genuine knowledge of what the virtue consists of in the first place.

5. *Worth-conferring*. Another link is that some qualities are constituted as virtues only within particular communities. One could not see the quality as virtuous—or even really understand what the quality was—except by being part of the community in question. This point is analogous to MacIntyre's idea that 'practices' such as chess or portrait painting have standards of excellence internal to themselves which can be understood—and seen as excellences—only by someone initiated into the practice.[5] MacIntyre does not make this claim about virtues themselves, even though he sees virtues as involving producing goods internal to those practices, and as involving living up to the internal standards of the practice. (Moreover, a practice is distinct from a community.) Nevertheless, an analogous idea can be gleaned from his earlier example (under (4)) of communal forms of 'honouring' (e.g. one's parents). One can imagine that a certain activity or quality of character within a given community would count as 'honouring' only within that community, and would not be a virtue outside it.

<hr />

[4] MacIntyre, 'Patriotism', 9.   [5] MacIntyre, *After Virtue*, 175–8.

It is not clear if this is a distinct point from (4) or only a point about different levels of description. The point about content-conferring assumes that a quality is named as a virtue but that it is only within a community that one knows what that virtue actually comes to in a lived context. The worth-conferring point seems also to presuppose that there is *some* level of description of the activity or quality on which it can be seen to be a virtue; this is not incompatible with, and seems even to presuppose, the point of (5), that some qualities cannot be recognized to be virtues except within communities. Yet there may be a substantive difference, in that (4) envisions a principle with some (though abstract) moral substance, stated outside any particular communal context, which is the principle of an actual virtue; whereas for (5) what is statable outside the communal context is only the *name* of the virtue, without any specific (even abstract) content incorporated therein.

6. *Virtues sustaining community.* Some virtues—such as trust, civility, tolerance—are particularly well-suited to sustaining communal life in general.[6] And other virtues may sustain the particular forms of particular communities. Such virtues may or may not be 'worth-conferring' in sense (5).

I mention these possible links between virtue and community without attempting to assess how extensive such links are, or are being claimed to be. The 'learning' link seems plausible for all virtue. But obviously not *all* virtues are internal to communities in sense (5), nor do all virtues sustain community in sense (6). MacIntyre acknowledges that some rare individuals can sustain their own individual virtue without the support of a community in sense (2).[7] Still, without defending this proposition, I will proceed on the assumption that with the possible exception of (3) (agency-constituting), all of these links hold in cases of some virtues, and that this fact is significant for understanding the moral psychology of virtue. Yet much writing on virtue proceeds as if these links did not hold, or were of no particular significance. One gets the impression in much virtue writing that the social dimension of virtue—expressed in a sustaining, content-providing, or worth-conferring role—is of little consequence.[8] Perhaps this social dimension is not actually denied; and there

---

[6] Edmund Pincoffs refers to virtues that sustain associational life as 'meliorating' virtues, in *Quandaries and Virtues: Against Reductivsm in Ethics* (Lawrence, Kan., 1986), 86–7.   [7] MacIntyre, 'Patriotism', 10.

[8] Examples of influential writing on the virtues that generally lack this explicitly social/community dimension are J. Wallace, *Virtues and Vices* (Ithaca, NY, 1978); P. Foot, 'Virtues and Vices', in her *Virtues and Vices* (Oxford, 1978), 1–18; P. French, T.

may be a bow in its direction. Yet—in strong contrast to MacIntyre's work—the impression is given that the virtues and a life of virtue can be understood apart from particular forms of social life.

II

I want now to explore in some detail a particularly striking example of virtue tied to a community—in several of the senses above. Before doing so I must distinguish between two ways that 'virtue' is understood in moral theory and everyday life. In one sense the word 'virtue' refers to a quality of character which is *especially admirable*. It is especially admirable because it issues in actions, and expresses itself in emotional reactions, that go beyond what is normally expected of people and for which they are not thought to warrant special esteem. I will call this 'noteworthy' virtue.

The second conception of virtue, however, is of *any* valuable trait of character—not only noteworthy ones but also ones issuing in actions and feelings which, while morally worthy, are simply what are to be expected of a normal moral agent. The latter are thus not regarded as meriting distinct praise or esteem. Many acts of honesty, compassion, temperance, and other virtues are of this sort. Virtue here is *good* but not (necessarily) *especially*, or notably, valuable; I will call this 'ordinary' virtue.

While one sometimes finds the term 'virtue' used in a way that restricts it to noteworthy virtues, the distinction is best seen as a classification of acts of virtue rather than of entire virtues themselves; some virtuous acts are especially worthy and some are only 'ordinarily' worthy. It may be that acts of some virtues—e.g. courage—are *generally*, or even always, noteworthy. And perhaps others—such as honesty—are generally of the ordinary type. Nevertheless, there are certainly some noteworthy acts of honesty in very adverse circumstances, and perhaps even some minor acts of what is still appropriately called courage that are closer to the 'ordinary' pole of moral worth. In general, I would suggest that every virtue has both noteworthy and ordinary manifestations, depending on circumstances.

Note that the ordinary/noteworthy distinction cannot be identified with

Uehling and H. Wettstein (eds.), *Ethical Theory: Character and Virtue, Midwest Studies in Philosophy XIII* (Notre Dame, Ind., 1988); R. Kruschwitz and R. Roberts (eds.), *The Virtues: Contemporary Essays on Moral Character* (Belmont, Calif., 1987).

the duty/beyond duty distinction. Generous acts, for example, always go beyond what the agent owes to the recipient; they are always 'beyond duty'. Yet some acts of generosity are so minor that they would fall under the 'ordinary' rather than the 'noteworthy' rubric.

The example I will explore is the oft-cited case of the village of Le Chambon, a French Huguenot enclave (in Vichy France) which during the Nazi occupation of France sheltered about 3,000 refugees (mostly Jewish), a number roughly equal to the population of the village. The aspect of this fascinating historical episode that I want to focus on here is the communal nature of the rescue enterprise—the way that the community as a whole had an impact on the decisions of its individual members to help with the rescue activities.[9]

Scores of individuals made individual, or family, decisions to help the refugees. Such decisions carried great risks. To aid refugees, and especially Jews, was punishable, sometimes by death (though the punishments were not as severe nor as stringently enforced as in other areas in Europe, e.g. Poland). Three of the village's leaders were jailed for a time for engaging in these activities.

There were many different forms of participation in the rescue activities. Often a refugee would simply show up at someone's door, and that person would have to decide on the spot whether to help, either by taking the refugee into their own home or trying to find other shelter for her. Obtaining false identity and ration papers, moving refugees, getting food, and sometimes smuggling persons out of the village toward Switzerland were also essential tasks. Simply contributing to keeping up the façade that nothing worthy of the Nazis' attention was going on was a task shared by all. The failure of anyone in the village to attempt to blow the whistle on the whole operation—by informing the appropriate Vichy or German officials—was a precondition of its remarkable success. Hallie says,

Le Chambon became a village of refuge not by fiat, not by virtue of the decision Trocmé [the town pastor, discussed below] or any other person made, but by virtue of the fact that . . . no Chambonnais ever turned away a refugee, and no Chambonnais ever denounced or betrayed a refugee.[10]

---

[9] My sources on Le Chambon are P. Hallie, *Lest Innocent Blood Be Shed* (London, 1979); and Pierre Sauvage's film, *Weapons of the Spirit* (distributed by Friends of Le Chambon, 8033 Sunset Blvd. #784, Los Angeles, 1987). Sauvage, an American filmmaker, was himself born in Le Chambon, of refugee parents, during this period. His film contains interviews with several villagers who were involved in one way or another with the rescue activities, including the people who sheltered him and his parents.

[10] Hallie, *Lest Innocent Blood Be Shed*, 196.

The rescue effort was not a collective enterprise of the town in any explicit sense. Both Hallie and Sauvage claim that people never talked about it openly.[11] There was no clear and publicly visible form of sanction brought against those who did not participate. An individual could refuse to help without penalty or ostracism. While help often took the form of responding to a request from another villager—not always directly from a refugee herself—whatever individual disapproval one might experience for declining to help was overwhelmingly outweighed by the risks involved in complying.

There was one significant public forum in which the rescue effort was referred to, if only obliquely—the sermons of the town's pastor and spiritual leader, André Trocmé. Trocmé was a central organizer of part of the rescue effort. In his sermons he called people to the true teachings of Christianity as he understood them—to love one's neighbour, to cherish human life, not to consort with evil, to be non-violent. Though only indirectly, he made it clear that he took the providing of refuge as instantiating these teachings.

That Trocmé's (and his wife Magda's) moral leadership and organizational efforts were essential to the scope of success of Le Chambon's rescue activities is undeniable.[12] While this may be part of an explanation of the virtuous activities of the villagers, it is not an explanation at odds with that claim to virtue. It is impossible to explain the widespread collective participation without attributing to most of the villagers motives of compassion, a concern for human life, a sense of Christian (or non-Christian) duty, a concern not to co-operate with evil, an eschewing of violence. Hallie says that key decisions regarding rescue were made 'in kitchens', and Sauvage also emphasizes (even more so than Hallie) the grass-roots nature of the rescue enterprise.[13] Indeed, one thing that moral leadership (in contrast to demagoguery, manipulation, mere charisma) does is precisely to help people to find their better motives, to impress upon them moral truths which, for example, fear, the authority of the French collaborating government, a reasonable concern for one's own and one's family's welfare, and the like could easily lead one to turn oneself from. Hallie's account makes it clear that this form of moral leadership was André Trocmé's particular gift.

---

[11] Ibid. 197.
[12] My 'Moral Exemplars: Reflections on Schindler, the Trocmés, and others', *Ethical Theory: Character and Virtue*, 196–221 (also in L. Blum, *Moral Perception and Particularity* (Cambridge, 1994)), further explores the moral psychology of both André and Magda Trocmé as moral exemplars.   [13] Hallie, *Lest Innocent Blood Be Shed*, 8.

Le Chambon is a clear case of a 'community of virtue'. The tremend-
ous dangers involved plus the absence of mechanisms of direct social
pressure imply that the individual decisions to help the rescue effort can
plausibly be inferred to be virtuous ones. Sauvage's and Hallie's interviews with the villagers confirm this impression. Note that the rescue
efforts required much more than an initial compassionate response. Sustained follow-through was required, and most individuals engaged in
some form of direct participation for months or even years.

To speak of the Chambonnais as exhibiting virtue is not (necessarily)
to say that they possessed deep-rooted virtues (in the noteworthy sense),
in the sense of traits that would exhibit themselves in almost any circumstances. It is not that the fleeing refugees had the good fortune to discover a village peopled by saints, or moral exemplars. In fact, after the
war there was little to distinguish Le Chambon from many other villages
of similar size and composition.

This may seem a problem for the attribution of virtue to the villagers.
For if we cannot say that the villagers were people of fine character,
then how can we attribute (noteworthy) virtue to them? Because by
'virtue' I refer here to virtuous conduct, with virtuous motives, carried
out over a substantial enough period of time to ensure that those motives
be reasonably stable ones—not just impulses of compassion, or moment-
ary calls to conscience.[14] I thus do not include here a person who from
a good impulse offers to help but soon after regrets her decision, and
perhaps tries (successfully or not) to extricate herself from the rescue
activity she has undertaken. The stability of virtuous motives required
for the Chambonnais's rescue activities need not have been as deep-
rooted as an actual trait of character.[15]

Note that to attribute virtue to the Chambonnais is not to attribute
every sort of virtue to them. In *Weapons of the Spirit*, Sauvage interviews
a deeply religious fundamentalist Christian (most of the villagers were
not fundamentalists) who brings this out. This woman's religion allowed

---

[14] Also, I do not, of course, mean to suggest that the behaviour of the Chambonnais
during the war had nothing to do with their characters. Their characters must have been
such as to contain the *capability* for the relatively stable virtuous motives operative
during the Occupation.

[15] The motives which sustained someone in this 'follow-through' were not necessarily identical to those which prompted someone to help a refugee in the first place. For
example, once a villager took a refugee into her home, or became otherwise involved in
assisting her, a commitment to that specific individual (and/or to other villagers who
might also be involved in helping that person) might well contribute to motivating continuing help.

her to see absolutely clearly the evilness of the Nazi social order, and to recognize the Jew as a fellow creature, whose life was as valuable as her own. And yet in other contexts this woman may well have evinced rigid, narrow-minded, and even (what many would regard as) immoral sentiments and conduct. The great virtue of the Chambonnais in risking so much to save lives was still in many ways a quite specialized sort of virtue, one which would not directly or necessarily carry over into many other life situations.

What relations between community and virtue do we see here? First, there seems a 'content-determining' relationship. While many of the villagers might have professed belief in general moral precepts such as resisting evil or cherishing human life, it was the community mode of life (helped by pastor Trocmé's sermons) that filled in what it was to realize those principles in action. Outside a context of action, one would hardly expect widespread agreement among persons professing the value, say, of cherishing life, that this value requires them to engage in rescue efforts likely (though not certain) to save someone's life but at great risk to their own freedom and even their own life. Contemplating that value or principle from a dispassionate point of view, they might just as readily aver their agent-centred prerogatives, which limit how much can be demanded of one in the way of personal sacrifice.[16] They would then conclude that no moral principles can *require* so much of a moral agent. Yet, living in Le Chambon influenced large numbers of Chambonnais to come to believe that these risks are precisely what believing in the cherishing of human life or resisting evil *did* entail.

The community also played a crucial 'sustaining' role in relation to the villagers' virtue. On the most basic level, knowing that one's neighbours are doing something especially difficult but worth while makes it easier for us to feel that we too can do it. This must be part of what MacIntyre meant by saying 'I need those around me to reinforce my moral strengths and assist in remedying my moral weaknesses.'[17] Note, however, that this is not simply conformity—engaging in action only because one's neighbours are doing so, in order not to be 'left out'. For the latter assumes no, or very weak, independent motivation to engage in rescue, a motivation then supplied by the lure of doing what others are doing; while MacIntyre's statement assumes

---

[16] See S. Scheffler, *The Rejection of Consequentialism* (Oxford, 1982), ch. 3.
[17] MacIntyre, 'Patriotism', 10.

that the villagers already and independently saw the worth in these activities of rescue, but knowing that their neighbours were doing them made it easier to bring themselves to choose to do them in the face of the risks, and to be firmly convinced of the worthwhileness of these endeavours.

So one reason not to place too much weight on moral conformity in the villagers' motivation is that there is too much evidence that the villagers independently grasped the moral worth of the acts of rescue in a way denied by this form of motivation. But a second reason is the aforementioned lack of visibility of the rescue effort itself, the fact that it was seldom publicly discussed or referred to, that one was not always *entirely* certain which of one's neighbours were currently doing what for the effort, and that even when one was part of a small group organized for a specific task (e.g. securing false papers) one was often aware *only* of that particular group and not others.

The 'sustaining' relationship here has two components: (1) the community's helping the villagers individually to have a firm conviction of the rightness of the rescue effort in the first place, and (2) the knowledge that (some) others were taking part's helping to reinforce the continual translation of that conviction into action.

One significant piece of this sustaining structure concerned the Chambonnais's intense awareness of themselves as a religious minority (Protestants in a Catholic country), with a history of religious persecution and of resistance to that persecution. Sauvage's film depicts a moving ritual—apparently regularly performed—of a large gathering of Chambonnais singing a song of historical resistance to persecution. This self-conception can be seen as part of the village's moral tradition. But how did this tradition and historical memory operate to sustain the rescue activities? There seem to be two dimensions. One was to supply the motive of resisting an evil perpetrated by the state and state authorities. That form of motive directly linked resistance to their own persecution as Protestants with the persecution of Jews by the collaborationist French state. It was as if that motive of resistance to state-sponsored evil was made salient through historical tradition and memory, reinforced by ritual.

But there is a second, more indirect way in which the self-conception and historical memory of the villagers as a religious minority may have helped the rescue effort. That was to remove one important obstacle in the way of fully experiencing the Jews and other refugees as fellow human beings, rather than as an alien 'other'. That obstacle was the view of the Jews propounded by Pétain's national government.[18] In laws restricting Jews' participation in French life, in national propaganda (chilling footage of which can be seen in Sauvage's film), and (ultimately) in co-operating with the Nazis' 'final solution', the French government aimed to make it easy for ordinary citizens to see the Jew as 'other', to confuse and undermine natural human sympathy for the persecuted, and to couch this immorality in terms of an ostensibly worthy larger patriotic goal.

The Chambonnais were particularly well-equipped to resist this state-sponsored moral obfuscation. Their tradition of resistance to persecution made them generally sceptical of the state itself. In this regard, their moral traditions operated not so much to provide a direct motive to rescue but to *remove* an obstacle to a clear grasp of the moral truth of the equality of all persons.[19]

This latter point suggests a useful framing of the way that the Chambon community helped to sustain its inhabitants' virtue—that is, by helping to construct and shape their 'moral reality'. The community's moral traditions and the moral atmosphere there during the Occupation kept the reality of the plight of the refugees in the forefront of people's minds; it reinforced for the villagers the salience of their danger and suffering.

Though the virtue of the villagers was internal to the community in the sustaining and the content-conferring senses, it was *not* internal to the community in the 'worth-conferring' sense; nor did it, in MacIntyre's conception, produce a good internal to its practice, or to the community itself. On the contrary, the good in question—the saving of endangered persons—is very much an 'external' good, that is, a good *for non-members* of the community. As well, it is a universal good of which anyone (inside or outside the community) can see the value.[20]

[18] Hallie, *Lest Innocent Blood Be Shed*, 39.

[19] The notion of an 'obstacle' to moral perception and moral motivation is discussed in my 'Moral Perception and Particularity', *Ethics* 101 (1991), 701–25, pp. 717–18 (also in Blum, *Moral Perception and Particularity*, 48–9). The notion is taken from I. Murdoch, *The Sovereignty of Good* (London, 1970).

[20] When MacIntyre talks about 'external goods' he generally means competitive goods such as money, power, and status: see *After Virtue*, 176, 181, and *passim*. This conception is part of what allows MacIntyre generally to portray goods internal to practices as somehow more worthy than goods external to them, though MacIntyre does not entirely denigrate these competitive goods. That MacIntyre neglects 'positive' external goods (like saving the lives of people not in the community), the virtues which produce them, and the communities in which they are promoted is part of what underpins his pessimism, his sense of extreme moral fragmentation, and his notion that moral renewal can come

III

Yet the MacIntyrean idea that a quality constituting virtue to members of a community is nevertheless not seen as a virtue by those outside the community contains an idea of insider/outsider *moral asymmetry* that is suggestive for the case of Le Chambon. When (separately) Philip Hallie and Pierre Sauvage went back to interview the Chambonnais several decades after the events in question took place, they found that the rescuers did not regard themselves as having done anything worthy of special attention or praise. They were uncomfortable with Hallie's and Sauvage's questions about 'why' they acted the way they did, rightly taking it to imply something in special need of explanation, of special noteworthiness. The Chambonnais did not see their actions and practices as having been virtuous in the 'noteworthy' sense. When pressed to say why they helped the refugees, they said, 'It was simply what one had to do', 'She [a refugee] was standing at my door; how could I fail to help?', and things of that sort.[21]

However, from the outside we very much *do* see the Chambonnais as having been virtuous in the noteworthy—and not only the ordinary— sense. There could hardly be a clearer example of collective virtue in the noteworthy sense. The Chambonnais did what few Europeans did or felt called upon to do. Yet the fact that the Chambonnais did not themselves see it that way themselves is significant, and perhaps is part of how we are to understand the potential virtue-sustaining function of community. For part of the state of mind involved in the villagers' being able to carry on these rescue activities day after day must have been precisely that they did come to regard these activities as something like normal, unremarkable acts—acts that could simply be expected of an ordinary person. To see them as worthy of special praise is to

only through relatively self-contained communities unconnected to a larger social order and to each other: see, e.g. p. 245. (These views are not so pronounced in MacIntyre's later writings.)

In fact many entities with communal features can *only* be understood as, at least in part, serving ends that are 'external' to them. Educational or medical communities are examples of this. Medical communities have in some sense their own 'internal' standards, authorities, traditions, initiation rites, and the like. Yet one cannot understand the point of a medical community without seeing it as serving its clients and the society as a whole—as serving 'health', a good 'external' to the medical community as defined solely by its practices. So standards for judging a medical community must come at least partly from how well it does in fact produce this external good.

[21] See e.g. Hallie, *Lest Innocent Blood Be Shed*, 154. This point is made more fully in Sauvage's film.

emphasize them as something that could not be expected of anyone, as something engaging in which put one beyond and apart from the ordinary person. The weakening of the sense of one's actions as 'to be expected' can in turn (though it does not necessarily) weaken the will necessary to carry out the virtuous actions under adverse circumstances.[22] And the fact that others *were* engaging in, helping, and supporting the rescue activities—even though this was seldom directly discussed—is part of what helped the villagers to define them as 'ordinary' and unremarkable.[23]

Community, then, can support (noteworthy) virtue by helping its members to experience as ordinary and 'to be expected' behaviour which for others goes *beyond* what can be expected. A major factor making a course of action too much to expect or demand is that it is unduly burdensome. In one way or another the notion of 'undue burden' is frequently built into accounts of duty. Acts which unduly burden people are good but cannot be expected as duty. Thus Sidgwick: the common-sense duty of beneficence is the 'positive duty to render, when occasion offers, such services as require either no sacrifice on our part, or at least one very much less in importance than the service rendered'; and Rawls: 'Supererogatory acts are not required, though normally they would be were it not for the loss or risk involved for the agent himself.'[24]

---

[22] I am not claiming that one *must* have a supporting community in order to engage in noteworthy virtue; the numerous examples of rescuers during the Holocaust who were relatively isolated from their communities, depending on the help only of their families and in some cases working independently even of them (or not having families), testify to the contrary. It is fair to say, however, that such virtuous activities are much more likely in the context of supporting communities than in the absence of them. This echoes MacIntyre's point: 'Of course lonely moral heroism is sometimes required and sometimes achieved. But we must not treat this exceptional type of case as if it were typical' ('Patriotism', 10).

[23] The potentially powerful effect of community can be seen as much with regard to vice as to virtue. There can be communities of vice as well as virtue, where the community helps to shape a sense of moral reality toward, say, corruption, rather than compassion. The narcotics squad of the New York City Police Department, as portrayed in the film and book *Prince of the City*, illustrates this (R. Daley, *Prince of the City* (London, 1979); *Prince of the City*, directed by S. Lumet, distributed by Orion Pictures (Los Angeles, 1981). Being a member of those units helped to shape a sense that corruption was an everyday, expected thing—not that it was morally right or permissible exactly, but just that it was an appropriate mode of operation.

[24] H. Sidgwick, *The Methods of Ethics*, 7th edn. (London, 1907), 253; J. Rawls, *A Theory of Justice* (Oxford, 1971), 117; cf. p. 439, where 'reasonable self-interest' is the operative excusing condition from what would otherwise be a duty. Note a not insignificant difference between two constructions of both these formulations. The first is that one should offer aid to others when the cost to oneself is *negligible* or *minimal*. The second, more demanding view (that is, more is demanded in the way of duty), is that the cost to

However, what people regard as 'undue burden', and hence as 'what can reasonably be expected', is quite variable and can be deeply affected by one's communities. Let us illustrate this with an example in which much less is at stake than in the Le Chambon case. A faculty member switches jobs from one college to another. At her former college, Professor Martinez's department made limited demands on her. Departmental meetings were infrequent and responsibilities few, beyond teaching one's classes. In her new department, however, the demands are substantially greater. Meetings are more frequent; there are more departmental responsibilities on top of teaching—discussions of pedagogy, re-evaluations of programme, expectations of being informed regarding various campus concerns that impinge on students' lives, greater involvement in advising, and the like.

At first Professor Martinez experiences this increased load as unduly burdensome, and more than is reasonable to expect of a faculty member. It certainly would have been regarded as such in her previous department, whose construction of 'burdensomeness' Professor Martinez is here reflecting. In time, however, several factors change her outlook and her experience of burdensomeness. She realizes that not insignificant matters slipped through the cracks in her previous department. She sees how in her new department the programme is improved and the students better served because of the greater work she and her colleagues put in. Her teaching is itself improved because of the improvements in the programme and because of her greater understanding of issues affecting the students. Professor Martinez comes not only to recognize this superiority in her current department but to care about and positively value it as well. She comes to care that students in her department are better served, that tasks are responsibly carried out, that difficult issues are faced and dealt with in a collegial manner.

In time Professor Martinez comes no longer to experience the departmental work-load at her current institution as unduly burdensome. It is not that she experiences it as unduly burdensome but resignedly accepts the load—with that undue burden—as part of her new job responsibilities, hence something she sees herself as obliged to bear. That would be one possible reaction to the new situation, but is not the one I am envisioning. An important part of what enables Professor Martinez to

oneself be minimal *in proportion to the good being rendered to the other person.* The latter construction would require more sacrifice as a matter of duty than the former in cases where the good to be promoted (or evil to be prevented) is very great. Both Sidgwick's and Rawls's formulations are somewhat ambiguous on this issue.

come *not* to experience her work-load as unduly burdensome is that her colleagues appear not to regard it thus (which does not mean that they, and she, *never* mind or resent it). Their already existing sense of the naturalness and to-be-expectedness of the work-load of the department, their belief in the values of the programme, and their sense of responsibility toward it help to construct a collective reality for Professor Martinez (and for themselves) within which the value of the programme is made salient—with the attendant impact on the experience of the work-load as perhaps demanding (and certainly more demanding than in her previous department) but not 'unduly burdensome', not 'beyond what can reasonably be expected'.

Both this and the Le Chambon case illustrate how communities can powerfully shape members' sense of undue burden, and hence of what they regard as 'reasonable to expect', and, through this, their ability to sustain a level of virtuous conduct beyond what in some other contexts would be regarded as too much to expect (though good and admirable). This insider/outsider asymmetry is an important element in the person whose noteworthy virtue is grounded in community.

IV

Let us look now at some familiar attempts to describe what is going on when an individual's moral behaviour is notably virtuous. I will argue that these attempts fail to grasp the significance of insider/outsider asymmetry and thus give an inadequate picture of the psychology of the particular sort of morally excellent person I am concerned with here.

The first place to start is with the notion of 'supererogation'. Various somewhat distinct analyses have been offered of supererogatory acts, but I will first consider David Heyd's, in his comprehensive work, *Supererogation*.[25] For our purposes, Heyd's analysis is that supererogatory acts are good to do but not bad or blameworthy not to do; in not being wrong not to do, then, they are 'totally optional and voluntary' and their being optional in that sense is part of what gives them their value.[26]

[25] D. Heyd, *Supererogation* (Cambridge, 1982). A more recent, usefully comprehensive treatment is G. Mellema, *Beyond the Call of Duty: Supererogation, Obligation, and Offense* (Albany, NY, 1991).

[26] Heyd, *Supererogation*, 9, 173–6. J. Fishkin, *The Limits of Obligation* (New Haven, Conn., 1982) uses a similar concept, 'morally discretionary', to define supererogation (p. 5).

Describing noteworthy virtue as 'supererogation' in this sense does not capture the way that the (notably) virtuous agent sees her own action. She does *not* regard her act as morally optional; rather, she feels some sense of moral compulsion to perform it. This sense of moral compulsion need not be straightforwardly that of *duty*; that is, the virtuous agent may feel that she 'ought' to perform the virtuous act, without necessarily regarding that act as a duty or obligation. On the other hand, the virtuous agent *may* regard the act as her duty. Both duty and non-duty forms of virtuous action can be found in the Chambonnais's reasons for action. For some the presence of a refugee, of someone in need, aroused a compassion in which the refugee's plight constituted a direct reason for them to act—a reason possibly involving an 'ought' but not a duty; while for others, a sense of duty was evoked. But in neither case did the villagers see the action as 'optional' in the sense of Heyd's analysis.

It is true, perhaps, that the villagers saw their actions as 'voluntary', in the sense that there was no organized social or legal pressure or threat involved in their performing the act. But that situation does not distinguish such actions from many instances of compliance with ordinary duties, in which the agent feels a moral compulsion to perform the action, but in which there is no other sort of pressure brought to bear, or even implicit. Heyd's use of the term 'voluntary' is thus misleading as a way of distinguishing supererogatory action from ordinary duty, leaving 'morally optional' as the crucial characteristic distinguishing supererogatory from dutiful action.

A slightly different formulation is that the supererogatory act is 'morally recommended' or 'encouraged'—in contrast to what is *required* by morality as duties, or as obedience to certain moral rules or principles.[27] Yet it would also be misleading to see the communitarianly virtuous person under this rubric. For, while the idea of 'morally recommended' may go a bit beyond the idea of a purely voluntary or morally optional act (toward some degree of moral pull or compulsion), it does not incorporate the strong moral pull experienced by the notably virtuous agent. In the idea of a 'moral recommendation' there is still too much implication that the agent can choose to reject the recommendation without a sense of having morally failed in any substantial sense. But the virtuous agent *would* regard herself as having failed in some way

---

[27] Heyd uses the concept of 'morally encouraged', and B. Gert, *The Moral Rules* (Oxford, 1966), the notion of 'morally recommended'.

were she not to perform the action. (This is not to say, however, that she would necessarily regard herself as being *blameworthy*, if that is taken to mean that other persons would be justified in blaming her, or that she would regard them as justified. The issue of blame and blame-worthiness needs to be disentangled from the idea of regarding oneself as having morally failed.)

Another variation on this general approach is the idea of noteworthy virtue as a *personal moral ideal*—that is, a moral project taken up by an individual and seen as having a moral claim on her only because she has chosen it as her ideal.[28] Again, this does not seem an accurate depiction of the notably virtuous agent's actions either. For she sees herself not so much as choosing to take up a project as feeling compelled to engage in an endeavour. The Chambonnais villager saw herself as responding to a given moral reality—the refugee's need for shelter—not as acting out of a sense of personal value or as following an ideal. As mentioned earlier, the villagers did not in general regard their actions under the rubric of an 'ideal', if that is taken (as it is normally meant) as a set of principles higher than the ordinary.[29]

In addition, the villagers' virtuous endeavours had a *collective* char-acter not captured by the idea of an individual moral ideal. The difference is not merely a matter of an enterprise shared with others rather than simply performed alone. It is also, as we have seen, that the community was essential in shaping the agent's (thus shared) sense of moral reality, and in sustaining her virtue partly though the knowledge that the vir-tuous activities were also being carried out by others.

A quite different approach to the psychology of the (notably) virtu-ous agent is taken by A. I. Melden in his 'Saints and Supererogation'.[30] Melden sees what he calls 'saints' as acting from a sense of duty, but one not construed universalistically, as applicable to all. Melden explains this non-universalistic sense of duty by saying that the saint sees him-self as morally different from others, and thus as being bound to a different set of standards from other persons. The saint has a kind of

[28] Gert, *The Moral Rules*, extensively develops the notion of a 'personal ideal'.

[29] This description does not, I think, hold for André Trocmé, whose involvement (and leadership) in the Chambonnais rescue effort can be thought of as stemming from his 'personal ideals'. This feature of Trocmé's moral psychology is discussed in my 'Moral Exemplars'. Yet even here the notion of personal ideals would not involve a personal set of values that Trocmé would have seen as clearly 'going beyond' what ordinary morality required.

[30] A. I. Melden, 'Saints and Supererogation', in I. Dilman (ed.), *Philosophy and Life: Essays on John Wisdom* (The Hague, 1984), 61–81.

personal moral calling, though this is different from the personal moral ideal just discussed in involving a sense of duty rather than a morally optional project.

But the Chambonnais did *not* see themselves as morally distinct from ordinary persons, as having a distinct moral calling. They did not see themselves as bound to a morality *for themselves alone* (as Melden's analysis implies). While nothing in their lives compelled them to face up to this question, it seems clear that they would never have positively affirmed that the ethic which guided their actions was *not* applicable to others in comparable situations. Note that it does not follow that the Chambonnais did see their ethic in *universal* terms, as distinctly applicable to all others. That is, they gave no evidence of positively believing that the ethic that guided their actions was an appropriate standard for all persons, everywhere, so that any failure to live up to that standard would be wrong or blameworthy. It is perfectly consistent to say—and seems in accordance with the portrayal of the Chambonnais in Hallie's and Sauvage's treatments—that the Chambonnais affirmed *neither* the universality *nor* the exclusivity (to themselves, as in Melden's view) of their ethic.

It might be thought, however, since for many of the Chambonnais it was a specifically *Christian* morality that informed their actions, that their morality was a universal one. This is true, in so far as their Christian morality prescribed a sense of duty or other moral requirement toward *all* persons, and not only toward members of one's community or toward Christians. But this is not the sense of universality embodied in the philosophic tradition (which Melden is contrasting with his view of duties for specific persons or groups) that sees duties as applicable to all agents. This latter notion of duty involves the idea that when one conceives of oneself as having a duty, one sees oneself as doing so because one accepts the universality of that duty, and thus implicitly accepts the idea that such duties are binding on all other agents (relevantly similarly situated). There is no evidence that the Chambonnais looked at their own behaviour in this way. In fact, the notion of a specifically *Christian* morality is precisely that of a morality *for* Christians only—with no necessary claim to validity for non-Christians—though *toward* all persons, Christian and non-Christian.

It is possible, of course, that some of the Chambonnais *did* regard their actions as incumbent upon all moral agents similarly situated; that is, they in a sense regarded the rescue activities as a matter of 'ordinary', universalistic duty. Even if that were so, we would still need an explanation for what in their psychology caused them to take this (not only theoretical but lived) view of ordinary duty, when so few other Europeans at the time did so. And here we seem compelled to appeal to their community as helping to shape that particular sense of duty, just as for other villagers it shaped their sense of what they morally ought to do without couching that in terms of universalistic duty, or even duty at all.

Thus, none of the philosophical attempts succeeds in expressing the psychology of the (notably) virtuous agent. A major weakness in the 'morally optional', 'morally recommended', and 'personal ideal' views is that they all aspire to something like a purely objective account of where one draws the line between the ordinary and the noteworthy (or between duty and supererogation, not that these are precisely the same thing). But a key feature of these accounts—the feature that draws the line in question—makes reference to something like 'undue burden' or 'what can be expected' or 'reasonable self-interest'. But these factors are experienced and regarded entirely differently from within different communities. (More generally, they are regarded differently by different individuals, but I am focusing on the communal setting here.) What one group regards as an undue burden, another sees as what can reasonably be expected.

In a sense the 'morally optional', 'morally recommended', and 'personal ideal' accounts of the ordinary/noteworthy distinction do succeed in capturing the psychology of ordinary virtue—but not that of noteworthy virtue. That is, the person of ordinary virtue does see herself as acting from what is incumbent upon her and as eschewing the higher flights of morality which she may see as admirable but *not* incumbent upon her; from her vantage point the notably virtuous person *is* acting from an ethic that is optional, perhaps morally recommended (but not required), or constitutes a personal ideal for that individual.

What these accounts do, then, is to describe what both the ordinarily virtuous person and the notably virtuous person look like *from the vantage point of the ordinarily virtuous person*. But they do not capture what the notably virtuous person looks like to herself. (By contrast, Melden does genuinely attempt to do this, but his account is incorrect.)[31]

[31] These remarks should not be taken as an attack on the notion of 'supererogation' itself. They might be taken as such, for anti-supererogationists sometimes use the argument that no firm line can be drawn between duty and supererogation, and also (somewhat following upon this point) that what people may think of as the higher flights of morality are nevertheless no less actual moral requirements than the more ordinary duties. But I agree that there are some actions that go beyond what can be reasonably expected, and that these are deserving of particular praise. I just do not think that a

A natural response to recognizing this variability in the ordinary/noteworthy distinction might be to attempt explicitly to *relativize* that distinction to particular communities, instead of seeking a strictly universal account. Thus, one might say that what *are and are not* undue burdens are defined *for* particular communities. Hence what appropriately counts as undue burden is given by one's community. But this view will not do, for it turns a *descriptive* truth—that a sense of due and undue burden tends to be shaped by and is relative to one's communities—into a *normative* one that would involve *affirming* the validity of every community's standard of undue burden, no matter how undemanding.

The abandonment of the 'communal relativist' affirmation of each community's standard of reasonable expectation and undue burden, coupled with the abandonment of a trans-communal or universal standard, entail, perhaps, that we cannot say that the notably virtuous person's view of burdensomeness is *correct* as against the less demanding standards of other communities. Yet what we are still enabled to do is to describe the psychology of the notably virtuous agent, and say that her virtue is more admirable than that of ordinarily virtuous persons. That is, we can still say—as we must—that the villagers of Le Chambon set a standard for moral excellence that applies to us all. And we can recognize a truth important for moral philosophy as well as moral education—that particular sorts of communities can play a crucial role in sustaining that moral excellence.[32]

general formula can be provided that allows us to sort actions into these two categories independent of the particular moral communities within which people function. I do think, for example, that even in Le Chambon during the period of rescue, there might well have been actions generally regarded by the villagers as above and beyond what could reasonably be expected, and thus deserving particular praise, even if their standard of 'reasonable expectation' was itself so much more demanding than in other communities.

[32] I wish to thank David Wong for support and helpful comments on an early draft. I thank the participants in the 1st Annual Riverside Colloquium on the Virtues for helpful comments on my presentation there. Thanks are due especially to Charles Young, whose remarks as commentator on this paper at the Colloquium were particularly thoughtful and helpful. A longer version of this paper appears in my *Moral Perception and Particularity*.

FURTHER READING

A huge amount of literature on the virtues has appeared over the last three decades. The following brief list is intended as a guide for those who have begun thinking about the virtues and wish to go further.

Books

ARISTOTLE, *Nicomachean Ethics*, tr. T. H. Irwin (Indianapolis, 1985). Contains handy notes and glossary. Must be read: do not accept second-hand accounts.

BAIER, A., *Moral Prejudices* (Cambridge, Mass., 1994). Thoughtful essays on issues in moral theory, including trust and love.

BLUM, L., *Friendship, Altruism, and Morality* (London, 1980). Defence of importance of altruistic emotions against Kantianism.

FLANAGAN, O. (ed.), *Identity, Character, and Morality: Essays in Moral Psychology* (Cambridge, Mass., 1990). Important collection of contemporary papers.

FOOT, P., *Virtues and Vices* (Oxford, 1978). A collection of classic articles by one of the most influential writers on the virtues.

FRENCH, P., UEHLING, T., and WETTSTEIN, H. K. (eds.), *Ethical Theory: Character and Virtue, Midwest Studies in Philosophy XIII* (Notre Dame, Ind., 1988). High-quality collection of papers by various modern writers.

GALSTON, W., *Liberal Purposes: Goods, Virtues, and Diversity in the Liberal State* (New York, 1991). Discusses virtue within context of modern liberalism.

GILLIGAN, C., *In a Different Voice* (Cambridge, Mass., 1982). Defends suggestion that there is a feminine ethic.

HAMPSHIRE, S., *Morality and Conflict* (Oxford, 1983). Collection of related papers by influential writer.

HUME, D., *An Enquiry Concerning the Principles of Morals*, ed. L. A. Selby-Bigge, rev. P. H. Nidditch, 3rd edn. (Oxford, 1975). Classic naturalistic account of the origin and content of a morality revolving around the virtues.

KRUSCHWITZ, R., and ROBERTS, R., *The Virtues: Contemporary Essays on Moral Character* (Belmont, Calif., 1987). Useful collection of already published articles; contains bibliography.

MACHIAVELLI, N., *The Prince*, tr. G. Bau (Harmondsworth, 1961). On the question of political *virtù*.

MACINTYRE, A., *After Virtue* (London, 1981). An immensely influential and stimulating book.

MURDOCH, I., *The Sovereignty of Good* (London, 1970). Short and profound.

NODDINGS, N., *Caring: A Feminine Approach to Ethics and Moral Education* (Berkeley, Calif., 1984). Good introduction to the ethics of care.

PLATO, *Republic*, tr. G. Grube, rev. C. Reeve (Indianapolis, 1992).

SLOTE, M., *From Morality to Virtue* (New York, 1992). Defends virtue ethics against common-sense morality, utilitarianism, and Kantianism.

VON WRIGHT, G. H., *The Varieties of Goodness* (London, 1963). Contains chapter on virtue.

WALLACE, J., *Virtues and Vices* (Ithaca, NY, 1978). Neo-Aristotelian perfectionist virtue ethics.

WILLIAMS, B., *Ethics and the Limits of Philosophy* (London, 1985). Powerful critique of modern ethics.

Articles

ADAMS, R. M., 'Motive Utilitarianism', *Journal of Philosophy* 73 (1976), 467–81. Useful when thinking about relation of utilitarianism to virtue ethics.

ALDERMAN, H., 'By Virtue of a Virtue', *Review of Metaphysics* 36 (1982), 127–53. Defends primacy of character and virtue in ethics.

ANSCOMBE, G. E. M., 'Modern Moral Philosophy', *Philosophy* 33 (1958), 1–19. Started many balls rolling, and continues to do so.

BAIER, A., 'What do Women Want in a Moral Theory?', *Nous* 19 (1985), 53–63. Advocates supplementing the concept of obligation in moral philosophy with those of 'appropriate trust' and its related virtues.

COTTINGHAM, J., 'The Ethics of Self-Concern', *Ethics* 101 (1991), 798–817. Defence of virtue ethics within framework of Aristotelian self-love.

FRANKENA, W., 'Prichard and the Ethics of Virtue: Notes on a Footnote', *Monist* 54 (1970), 1–17. Early and critical discussion of virtue ethics.

GARCIA, J. L. A., 'The Primacy of the Virtuous', *Philosophia* 20 (1990), 69–91. Argues that concepts such as 'right' and 'wrong' action have to be understood in terms of virtue concepts. This volume of *Philosophia* contains many other good articles on the virtues, with special reference to the work of Philippa Foot.

HERMAN, B., 'On the Value of Acting from the Motive of Duty', *Philosophical Review* 90 (1981), 359–82. Defends Kantianism against the charge that it undermines the value of acting from sympathy and concern for others.

LAIRD, J., 'Act-Ethics and Agent-Ethics', *Mind* 55 (1946), 113–32. Old but still important.

MCDOWELL, J., 'Virtue and Reason', *Monist* 62 (1979), 331–50. Highly significant piece, combining Aristotle and Wittgenstein.

OLDENQUIST, A., 'Loyalties', *Journal of Philosophy* 79 (1982), 179–93. Insightful discussion of personal moral relationships.

O'NEILL, O., 'Duties and Virtues', *Philosophy* 35, Suppl. (1993), 107–20. Argues that the concepts of duty and virtue are not in opposition.

PINCOFFS, E., 'Quandary Ethics', *Mind* 80 (1971), 552–71. Critical of modern concern with ethical dilemmas.

SCHNEEWIND, J., 'The Misfortunes of Virtue', *Ethics* 101 (1991), 42–63. Argues that virtue ethics was tried and found wanting in the relatively recent past.

STOCKER, M., 'The Schizophrenia of Modern Ethical Theory', *Journal of Philosophy* 73 (1976), 453–66. Particularly powerful statement of the alienation charge against modern ethics.

TRIANOSKY, G., 'What is Virtue Ethics All About?', *American Philosophical Quarterly* 27 (1990), 335–44. Brief and systematic introduction to the territory.

WILLIAMS, B., 'Persons, Character, and Morality', in A. O. Rorty (ed.), *The Identities of Persons* (Berkeley, Calif., 1976), 197–216; repr. in B. Williams, *Moral Luck* (Cambridge, 1981), 1–19. Critique of impartiality as embodied in utilitarianism and Kantianism.

INDEX